IF YOU KNEW SUSIE ...

IF YOU KNEW SUSIE ...

'There is always some moment in Childhood when the door opens and lets the future in'

The Power and the Glory (Graham Greene)

Susan Uebel

Published by Susan Uebel

A CIP catalogue record for this book is available from the British Library.

ISBN 978-1-9996988-0-5

Book layout and cover design by Clare Brayshaw

Prepared and printed by:

York Publishing Services Ltd
64 Hallfield Road
Layerthorpe
York YO31 7ZQ

Tel: 01904 431213

Website: www.yps-publishing.co.uk

DEDICATION

I dedicate this book to all those who have, through their love, friendship, expertise and kindness helped me to become the woman I am today.

UNFAILING BELIEF OF DEAR FRIENDS

Alessandra and Roger Richards
Jonathan Sampson
Ian Geldart
Andy and Chris Shelton
Paul Andronikou
Angela Scott

INTRODUCTION

"Ronnie, one would think that I didn't have a life before you came along". This was a well-worn phrase in our house. Some of you may have met my Actor husband, Ronnie. My first book was a gift of applause for him. This one is about me. Ronnie's aura remains and is a constant in my life, although he left me many years ago; he died in 2004.

I could not write about my yesteryears, the days of yore, without knowing that Ronnie would be by my side. He is. I hope his imagined interjections will not be intrusive. He and I were in tune. I know he would not be able to resist the temptation to interfere, to add-on and always – to laugh.

'Yes, petal, you did have a life...'

ANLABY

1939

'I remember, I remember, the house where I was born...'

(Thomas Hood)

I was born on 2 October 1939 in the village of Anlaby. The Yorkshire seafaring city of Hull, almost ten miles away, was lost in the distance. Unspoilt meadows, hedgerows and trees lay between.

My village was a venerable mix of lanes, thatches, trees-to-climb, grassy knolls, pasture and – Miss Johnson's grocery store on the main street. My address was Fifth House, Lowfield Road, a leafy offshoot from the pivotal thoroughfare.

Voases Lane separated our house and four others from three on the other side. The houses were newly-built: red brick, smart, three bed-roomed dwellings. The back gardens spilled on to farm land and the grand grounds of Anlaby House, a lofty stately home of the day.

My father, Charles Henry, affectionately known as Charlie, was a butcher. His shop was located on Porter Street in Hull; a thriving, established business which attracted trade from far-reaching corners of the East Riding. Pork Pies and all things Delicatessen, displayed with appetising flair, made up the window-dressing. The Uebel family was comprised of my Daddy and three sisters:

Annie – in her opinion, 'Anne' was more appropriate – Elsie and Laura.

Laura, it seems, was the favoured youngest sibling.

'Oh God, what did Jessica think to that?'

I'm coming to that, Ronnie...

Grandfather Uebel, Christian, died before I was born and Grandmother, Sophia, passed away two years after I came into the world.

My mother, Jessica, was an only child. Her parents, Harry and Annie (who didn't mind being called 'Annie') lived a stone's throw away on the Anlaby Road, a main highway into Hull.

My Mother and Father were a golden couple. Both were beautiful. They married in September 1938 and, I suppose, their Wedding was a Society gathering of the day. My Mother was a ballet dancer. Photographs reveal a graceful, delicate vignette. Her chestnut hair was enclosed in a loose chignon at the base of her neck while a luminous complexion, flawless in texture, enhanced an unforgettable image.

Charlie & Jessica

My Mother Jessica

'I sense sadness...'

Yes... it remained there forever.

My Father – dark, handsome, and dashing – was thirty-three when he married and five years older than my Mother. Rumour had it that there had been a history of moderate philandering; not enough, however, to warrant the sobriquet of roué. Many years later, my Mother, in moments of pique, did spill the beans about his gambling.

'Oh eck!'

Newlyweds, my Parents set up home in what was to become a residential area. I can recall that my early years were spent in considerable comfort. The house was compact but furnished with flair, discrimination and style.

The kitchen was a spotless white and equipped with labour-saving devices of the era – a Dolly-tub comes to mind, complete with Posher! I'll explain, before Ronnie does! The Dolly-tub was a large washing vessel made of metal. The weekly wash could be left to soak in it while, from time to time, the Dolly Stick or Posher would be dunked therein thus moving the contents to and fro.

Red fitted carpets covered the hall and stairway. The room at the back of the house was known as the Dining Room and housed oak table, chairs and sideboard. Two high-backed easy chairs reclined in front of the fireplace. The Front Room, reserved for special occasions – visits from the Vicar or consultations with Dr. Mackintosh our family Doctor, warmly referred to as Dr. Mac., was furnished with a chintz-covered three-piece suite and matching curtains. It certainly demanded respect! Both Reception rooms were heated with coal fires. My Mother was an expert fire-maker. This daily chore was referred to as 'laying the fire'; first, screwed-up newspaper, then the wood and finally lumps of coal. Jessica was not satisfied until the fire was roaring. One of the most heart-warming recollections of my early life was returning from school and glimpsing its glow through the window.

'Little golden-curled Susan...'

One of Ronnie's musings when pandering or coddling – always teasing.

Neighbours on either side were varied; some friendly, some cautious or wary, some decidedly mistrustful. This was understandable. In 1939, the country was on the brink of War and my Father was of German descent.

My Grandparents came to England unknown to each other and from different parts of their country. They met at Hull's German Church, married, settled and built up a booming business where cuisine, relishes and delicacies for the table were greatly appreciated. My Father inherited their gifts and he and his Sisters toiled from morning until night to serve of their best. Auntie Elsie worked tirelessly in the kitchens, single-handedly managing the sweating, cavernous ovens and turning out the incomparable home-made Pork Pies.

'I would have made a great friend of your Auntie Elsie...'

My Father left for work at 5.00 a.m. and often did not return until after 7.00 in the evening.

Unrest must have been accelerating at that time and the country's tendency shifting, so there was little wonder that my Father was regarded by some as a threat. I can only imagine my Mother's fear, for in the first year of her marriage, she was pregnant.

My Father was a provider, a supplier of a necessity – food. Therefore, he was exempt from serving his country. He faced his own frontline on a daily basis with the possibility of conflict, damage to his premises or internment. After all, this had happened to many of his compatriots. His fellow countrymen had been faced with bricks and smashed shop windows.

Daddy joined the Home Guard.

My Mother, tiny and apprehensive, gave her trust to Dr. Mac and together they delivered me into an uncertain world.

'Poor love...'

~

I remember little of the first years of my life. I know there was an Air-raid Shelter in our back garden. My Mother had a very definite procedure when the sirens could be heard. A rug was kept on my Parents' bed. My Mother would roll me within it, squirming, whimpering and half asleep, before spiriting me away to safety. I can see, in my mind's eye, my Father and Grandpa standing at the garden gate, gazing at the rosy red lights of Hull as it burned. I was safe....

'Mam always knew when it was one of ours – "He'll get the buggers", she'd say...'

Gran and Grandpa spent much time with us. Gran was a daily visitor and Grandpa, a Cargo Supervisor, came when he could. The arrangement was useful. My Father rested assured that help at home was at hand. He unwound with a pint at the Red Lion. All would be Blackout by then and the leafy lanes of Anlaby shrouded in murk and mist with only chinks of light visible from a careless torch.

The Red Lion was a thatched Pub in the centre of the village. I remember overhearing scraps of conversation about its interior which seemed to be small and cosy. All who had a penchant for the sharing of intimate secrets, facts, figures and data propped up the bar or found a shady corner to share the doings of business or farming acumen. The War and its overtones must have flooded the contemplation and notions of all. This is pure supposition: the projections of me the adult. Then, I was only five years old, or thereabouts.

The Church was situated on Wilson Street. It nestled between weaving, twisting lanes and pathways. There, I was Christened. Gran would trundle me along to see Weddings. The dresses, presumably scrambled together with Wartime dearth and deficiency were, to me, sumptuous pictures of fairytale mystique.

Miss Johnson's grocery store was next to the Toc H. I liked the word Toc although never really knew what the Toc H was. Much more tempting and enticing was Miss Johnson and her dim, shelf-filled shop. The wooden counter dominated and behind it Miss Johnson presided over the doling out of rations, cutting of coupons and measuring of sweets: dolly mixtures, aniseed balls, liquorice allsorts and barley sugar. Giant jars, glass and filled with goodies, lined the shelves and it was difficult to make up your mind. Miss Johnson was stout, untiring and dogged in strategy. She would not be messed about. Clad in pristine white apron which reached the floor, she would weigh her sweeties prudently, decanting them, jangling, into cone-shaped paper bags: ever watchful for the odd gobstopper which could escape her red, work-worn hands and drop to the floor where Foxy, her vigilant terrier, would pounce.

'Did she sell bullets? We always had bullets in Hartlepool...'

She did have a slab of toffee which she broke up with a hammer.

On sweltering Summer days, the air was pervaded with the pungent, acrid smell from Rawsons, the pig breeder's domain.

'Pig shit, eh?'

Thank you, Ronnie. I was trying to be polite. The odour was almost as penetrating and intrusive as Hull's Fish Dock on a foggy day. As the years rolled by, the stink of Fish Meal and the beloved Docks meant home to me. The whiff and the reek was akin to pulling on a comfy, worn-out slipper.

A Blacksmith resided on the corner of Lowfield Road.

'Under a spreading chestnut tree, the village smithy stands...' that's Longfellow, you know....Mmn...I'm a short fellow!'

His workshop drew me like a magnet. Watching him at work and taking in the tenor of his surroundings filled me with anticipation, excitement and gladness. The quintessential remembrance was the scent of horses: musky, patent and steadfast. That unmistakeable air has remained with me all my life. My love of horses has never diminished.

'What about Daisy and Violet?'

Ah, you remembered Ronnie....

There was a huge meadow at the rear of the Lowfield Road houses. It was filled with wild flowers and rich grasses.

This field, laden with buttercups, the delicate blue cuckoo flower and celandines, became for me and my playmates a source, a spring for adventure, exploit and escapade.

It was also the grazing ground for Shire Horses, Daisy and Violet. Mother and Daughter, they roamed at will. I remember Violet the foal and watched engrossed as she grew, her glossy coat turning from a dusky brown into the jet black of her Mother's. From time to time, both would hang their heads over the fence at the bottom of my garden and I would just be able to reach the velvet muzzle of each.

Daisy and Violet visited the Blacksmith. I would nag Grandpa to go and see! If I was lucky, the Blacksmith would hoist me on to Daisy's vast, broad back, my short legs hardly able to straddle. Grasping and hanging on to handfuls of Daisy's mane, I would ride all the way home, so high that I could look over gardens, roofs and the branches of trees. It was the pinnacle of my childhood delight; little did I know then that horses, my gentle, noble beings, would become the focus, highlight and hub of my formative years.

~

Susie & Rattler

Our best-loved and immediate neighbours were the Wheldons. The Family consisted of Mrs. Wellie (much easier to say than Wheldon), her husband and children: Sydney, Gordon (Gordie to me) Terry, and Rita. Mrs. Wellie nicknamed her daughter Rattler for Rita was noisy. She could be heard slamming doors, banging drawers and bolting down the stairs two-at-a-time. The eldest son was Sydney and a pilot. He brought home our very first banana!

I think it would be fair to say that I spent most of my early life at the Wellies' house. Mrs. Wellie made the most delicious scones, known to her as Rakkies, and kept chickens in the back garden. She had names for all: Shassy, Beryl, Jennifer and some I just cannot remember…oh yes, Beattie…

Neighbours on the other side, the Holmes', were not so celebrated or well-liked. According to my mother, Mrs. H. was a nasty piece of work. It was many years into the future when my Mother elaborated on what seemed to have been a particularly disagreeable encounter. Apparently, my poor Mother had been of ungainly proportions during her pregnancy and the malicious dweller next door had remarked "It's going to be a real fat little German"!

'What a cow!'

Thank you Ronnie, my sentiments exactly. Needless to say, from then on the rot had set in and being on speaking terms with "those people" was out of the question and I grew up to accept that The Holmes', including their innocent daughter Anna, were very much out of bounds. This was tricky for our ten foots backed on to each other and so for my Parents it was an ongoing nuisance to be within sight of the enemy and often difficult to avoid eyes meeting inadvertently.

'Oh yes, driveways could measure ten feet then...'

Mrs. H. had auburn hair, ginger as my Mother would have it, so, subsequently, every person she encountered, who had the misfortune to possess similar colouring, would be tarred with the same brush as Mrs. H.

Further along our side of Lowfield Road lived Mr. & Miss Hyde. They were vague, obscure figures and kept themselves very much to themselves.

'Maybe because they were Mr. and Miss....er...you know...'

No, Ronnie, I don't know – what are you implying? When I was little, it never occurred to anyone to question their way of life. I remember them smiling and nodding as I passed with my doll's pram.

'Hmn, thereby hangs a tale...'

Mr. Kirkwood, the coal merchant, resided on our corner of Voases Lane. Opposite, Frank Armstrong, an Artist and Portrait Painter, lived. His son, Warwick, was a playmate of mine.

'Playmate? Yes, I can imagine...'

Well don't Ronnie. We were nearly five or six years old at the time. As a matter of fact, in due course, my parents approached Mr. Armstrong with a commission to paint me in oils. Don't say a word Ronnie!

I remember sitting still for what seemed an eternity; in a mustard Moygashel linen dress which I disliked intensely. I discovered much later that this material was really high end and produced in a small Northern Irish village of Moygashel, County Tyrone, for Dior no less!

'Posh!'

The portrait now hangs in the hallway. I've been told that Mr.Armstrong did capture the essence of something quite unusual in such a young participant.

'The eyes are the window of the soul – an old soul looking out, perhaps?'

The last house to be built on Lowfield Road belonged to the Sawdons.

Mr. Sawdon was very tall and smiley. Whenever he saw me tottering by wearing my Mother's high-heeled shoes he would wave and call "Hello, blue eyes!"

Dressing up and playing shops was a very favourite pastime. I would spend many hours voiding my Mother's chest of drawers and unveiling the contents, mostly items of lingerie, on the bed. I would be shop assistant and Gran, very obligingly, a long-suffering customer.

"Good afternoon, may I help you?" Then there would be a lengthy discussion about colour preference or availability of the chosen garment. Sometimes, the shop would sell groceries, so I went all out to reproduce a very detailed character study of Miss Johnson. I would weigh dried peas – a useful substitute for aniseed balls – into cones of newspaper. Grandpa would be roped in on paper-bag detail.

'God, the patience of Job....you know... I think I'd have been a good Grandpa...'

Travelling by bus was always an exciting adventure. I paid great attention to bus conductors, their ticket machine and pressing the bell for stops. So, the stairway at home became my upper and lower deck. Gran and Grandpa would take their stair seats, very cramped and uncomfortable, while I issued tickets with the help of a pair of scissors and pieces of cardboard. Improvisation ran riot and I was totally absorbed in a land of make-believe, especially when Grandpa was able to make a very convincing bus engine noise and acquired a piercing bicycle bell for stops.

Gran and Grandpa played a very significant part in my life. Their home was a snug adventure playground and I loved being there. The back garden was long and large. There, Grandpa grew his vegetables: peas, beans, potatoes and carrots. A further delight was the fruit bushes. In the hot Summer sun they would groan under their heavy load of raspberries, red and black currants and loganberries. My fingers would turn pink and my tongue blue with constant tasting of berry and bramble. In those days Summer was Summer and Winter was Winter. One awoke knowing that the sun would shine or the snow would snow.

Grandpa

The foremost garden faced the main road, the Anlaby road; there grew Grandpa's collection of Roses. I would help as he cut Gran's favourites for the front room. Grandpa had long fingers. His nails were neat. I remember sitting, engrossed, while he pared them with a penknife. Often, that would be in the evening, after tea. Mealtimes, in those days, consisted of three substantial spreads: breakfast, dinner (at lunchtime in the North), high tea and sometimes supper. It was not unusual to see Grandpa tuck into bread n' cheese before bed. Perhaps one of my dearest memories would be sitting on Grandpa's knee listening to a nonsense song, totally ridiculous sounding words accompanied by an equally silly, zany and farcical tune:

"Mootin-mah,
Wingy-wah
Culliberri-wongi
Wingi-wah...."

'Hell's teeth, I don't believe it!'

Perhaps that's why I appreciate your daftness so much Ronnie. I had a good grounding!

Before home time, I would be allowed to play horses on the arm of a very solid, sturdy couch. This was an ancient, black, horsehair sofa with enormous appendages which served very well as a saddle for an excited six year old.

'I'm glad I didn't know all this before I married you! How did you know it was horsehair, Alice?'

Because little bits of wiry stuff would stick through and prickle my legs so I asked Grandpa what it was.

'Dear God!'

Daddy would appear soon to collect me and it would be time to go home.

I loved my Gran and Grandpa. Gran was special. She spent much time at Lowfield Road and I could never visualise life without her. She was a stalwart, dependable, tried-and-true presence and supreme story-teller. Here began my life-long love of books. I struggled through several Childhood illnesses. Measles seemed to be the worst. Dr. Mac visited daily and the front room was given over to my nursing. The curtains were drawn and a bed was heaved down from above. In feeble state I kept hearing "delirious" but then was wafted away into a dream world where strange beings lived. I was frightened. Gran would sit beside me.

As the stories began I would reach up and my feverish fingers would rest beneath her chin. It was cool there.

'Oh darling....'

A rich and enchanting memory of my Gran days or rather, evenings, was when my Mother and Father were dressing for Grand Balls.

'Whose Grand Balls?'

I'll ignore that, Ronnie. These probably came under the nom de plume of Master Butchers, Master Bakers or Master Fish Merchants. They were very notable events and gear was for nothing short of grandee occasions.

My Mother had a skilful Dressmaker by the name of Mrs. Sizer. Apt title, for, as I recall, the lady was of commodious expanse. She wore plunging necklines and it wasn't until she came to rest on her fitting-stool that I was able to peep down and observe at close quarters huge mounds of flesh which at the time seemed a mysterious and somewhat unwieldy load to haul around. Judging by her difficulty in manoeuvring these anatomical bits, her whole carriage seemed dicey when picking her way through paper patterns, tape measures and pins. She did not steer a true course.

'That's an evil description...'

Mrs. Sizer created glorious gowns for my Mother and my Mother was glorious when wearing them. Tulle was fashionable then and fairytale splendour encircled my beautiful Mother with yard upon yard of its diaphanous folds. An abiding, adored memory was of a full-skirted, floor-length black concoction. Its minute waist was emphasised by a corsage of white flowers, matched only by the snowy-flowered snood which encompassed my Mother's chignon at the nape of her neck. The whole was complemented by white kid gloves. She was magical. Gran and I watched as this Cinderella awaited her coach.

'That's a bit over the top, Alice...(Alice was a baffling diminutive used by Ronnie on manifold occasions)*...now what about your Father?'*

Well, he was also a sight to behold. He would have a tail-coat and starched cravat. All accompanied by white silk scarf and patent black shiny shoes. When all was assembled, he would then fill his silver cigarette case with untipped Senior Service. Gran told me that they were accomplished dancers and others would watch as they moved effortlessly over the floor.

Then it was bedtime and I would fall asleep remembering and anticipating the finding of after-dinner Petit-Fours that my Mother would have secreted in her evening bag.

~

Auntie Anne and Uncle Erbie were regular visitors.

'Who were they?'

Old friends of my parents. I liked them. Uncle Erbie – his real name was Herbert – was a plump, good-humoured, jolly man. Now he really was a genial, patient soul, for he would let me play hairdressers, using his pate as a model. I would stand on a stool behind his chair and ask him to describe the style he preferred. Auntie Anne would then produce a tail comb from her capacious handbag and I would give Uncle Erbie a centre parting, then attempt to curl the side strands. Apparently, I could call to mind hairdressing jargon quite expertly.

'What was the state of Erbie's head?'

Well, it did look a bit pulled about but he never stopped smiling and never complained.

'The people you have persecuted....'

Oh give over. The visits of Auntie Anne and Uncle Erbie were always good. I suspect Gran and Grandpa could be a little jealous....they always seemed somewhat tight-lipped when praise was being meted out.

Auntie Anne was rather peculiar to look at. Her bottom lip fascinated me. It seemed to droop. I thought it must be rather difficult to position when putting on lipstick. Having said that, she never seemed to miss. Auntie Anne was as indulgent and serene as Uncle Erbie. She was always there to help me do up my gaiters.

'Your what??!'

I wore gaiters instead of boots in Winter. Admittedly, they were something of an encumbrance. Made of leather, the side buttons had to be secured with the help of a button-hook, so there was much wriggling and giggling before the process was finished. They were accessory to a fake fur coat which met with widespread admiration on momentous occasions.

'I'm speechless!'

My Father was known to many in the world of business. In particular, he was acquainted with the Head Chef of Hull's Royal Station Hotel. So, for a special outing, I would be taken, clad in gaiters and fur, to a very regal Dining Room there.

'You couldn't make it up! And there was me in Hartlepool with a jam sandwich! Go on, Alice, what did you have? I mean, bearing in mind that this was Wartime!'

I had a Peach Melba!

At this point, I think Ronnie's remarks would be unprintable.

~

My Mother, as with many Mothers at that time, had a daily routine. She house-worked in the mornings. After setting both coal fires, there would be dusting and vacuuming to be done. This happened during the first half of every day. Once chores were completed and dinner had been served, it would be time for washing: often a swift operation at the kitchen sink and referred to by my Mother as "a lick and a promise". There followed a change of clothes: an afternoon dress, skirt or jumper. Next, it was time for shopping in the village. Fresh provisions were bought daily. These spins were happy occasions for me, but Mammy (much more common at that time than Mummy) was often preoccupied and thoughtful. She was, however, animated when meeting neighbours and friends. Mammy was strict when it came to dressing: I was never allowed to choose. I was told which dress I would be wearing.

'Had you started school then?'

No, but I was about to. I cannot remember being prepared for this substantial change which was going to take place. When the inevitable happened, I was deeply shocked at being separated from my Mother and the familiar trappings of home. I do recall my Mother recounting an experience she had had at one of the Schools which was being considered.

Tranby Croft Private School was lodged in an imposing house set in its own grounds which consisted of woodland and manicured gardens.

'Am I in for a bit of history here?'

Brace yourself Ronnie. The house was famous for the

baccarat scandal, also known as the Tranby Croft Affair of the late 19th Century, which was said to involve Edward, Prince of Wales. Baron William Gordon-Cumming apparently cheated during illegal card games.

The Wilson family, who owned the largest shipping company in the world, lived there. The building was a large Grade II listed Victorian country pile and estate at Anlaby.

Rita, from next door, would often take me on a "hike" as she called it. We would explore the house grounds and miniature lake. In later years, I would imagine it as Thornfield Hall and Mr. Rochester.

'Typical!'

After World War II the house was used by a School for Girls and chosen by many well-heeled, social-climbing parents for their offspring. My Mother was granted an interview with the then Headmistress, a Miss Jefferson, in the hopes that I would be given a place. Imagine how crestfallen she must have been when this formidable woman announced: "I'm afraid, Mrs. Uebel, we do not accept the daughters of Tradesmen here".

'What a bitch!'

My Mother was loving but unpredictable. Her behaviour could be very threatening. She was a proud Mother – proud of me, certainly. I was exquisitely, uniquely dressed and my golden curls were nurtured and treated with the utmost care. Consideration for the feelings of others and good manners were of paramount importance to Mammy.

'There's a but coming along....'

I was afraid of her. To this day, I do not know how I transgressed or offended her in those early times, but I must have done.

"What were you doing with Warwick and June? In the field?" She would accuse after I had been brought in from playing. (June was a friend the same age as me and we would spend our days together playing with dolls. She lived further along Lowfield Road and the garden boasted a mature Laburnum blossom tree. We would hold tea parties under its leafy canopy. June had a very beautiful doll, a baby doll called Gwennie. June was generous and quite content to share hugs with Gwennie. (Friend Warwick absented himself on those occasions!)

"I wasn't doing anything...."

I will never be able to erase the shock. The shock of being pinned against the kitchen wall and....

'Did she hit you?'

Yes, but her face was terrible. It seemed to twist and become something else, something that wasn't Mammy. I felt the blows, the shocking impact, but I will never forget her face at those times. It was as if she purposefully contorted her expression to terrify. It was as if she hated me at that moment and suddenly, her beautiful features became that of another being. Surely, my face must have been etched with fear. How can a Parent ever forget that? Knowing you have hurt a child – your own child...

Sometimes, Mammy would hide and I wouldn't be able to find her. That was terror of a different kind. Once, when I didn't know where she was, I ran to Mrs. Wellie, scared and tearful. While waiting in the front room, I saw my Mother passing the window outside. She looked at me and transformed her face once more into something savage. Mrs. Wellie must have pacified her. I was not touched that day.

"You're asking for a good hiding" or "I'll jowl your head against the wall" were phrases commonly used. I still don't know what "jowl" meant. How do you "jowl"?

'Never mind, pet, she may have been unhappy. Mam was unhappy too but it didn't stop her laying into me... where was Charlie when all this was going on?'

At work, I suppose. I cannot recall him being there. I cannot recall Gran being there either.

It can never be right to strike a child. I was afraid of my Mother for the rest of my life: there was fear to make decisions without her approval, fear to venture far from home, fear of her opinions knowing that on occasion they would be different from mine. Fear of the guilt that was always with me. There was a time when I feared that Mammy may die before me. Then what would I do?

Well – I met you, Ronnie.....

Jessica was beautiful, Jessica could be very kind, Jessica was benevolent, Jessica was lonely, unhappy and sometimes cruel, but Jessica was my Mother and there was love for her....

'Did Charlie know that your Mother was unhappy?'

I think he did. There were rows. There was shouting and harsh tones. My Daddy was a talented man. He had wished to become an Architect, but Grandfather Uebel insisted that he worked in the business. It was common in those days. The youngest in the family, he was reared by a Nanny to whom he was devoted. Suddenly, when Charlie was older, she, presumably, was sacked – no longer required. Charlie was devastated.

When Christian Uebel died, Charlie inherited the enterprise. Grandmother Sophia thereby laid down the law and pressed Charlie to take his eldest Sister, my Aunt Annie, into partnership.

'Bugger...'

Yes, Ronnie, his independence went overnight. Annie controlled and in no time the establishment was supporting four households: Sister Laura, Aunts Elsie and Annie and ours. Needless to say, my Mother was furious. As I understood it, there were occasions when Sisters' welfare took precedence over that of Charlie's Wife and Daughter.

'Talk about driving a wedge...'

I think it was more than a wedge, but this is pure speculation; I guessed that there was much more cause for unrest in my Parents' relationship...

All the while, Daddy was a lovely man. Yes, handsome, but also funny and warm-hearted. He was popular with friends and contemporaries for his sense of humour and cordial disposition shone. Most important of all, I did not realise how much he loved me.

'But you do now, petal, and that means everything...'

I remember snuggling into his neck when I was little. I can still visualise his neck of all things. As I sat in the back of the car I would look at how his hair curled over his collar and think how nice it looked. I have never forgotten...

'You've never looked at my neck like that – and I always keep it clean...!'

I would not presume to know what troubles my Mother and Father had but I still feel the effect of bickering and unrest which permeated my childish world at the time. All was not well.

I recollect a heated moment at my Mother's bedside when there was shouting going on. My Father was holding me in his arms as he hissed "Well, you're not having this!" I suppose the "this" was me.

'Darling, you could never be a "this'"- er – you might have been a "that"! '

A drama followed this exchange. My Mother parcelled me off to Gran and Grandpa's. Desperate-sounding arguments then began there. After a few hours, who should appear on the doorstep but my Auntie Annie! Whispered, urgent discussion ensued. After, without more ado, I was parcelled off once more – home!

'Jessica had obviously left him but she was got at. Divorce was not on the cards in those days...'

Things settled.

Daddy made sure I visited his family, especially at Christmas. Usually, it was for a small gathering at Auntie Laura's house. I don't remember my Mother ever coming along, so I came to understand that relations between Laura and Jessica were somewhat fraught. I enjoyed these meetings and everyone seemed to like me. These were outings and I liked outings! It's a shame, Ronnie, that you did not meet my Father. You would both have had much in common. He was a Gardener and also, of course, very knowledgeable about food. You'd have got on like a house on fire.

'I like Charlie...but I like Jessica...why was she not smiling on her chic wedding photographs?...Most Brides are radiant...Jessica was sad....hmn...'

Daddy created a picturesque garden at Lowfield Road. Artistic, like him, it was filled with flower surprises around every corner. French windows at the rear of the house opened out on to a rockery. The stones were large and pink in colour. Alpines, within the gaps, filled the space with hue and texture. If I was lucky, I could glimpse a shy toad venture forth.

A low York stone wall formed a boundary before a lawn which made up the middle play area. There was a swing! At the bottom of the garden Daddy had planted a small apple orchard. There grew the tastiest apples ever! Another swing hung from the tallest branch of the tallest tree....and it was my secret place...my refuge, haven and retreat.

I almost forgot to mention...

Scotti was my Mother and Father's first pet. I do not remember him because I was "a babe in arms" Mammy said. Scotti was a Scottish Terrier.

'Surprise, surprise, Alice...'

The village had its own Road-Sweeper. The story goes that Scotti took a marked fancy to this lady and kept following her, doggedly, all the way home.

The culmination of this tale being that my Father, fed up with repeatedly tracking, retrieving and restoring Scotti to No. 5, bestowed him as a gift to this worthy woman. Scotti took up his new position without a backward glance!

Scotti was the first of many animal companions. Here, I inherited my Parents' deep love for all creatures great and small. Many would follow...

FOXDALE

1944

'You can never be overdressed or over educated'

(Oscar Wilde)

Foxdale was a Kindergarten in the neighbourhood of Kirk Ella, a few miles from Anlaby and several miles from Hull. Kirk Ella was up market. Every city has a Kirk Ella: a vicinity, an environs to where some may say the superior or more wealthy members of society would gravitate.

'You mean where the nobs hang out?'

Ronnie, no one could have summed it up in more succinct terms than you! Unfortunately, being wealthy did not always sit comfortably with rank.

'You're talking about snobbery!'

Perhaps I am. There was certainly a false and pretentious air of elitism.

I suppose I can compare such Yorkshire suburbs to Hampstead, Knightsbridge or Mayfair in London.

'I'm remembering The Bishop's Avenue in Hampstead... often gross!'

Originally, Kirk Ella and West Ella were small, very seductive and appealing settlements in the rural areas of Hull. Lattice-work windowed cottages opened their carefully-tended gardens on to illustrious and fetching avenues and walkways. All were well preserved over time and houses were occupied by Fish Merchants, Trawler Owners and august Directors of Commerce. There was a smattering of Professional folk: the odd Solicitor or Doctor. And – if you happened to reside on the Kemp Road, Swanland, then you were really rubbing shoulders with the echelons of society!

Nevertheless, mine was a charmed childhood. I grew up within sniffing distance of these opulent confines, these auspicious surroundings and my Mother was not oblivious to the promise such a scenario could foster or nurture.

'So Jessica wiped the memory of the odious Miss Jefferson from her mind?'

Oh yes, Ronnie, I came to learn that Mammy was not backwards in coming forwards. She didn't suffer fools. So, there were other fish to fry.

The Headmistress of Foxdale, the genteel Miss Sugden, ran her Primary School on the ground floor of a large private house in Kirk Ella.

Presumably, she lived on the first floor which was also home to her elderly Mother. The residence was bay-fronted, detached and spacious.

'It needed to be with plundering, marauding youngsters roaming around!'

The back and front rooms were given over to classes. Small wooden desks...

'Oh God, it takes me back to Miss Robinson, who made me the flower monitor...'

Yes, my darling, I remember that story...!

As I was saying, small wooden desks furnished the room and we were kept warm by yet another coal fire.

'No 'elth and safety in those days...bliss...'

No provision was made for food, but we were provided with small bottles of milk at half-time.

'I really looked forward to that in Hartlepool. We didn't get much of it at home.'

Then, weather permitting. we would be let loose on a very expansive back garden, well fenced in but without too many plants for voracious children to...

'Destroy...?'

Thank you, Ronnie.

My first morning at School is indelibly printed upon my memory. Now into old age, I look back on that time as one of the first traumatic episodes in my life.

The morning was quite ordinary. My Mother, dressed as usual with unerring taste, not a hint of over-dressing, was assembling my school uniform. What was that? Once all was marshalled together, I heard the words: "You're going to School today".

I was five and dumped brusquely and dumbfounded in the Front Classroom at Foxdale. The kindly Miss Sugden attempted to comfort but there followed such a torrent of anguish that no person, other than my Mother, could have quelled. It continued throughout the morning. I had been deserted and abandoned by her without a hint of explanation. The fear beggared description. I had never been separated from either of my Parents before that day. In the melee that followed, another Teacher tried to pacify and partly succeeded. I came to learn that this young, raven-haired mistress was Olive Airey, a gentle and compassionate saviour.

I made friends easily and Foxdale School became a preserve of enlightenment, understanding and learning. My Teachers, Miss Airey and another, Marjorie Brier, were both youthful and gifted with inspirational aptitude.

Miss Sugden reserved the end of the afternoons for story time. Needless to say, it became my favourite interlude of the day. I loved listening to the words, the phrases and the imaginary pictures they created. I had learned to read very rapidly. I was eager to know the stories for myself, to savour them and delve into a world of fantasy and image.

'My best poem was Abou Ben Adhem (may your tribe increase)!'

Who wrote that, Ronnie?

'Leigh Hunt. There you are, Alice, you learn something every day!'

Miss Sugden was a gifted reader. She was also interesting to look at while reading. Her voice was mellow, but I noticed that she did not have much saliva.

'Spit...'

Er, yes Ronnie. So, small particles of er...spit...would collect in the corners of her mouth until she stopped reading, momentarily, to clear them with a lick. Consequently, her mouth was dry making her speech a little thick at times. Also, Miss Sugden was usually covered in chalk. Her skirt and jumper would show a day's work of chalk. Her fingers, parched and wrinkled, made a crisp, rustling sound as she turned the pages. Miss Sugden was very exact and particular about showing us how to turn the pages of a book correctly – no moistening the edges, pulling the leaves roughly or bending the spine. She reminded us that a book should always be treated with respect, taking into account others who may wish to read after. Most memorable of all, Miss Sugden would hold the book to her nose and then remark on the unmistakeable scent of that book and had we noticed how distinctive its aroma was?

Miss Sugden was distinguished. She was memorable. She was a Lady.

I discovered that I was clever. Each subject appealed to me and I had a thirst for knowledge, especially for English and Literature. Miss Brier must have noticed potential, a capability and flair for the spoken word.

'Didn't she mention this to your Mother?'

Oh yes, in fact she went as far as to suggest that Mammy allow me to have Elocution lessons with her.

'Old-fashioned word nowadays... I reckon Jessica saw the green light to push a bit.'

I admit it was likely that her ambition for my future began with Marjorie Brier.

'I went to tap classes because Mrs. Simpson gave me a few free lessons when I did her shopping for her.'

My Mother had already tried to boost enthusiasm for a ballet class, but I was bored rigid and somewhat inept, so she gave that up as a bad job. In due course, lessons with Miss Brier were planned and thereby a stamp was put on my future career, although no one knew it at the time.

Miss Brier lived on the Boothferry Road, Hessle, close to Anlaby. Lessons took place in the front room. She lived with her Mother and Sister: shadowy figures who kept a low profile. The Teaching room was somewhat cramped for an ancient, timeworn, upright piano presided gloomily over all movement and animation. Diffused and wafting over all was the mordant, sour smell of cat...

'Pee!'

Thank you, Ronnie.

Yes, the smell was somewhat invasive. Marjorie referred time and oft to "her pussy". Ronnie, be quiet!

Daddy would drive me, armed with a new, pristine exercise book, to my lessons.

Miss Brier kept dilapidated folders which contained various Speech exercises copied out on scraps of paper: Voice Production, Projection, Vowels, Consonants,

Articulation and Agility. She called this Theory. It sounded very important at the time. I came to realise just how significant it was. Other folders, equally olden, embraced Poetry collections. Over time, I came to recognise Prose and the writings of numerous Playwrights, including Shakespeare and the Bible.

I remember finding the sight of Marjorie's severely-bitten nails, as she thumbed through her papers, somewhat disturbing and wondered what she did with the bits after she'd bitten them. Childish, puzzling thoughts...they remained bitten down to the quick for evermore.

'Stress, poor lass...we never know what burdens others carry...'

The lessons were well prepared. First, Theory and the drilling of exercises. No stone was left unturned until mouth shapes, accuracy in Consonant shaping and Vocal Tone were proficient; adept. In conclusion, I was asked to choose a piece of Poetry from a given selection. I remember vividly Walter de la Mare's 'My Shadow', 'Cats' by Eleanor Farjeon and 'From a Railway Carriage' by Robert Louis Stevenson.

'Ahh....'

I learned the technique of speaking Poetry: where to pause and inflect. I never forgot and eventually that technique became a spontaneous, natural thing for the rest of my Professional life.

My Elocution book played a weighty part in Homework tasks: copying neatly my exercises and Poetry choice into it, trying to avoid smudges and mistakes. I loved taking great pride in attempting to imitate my Grandpa's italic style.

'Well, darling, there was the training that was to last you all your life – I believe that Marjorie Brier was meant to be.'

Mammy also realised my potential. She acted upon instinct and placed me in a situation where it could be recognised and nourished. I was given the opportunity, Ronnie. I was given the chance. I was my Mother's Daughter. She wanted me to succeed. She loved me.

Foxdale introduced me to a learning curve in more ways than one. I had made a friend, a close friend in Brenda. We seemed to like each other. Brenda's Father had a chain of fruit and vegetable shops and to all intents and purposes was well off.

Brenda and I frequented each other's houses on a regular basis. Our Parental excursions often took us to the swimming baths or cinema. We were firm friends.

I was in for a rude awakening. One Monday morning, Brenda refused to speak to me. This was for no apparent reason. I was cut out. Her cronies took their cue from Brenda and adopted the same attitude. Being ostracized by one friend is one thing, but being banished or put into exile by several other members of the class, is truly a drear and dreadful fate.

'Poor little thing – what were the cruel little shits up to?'

That's not all. A few days later, Brenda's Mother invited me to tea. Brenda behaved quite normally: we were forever friends once more. Euphoria! The following day, at School, my alleged friend reverted to her spiteful self and I was sent once more to Coventry! Not, however, before she announced: "I can't talk to you today anyway. Mummy's coming for me in the new Riley!"

'I hope you told her where to put the new Riley!'

No, I didn't. I was too upset. But – I didn't cry. I waited until I got home and then I cried. Mammy said, "Well what did you do to her first?" which wasn't exactly comforting. After she had heard the full story, Mammy was cross. She gave me a hug and dried my tears. Then, we went to Miss Johnson's for a jug of ice cream.

I went on to make a new friend, Ann, after that and she remained faithful and true until, sadly, she died at a very young age. I have missed her.

'How long did you stay at the lovely Foxdale?'

Until I was eleven, but much water was to go under the bridge before then.

Foxdale, for me, was a blessing. I left Miss Sugden's when I was at the top of my class in all subjects. Foxdale gave me a foundation. Foxdale braced and fortified me for what was to follow.

'If Jessica was here today, I think she would agree that the obnoxious, offensive Miss Jefferson did you a favour!'

MR PALMER'S

1945

'I'd rather have a goddam horse. A horse is, at least HUMAN, for God's Sake'

(J.D. Salinger – 'The Catcher in the Rye')

Frank Palmer's Riding School was in Cottingham or, rather, situated on Harland Way a road leading into Cottingham, East Yorkshire. Cottingham was known then as the largest village in the country. In later years, it became a sweeping suburb of Hull, just as the nearby Anlaby had done.

I was six when my parents, plagued with requests for a pony, thought it would be a good idea for me to have riding lessons.

'Why am I put in mind of Thelwell cartoons? Fat little girls on fat little ponies!'

Because, Ronnie, that is the way your mind works!

The large double-fronted, detached house which belonged to Frank Palmer and his wife Phil, stood back from the road. The driveway curled around the perimeter of the house and made its way to stables huddled a short distance away at the far end of a small paddock. It was a little girl's land of dreams...I think back....

As the car turned into the stable-yard, a stocky tweed-jacketed fellow came towards me. "Hello Susie," he greeted, "come and meet Ted and Bessie". Ted was introduced as Mr. Palmer's groom. He, too, was tweed-jacketed and as he smiled down at me, I noticed a missing tooth. He wore a time-worn, age-old cap, pulled down over one eye, jodhpurs and very dirty, leather knee-high boots.

I had jodhpurs. They took almost as long as gaiters to put on. The smell of straw and seasoned, balmy fragrance of horses hung in the air and I was enraptured.

"We keep the saddles in 'ere" said Ted. I found myself in the doorway of the Tack Room. I didn't know it was a Tack Room then. My eye roved over pegs holding bridles, saddles, martingales...

'Now who's riding a high horse!'

I went on to find out that they were straps fastened on to the bridle noseband to stop a horse rearing.

'Were you scared sweetheart?'

Oh no, being afraid never entered my head. I was just swept away with excitement. I was truly happy.

"Now, Susie, what do you think of Bessie?" said Ted. There, before me, a stable door was open. Beyond, I could see a stocky, squat Shetland pony.

"Talk to her, if you like...stroke her", joined Mr. Palmer. Then, he led Bessie out into the yard. She studied me. As I looked deep into her eyes, Ted adjusted her wee saddle. "Let's try that for size", said he. I was hoisted on to Bessie's back. I smiled as I had never smiled before.

'Oh, Susie, how I know Susie...'

Ronnie, it was such a precious moment and I have never forgotten it.

'Well, one thing's for sure, Jessica and Charlie must have been thrilled...'

Yes, they were, I could tell.

That evening, as the sun began to dim the stable-yard, I had my first riding lesson – how to hold the reins keeping my tiny hands still, how to sit in the saddle with straight back and knees tightly clutching Bessie's spherical girth. "Grip tight," said Mr. Palmer, "that helps her to know which way you want her to go and don't ever yank her mouth on those reins. Mouths on ponies are easily hurt if you yank".

'Even after all these years, you can remember Frank Palmer's words!'

They became an intrinsic, fundamental part of my riding culture.

So began the next eight years of equine ecstasy. The memory of them has lingered throughout my life and my love of horses has remained as an unforgettable legacy of those cherished years. Grandpa became chaperon extraordinaire, many a time serenading me with "If you knew Susie…like I know Susie.." on the way home.

'That man was a saint…'

True, Ronnie, but he loved me and I loved being with him. He was patience personified. He did seem to enjoy the airings to Cottingham and the meandering bus route through village and hamlet. Mammy or Gran would have concocted some tasty snack and so armed we would board the double-decker at Anlaby square.

I bring to mind so clearly those lazy, Summer days: the scent of stable, hay and mucking-out, the freshly-mown meadow and paddock, the creak of saddles and the bliss of feeling so special, so favoured. Now, an old lady, I look back with gratitude. I was sheltered. I was loved. I was carefree…

'While a faraway War was raging…'

Yes, my love, I lived at the end of the Rainbow….

Ted became surrogate Grandfather while the real one took a breather. Once he was satisfied that Susie was not going to end up on the deck, he promoted me to leading rein while he sat way up high on his mighty chestnut Hunter. A long rein was attached to Bessie's bridle so enabling me to trot alongside where Ted could keep an ever watchful eye on my riding prowess.

Soon, I was set free, free to walk, trot and gallop.

'Golden curls catching the wind, no doubt...I would have loved to know you then....'

It was a shining, halcyon time, Ronnie.

There followed other ponies. Brandy, a very beautiful black pony who had a penchant for throwing me off. Mr. Palmer, Ted and my poor Parents must have watched in horror as I was repeatedly, unceremoniously, dethroned and outsted on to the auspicious grass showing-enclosure at Gymkhanas.

Susie & Brandy

'No wonder you had to have your bloody hips replaced when you were fifty-three!'

"Get back on, Susie! You're all right!" was Mr. Palmer's encouraging shout.

He and Ted were always there to give me a leg-up – worried, I suppose, in case I lost my nerve. I never did, despite Brandy's terrifying bucking on the most unexpected occasions. I became accustomed to the ears going back, lying flat against his head and then – wallop, over I would hurtle. All with no thought to the danger I was in.

It did not transpire until some time later that Brandy had been broken to pull a trap, so whenever other horses or ponies sped up behind or beside, he panicked, saw the red light and deposited his baggage – me – on to the clod.

At the close of the riding days, Grandpa and I would wend our way home, yawning the while as the countryside sped by, before the bus conductor rang the bell and called "Anlaby next!"

"Fancy some chips, love?" enquired Grandpa.

'Go on, tell me about it – my mouth's watering...'

Blacker's fish shop was an esteemed emporium for post-riding chip feasts. "Two three-penn'orths, please", requested Grandpa.

'I can smell those chips now....were they in newspaper?'

Of course. Mrs. Blacker always put lashings of salt and vinegar on after she'd shovelled them into small, boat-shaped bags. Then you got a sheet of newspaper to put round, otherwise the vinegar ran out and trickled down your sleeve.

'Those were the days darling....'

As the years went on, I made many friends at Frank Palmer's Riding School. Friends' memory which has now taken its place in the annals of time: Margaret Anholm who had an astonishing Show Pony called Tit-Bits, lived in a prestigious manor house at Cottingham and introduced me to an irresistible absorption with Enid Blyton and the fictional St. Clare's boarding school! Billy Green, who galloped with me over the meadows and picked up the pieces when Brandy emptied me once more on to the turf. Dearest wickedly handsome Billy, who went on to be a Jockey and was killed in a motor accident at twenty-one. He was reaching the peak of his career.

I cannot forget Malcolm Wiley who taught me how to smoke my first cigarette when we took our ponies to shelter beneath a paddock oak tree.

As he moved into adult life, he developed a phobic fear of Cancer. I was told that he became so entrenched in his obsession that it caused his heart to fail and he died of cardiac arrest at the age of forty.

'We don't forget do we, my love…'

No, Ronnie, they helped to shape my early life, my shining years as you once called them…my lucky, blithe, untroubled years….

NICHOLAS CHARLES UEBEL

1946

'What strange creatures Brothers are!'
(Mary Crawford in 'Mansfield Park'
by Jane Austen)

No one told me that a Brother was coming. No one told me anything. Not even Gran and Grandpa told me.

It was the 27 September 1946 and five days before my seventh Birthday. I was looking forward to it. Perhaps there would be a new book about Ponies....

I remembered my sixth Birthday. I had a party and there was a big box for me to open.

'Go on, you lucky little thing!'

You'll never guess, Ronnie, but inside was a dolly – just like June's Gwennie! She was dressed in a crocheted dress and bonnet and was a real baby doll. Like the ones you often saw in a Draper's shop window.

'Yes, they were pot and fashioned in a very similar ways to real babies... I suppose you called her Gladys or Doris?'

She was Mary and I loved her until she started to grow old and was too old to be cuddled.

'I know the feeling!'

I learned many, many years later that Mary belonged to another little girl who had died during the War. Her

Mother had designed and made the dolly's clothes. She then waited until the time was right to part with her. My Mammy and Daddy had searched high and low for a dolly like Gwennie and when Mary was found, they knew how much she would be loved.

There was to be another party, but for someone else on the 27 September 1946 and I had been invited. The afternoon passed quickly with games and treats. At tea-time, the Birthday boy's Father took my hand and said, "Time to go home, Susan, there is a surprise for you! Daddy will be here soon."

'I wonder if it was, what I think it was, in a big box this time!'

I remember sitting on the settee, very quietly, not speaking. I was wondering ....wondering why I was going home early. It must be something important.

At home, I raced upstairs. Gran told me Mammy was in the front bedroom. "Look over there," said Mammy.

'I couldn't possibly guess....!!'

Ronnie, there was a cot. I had never seen it before. I looked inside and there was – a baby! A baby!

'Well fancy that – I couldn't possibly have known!'

Well, darling, I didn't know. I couldn't speak...a baby!

"He's your baby Brother, Susan," said Mammy. "We're going to call him Nicholas". "Nicholas" I whispered, "my own baby Brother".

I loved him. He was mine, my very own.

That night, Gran and I slept in the big bed in the back bedroom. Nicholas cried all night and Gran and I giggled all night. Nicholas made such a funny sound, a sort of mewing...in the dark....

There had been unrest, a quarrel and fracas on the morning of Nicholas' birth: between my Mother and Gran. I was unaware of argument, so the clash must have taken place out of my earshot. Perhaps I was in the garden...

'So how did you find out?'

My Mother mentioned it long after. It seems that resentment had been brewing. I suspect that two similar controlling forces were fighting for supremacy! The crossed swords had, according to Mammy, brought about Nicholas' somewhat earlier-than-expected arrival.

'Otherwise, he might have made it on your Birthday!'

Perhaps my Mother found Gran's close proximity suffocating. This was a strange dichotomy for Gran performed an integral role in the family format. There was reliance on her devotion, but frustration in the necessity of having to accept it. History repeats itself, for the selfsame dependence manifested itself in my adult relationship with Mammy. Such affrays or altercations were, however, rare for I was wary of my Mother. When pushed to the limit, I let fly, so the ensuing days would result in silent censure. I found myself avoiding confrontation and acquiesced to rule.

'You never acquiesced to my rule!'

Hmn!

I loved Nicky. He smiled and giggled his way through life so it was a constant joy to fetch and carry for him. He was quick to walk and nearly as quick to talk. 'Susan' must have been quite knotty to get your baby tongue around, so I became 'Nuna' and his best friend.

'Knackered Nuna, I guess!'

True, Ronnie. I was at beck and call. Soon, Nicky got the hang of screaming on demand and it was jump to it or face the consequences.

"Now what have you done to him...!" Mammy would accuse as I avoided a well-aimed swipe – often referred to as "a clattering"!

Life at No.5 Lowfield Road did become very different. For seven years my days had been filled with the needs of

Nuna, Nicky & Whisky

the only one – me. I was not jealous of Nicky. I suppose I could have been resentful, but I wasn't. I loved him, fretted about him and cuddled him when his eyes were frightened. His brown eyes could cloud with fear and uncertainty. I never knew why. Did anyone else notice this timidity, this doubt and this bewildered apology in his eyes; almost regret for being there?

'Perhaps you saw the soul looking out...searching...'

I know I protected him. I was Nicky's guard, his champion and his defender. It has always been so.

'What havoc were you causing while all this was going on?'

Gran and Grandpa continued to be central in my life. Both were Cinema-goers and visits to the Priory and Carlton on Anlaby Road were the highlights and thrills of my kingdom. Gran was partial to the Hollywood Musical while Grandpa plumped for Westerns. So, I became quite knowledgeable about both and about Film Stars. The glamour of Fred Astaire, Ginger Rogers, Ann Miller and

Virginia Mayo filled my whimsical thoughts and their visionary, fanciful dance routines were daydreamed about and then mirrored in the back bedroom.

'Did you have a feather boa or a pair of Judy Garland's red slippers?'

Well, no, but Gran always bought me the Film Review Annual every Christmas and I would sit by Mammy's roaring fire whiling away the hours; lost in a reverie of Hollywood swimming pools, Metro Goldwyn Meyer, Paramount and the lush lives of the American idol or luminary.

'I suppose the Western pin-ups were the likes of Alan Ladd, Randolph Scott and Jack Palance – he always played villainous Indians...'

I didn't know what a pin-up was in those days!

'Much more subtle than 'sex-pot'.

It was a long time before I knew what that was!

Ironically, many years later, when I began my years at University, the opening chapter of my Drama Degree Course was entitled The Hollywood Musical! Bliss!

'Did you tell them all about Gran and Grandpa, Busby Berkeley and 'Singing in the Rain'?

Well of course I did. Just shows, nothing is ever wasted.... Nicky continued to grow and his gait progressed from gripping tables and chairs for support, to tentatively grasping my outstretched hand. A peculiar vocabulary began to evolve: the Pottie became 'Julie' for some unknown reason -

'Who the hell was Julie?'

No one ever found out, but I suppose she came from a sound he had heard and felt comfortable with.

His Dummy (not often allowed) was a Dudas.

'Dear God, it gets worse!'

Nicky & Custard

Daddy found the most wonderful yellow bear. Custard was on four wheels and could be pushed around, rather erratically, by Nicky. I don't remember who christened him 'Custard' but it seemed appropriate at the time. I think shin-guards would also have been appropriate for most of us nursed sensational bruises after Custard had been at large.

'It wasn't all sunshine though, was it darling?'

No. Nicky began to have terrifying bouts of Bronchitis. We always knew when an attack was brewing, for he would start to be bothered by repeated coughing. Mammy knew what it was. She would say "Oh it's that peffing cough". It was an apt description: an intermittent, breathy intake of air. At first, it would be hardly noticeable but soon the little boy would fight for breath as his chest began to fill up with mucus. Mammy would pull the two dining-room armchairs together to form a bed and then a steaming kettle would take its place nearby. Mammy and Gran spent hours willing Nicky to recover. Custard and I kept watch....

Much to everyone's consternation, I began to sleep-walk every night.

'Poor little darling...'

Well, I didn't know what was happening but it seems I did some very strange and rather disturbing things...

'You don't say...'

Daddy found me trying to get out of the little bedroom window. I slept in the tiny box-room next to the master bedroom – usual in those Thirties houses. Mammy and Daddy needed to have that window firmly fixed after that. I was calmly steered back to bed, still sleeping and undisturbed.

On another occasion, I was found sitting on the lavatory in my nightie but also wearing my Panama Straw School hat!

'That goes a long way to explaining what I have to deal with...thank God you got out of the habit of wearing your Panama when you slept with me!

Well .....perhaps not....!'

It was decided that perhaps I needed a treat, some sort of diversion. So, a family foray was arranged. We were going to the pictures – to see 'Lassie Come Home'! I couldn't wait! Lassie was just about the most beautiful dog I had ever seen. What no one had bargained for was that disaster after disaster would befall poor Lassie. She ended up being dragged from her home, tied to a cart and dognapped. I was distraught! The whole celebration came to an abrupt finale when I had to be brought out of the cinema in floods of tears!

Mammy's life changed. Nicky's relentless and recurring illness changed all our lives, but Mammy's – perhaps

Daddy's – changed most of all. Mammy became focused on any factor which could precipitate an attack. Fog, mists or cold winds were the foe. Poor Nicky became a housebound prisoner: a protected but perhaps lonely little fellow. His Sister was his friend in need. Dr. Mac was a frequent visitor. When days were dire, a Nurse was summoned; not only to tend Nicky, but, I learned later, to tend my Mother. Mammy had pernicious Anaemia.

'Liver injections I presume? Poor love...'

Nurse Danby was a sight to behold. Nicky and I, when I was not at Foxdale, would kneel up on the front room window-seat and watch for her arrival. We could almost hear the huffing and puffing before her bicycle had crunched its way into the drive. By the time the front door opened and she was ensconced in the hallway, it was hard to tell who wheezed the loudest – Nurse Danby or Nicky.

Nurse Danby was middle-aged, or so she appeared to our young and inquisitive eyes. Stout, uniformed and resolute, she presented as an indomitable, baleful persona. Her leather Gladstone bag contained all manner of anomalous medical gear, instruments, documents and a superabundant amount of dust and fluff.

'Do you think she was a dyke?'

Well how would I know, Ronnie!

'Did she have moustache?'

I remember she fought her way through ice and foot of snow one Christmas and Daddy plied her with Gin n' Lime before she went off. Went off were the operative words for she wobbled her bicycle all the way down Lowfield Road and was very late when she arrived the next day!

Summer time did not present great threats to Nicky's welfare. Once the sun shone and relaxation prevailed, the family cruised along in a happier frame of mind.

Sunlit holidays were spent at Bridlington. Mammy and Daddy would rent a furnished house there, sometimes for as long as a month. How lucky were we! Fortunately, it provided an opportunity for Gran and Grandpa to join us. Daddy was fully occupied with the shop during weekdays but would drive over for weekends. It seemed to be an ideal arrangement.

Every day, our little entourage would be beach-bound; the South beach was a favourite and family friends of my Parents would often appear. Auntie Anne and Uncle Erbie, perhaps staying at one of the Hotels on the Front, Del Rio or Scarthoe, would be on deck-chair duty.

I recall a visit from Auntie Laura, her husband Uncle Len and their children, our Cousins, Christopher and Patricia.

'I thought they were a bit on the edge.'

Well, they were most of the time, but I suppose Mammy did have to hold out the olive branch now and again. I must admit, I didn't know my Cousins very well. Christopher could be somewhat unpredictable, I came to learn. Apparently, he had to be forcibly restrained during one beach visit when he took a metal spade and aimed it at my head!

'Little shit!'

I think that was a similar sentiment to the one my Mother held of him! She always put his obnoxious traits down to the fact that he was spoiled rotten by my Aunties Annie and Else. I suppose you could sympathise; he was the first child of their youngest Sister, Laura, and could not fall from grace in any shape or form.

'One good thing, little Nick must have thrived once warmed by the sun...'

Oh he did, Ronnie. Meantime, I was quite happily engrossed in Enid Blyton or The School Friend. When days were rainy, I could be found curled up somewhere quiet and absorbed by my silent friends – Books!

Daddy, at the start of the holidays, would always give me a £5 note. That was a huge amount of money in the Forties! Of course, later, when Nicky was older, he would have one also. These notes were large, white and covered in black lettering.

I think that most of my money was frugally spent on Books. Mammy would take me along to Garlands in Bridlington which was an enticing Bookstore housing all manner of alluring titles: The Mountain of Adventure, Five go to Kirren Island and Fifth Form at Malory Towers. I was reminded, constantly, of Miss Sugden as the whiff of new books and stationery filled my nostrils. Garlands was a treasure trove: pencils, rubbers, notepads, pens, folders gleamed from the shelves which groaned under weighty stores of Basildon Bond and the like. Colouring books and crayons, paint and brushes were playthings for rainy days. As the skies darkened and an indoors day dawned, the kitchen was cleared and endeavour prevailed. Nicky helped or hindered, giggled and made a mess.

The Follies had a lasting effect upon me, even at the tender age of eight or nine. Bridlington presented a Summer Variety Show in the Floral Hall. I could hardly contain my excitement at the prospect of a visit. I was entranced by the colour, costumes and fetching, enticing Artistes who graced the stage. An immaculate row of dancing girls high-kicked their way towards the footlights and I marvelled at faces bright with powder and paint. Maquillage! Magic! Various turns followed: Acrobats, Magicians and Sorcerers who mystified with dexterity and mystery, men who stood centre stage and told funny stories, and sometimes a Lady would appear with a troupe of performing dogs. Here was a whirlwind of dreams and enchantment. I was bewitched.

I had been bewitched before. A Christmas Pantomime presented at the Tivoli Theatre in Hull captivated me. I was spellbound as Fairies flew out over the Auditorium and threw flowers. My love of Theatre, the joy of imagination and fantasy, was born.

'Do you remember me telling you of my little Theatre? I made all my own Actor figures. Just think...when you were watching the Tivoli Fairies, little did you think there was another one waiting for you in Hartlepool!!'

Sometimes, the best gifts come in unusual packages!

My life revolved around Nicky, Foxdale, Mr. Palmer's Riding School and Elocution. I loved all.

Marjorie Brier continued to encourage expertise and professionalism. Soon, I was partnered with other pupils and Valerie and Barbara became my Acting pals. Valerie seemed to be studious and proper. She mastered all things Theory with skill and precision, while Barbara, although gifted with knack and know-how, proved to be something of a wild card! She excelled in Acting as opposed to the formality of Verse Speaking. So, I was blessed with friends who not only possessed a love of the spoken word but were becoming distinctive, contrasting connoisseurs. We three were promising to be an adroit triumvirate.

'I say, talking about agility and precision of speech, do you remember trying to crack 'Polish it behind the door' , which could be very questionable if one stumbled, or, 'Has the Doctor seen her, Fanny?'. For God's sake remember to put the comma in or you're in real trouble!'

Thank you, darling...I'll remember that...

~

Doctor Mac found himself visiting not only Nicky but me! He was about to retire and hand over to a young Scot by the name of Dr. Donaldson, but before doing so, he was consulted repeatedly for my painful and troublesome bouts of tonsillitis. "Those tonsils are septic most of time", he announced. "They'll have to come out". There was very little planning or talk, I remember, about them having to come out. I know I was promised a whole day at Mr. Palmer's and at least three new Enid Blyton adventures; bribery before I faced the knife!

I was about to contend with one of the most disturbing episodes in my early life.

My operation was to take place at the Victoria Nursing Home, Victoria Avenue in Hull.

'Sounds posh…'

Well, I was in no fit state to know that. All I knew was that I was going alone – no Mammy or Daddy. Even Enid Blyton did not banish the dread of being left in an alien room equipped with two beds. The other occupant was a crying baby, supposedly also forsaken in order to…

'Have something done…'

Spot on, Ronnie.

That night is indelibly imprinted on my memory. I was inconsolable and wept until first light. It was my first brush with desperate, distressing homesickness. I came to realise over the years that its term 'sickness' was an unerring, unblemished truth.

Everyone was very kind. Gently, I was escorted into a white room and asked to perch on the side of a bed. A small cloth was placed under my nose and a Gentleman said, "Now Susan, just count to ten." When I opened my eyes once more, a voice said, "All done, Susan. Now what did you dream about?" I remember replying "I went for a walk with you!"

'Typical!'

Everyone was laughing…I can't think why. Anyway, my throat was hurting so much, I couldn't take in much else.

'Did you have some ice cream?'

Oh yes. When Mammy and Daddy came to collect me, Mammy was crying. I think she must have missed me very much. She gave me a big bunch of Marigolds! That was when I first realised that poorly people should always receive flowers!

Nicky & Sue 'First Steps'

The grown-up Nicky!

NICKY AND ME

1947

'.....oh, Auntie Em, there's no place like home'

(Wizard of Oz)

The lingering doubt between my Parents did not disappear. It hung like a haze, a flutter or frisson of discord. This friction could combust and a trifling argument wrangle into flashes of discontent and bitter showdown. The toddler Nicky would sense distress and his frightened whimper was stilled only by Custard and a cuddle.

'Who was it that said "I smile because you are my Brother. I laugh because there is nothing you can do about it"?'

This ambiance, this misgiving did not spoil my life. I was very happy. Nicky was a centrepiece and minding him was a joy. He was included in most of my childhood larks and capers. When June and Gwennie came to play, he chuckled, got in the way and hurtled Custard around the back bedroom like a banshee.

'Hell's teeth, there's no end to it!'

The back bedroom in Winter, was cold. Jack Frost would have been at work and a myriad of icy images would veil the view beyond. On such a day, the hallowed Front

Room became our place of play. The fire was roaring and Mammy would have been careful to hoist the fireguard.

'You don't see many of those nowadays – huge gratings placed in front of the fireplace – Mam used to dry her bloomers over ours...'

I remember burn marks on Mammy's precious carpet where sparks had flown. Daddy was a smoker. It was a miracle that we were not burnt to a crisp . Scorch marks, where his cigarette had dropped from sleepy fingers as he armchair slumbered, oblivious to consequence, peppered the floor.

Bored with Gwennie, June and I passed the time gazing from the window, trying to catch sight of any intriguing incidents outside.

'No sign of the ubiquitous Mrs. Holmes?!'

No Ronnie. She lurked undetected most of time, but I did feel sorry for Anna, her Daughter. I think she would have liked to play.

Our attention was drawn to people walking by. Here was a reminder of the far-flung War. Some way down Lowfield Road, there was a Camp. Nissen huts, tunnel-shaped, concrete-floored and built with corrugated iron, occupied every inch of ground. Here were housed 'displaced persons'. Data supplied by Daddy who was trying to answer our probing questions.

We would see these poor displaced persons shuffling unsteadily along our road. Some were very strange to see. Our infantile eyes could only wonder and puzzle. Why did they have shaven heads? Why were their faces different in shape and colour from ours – broad, flat, yellowish faces?

'Mongolians, I wonder? Asian people....poor souls, whoever they were...'

I know Mammy always wanted to ask them to come in for a warm. She invited any Gypsies who came to the door to have a cup of tea. One day, I came home from Foxdale to find at least six lady Gypsies sitting in the ten-foot drinking tea!

'Perhaps she thought they would put a Curse on her if she refused to buy their pegs! I bet Mrs. Holmes wasn't very pleased'!

~

I was to take part in an auspicious event. Rattler Wheldon was going to be married! I could hardly contain my excitement when Rita asked me to be her Bridesmaid! She went on to say "you're going to have a dress that rustles when you walk!"

Oh Ronnie, what a day that was! My dress was made of white flecked organza and I had flowers in my hair. It was the underskirt that made the rustling sound and I kept moving about so that I could hear it all the time.

'I hope you were not upstaging the Bride!'

The Wedding was at Anlaby Church and everyone from the village came to watch. Even Miss Johnson!

'Did she wave and throw fruit gums – I hope Rawsons wasn't cleaning out the pigs on the same day!'

Afterwards, we went home and later on, Daddy brought fish n' chips and we listened to PC 49 on the Wireless. He always bought fish n' chips on a PC 49 night. Dick Barton was on every day and we never missed one episode. Well, Daddy and Grandpa never did…Mammy always said she had better things to do! I think she really did enjoy it just the same. They were lovely times. I was very happy. Nicky was very happy.

I look back at erstwhile, sepia photographs. I see pictures of a harmonious, contented family: glimpses of smiling, glad, devoted and constant Parenthood. Now, so much later, do I imagine contention and strife? I see visions, impressions and snapshots; passé, dated records of yesterday. Perhaps such transparencies record only the joy. The photographer looks for and expects peace, sincerity and truth before he clicks the shutter. It is only in the off guard moment, when life and mien is caught unawares, that a gleam of candour shines through.

'Beauty in the eye of the beholder...'

I never doubted the love. Nicky and I were cherished, treasured and held dear. Who knows what hidden suffering or wretchedness precipitated change of mood or countenance. My Parents, Grandparents and all those around them must have known the enduring uncertainty of the War; the abject fear and horror of a Nazi coup d'etat.

Nicky started school. He attended Kirk Ella Primary School which was administered by a married couple. According to Mammy, both seemed to be a somewhat colourless, dull, teaching duo. Perhaps choice of tuition was limited in the early Fifties.

Nicholas was a sensitive little boy, easily hurt and wounded. He had missed much of his early education through illness and found himself left behind. His early years of development presented many trials that were hard for him to bear. Mammy and I were his protectors, but were unable to rise to his defence in the classroom and the indifferent Heads were slow to offer emotional support for needy children such as my Brother. Mammy was very well meaning and would strive to comfort with "Never mind, Nicky love, I was never a scholar either". It was questionable whether this was the most favourable line of approach! He was tall in stature, handsome and seemingly robust, which perhaps gave the lie to any physical weakness.

'Well, Sue, we all know that some, particularly children, cannot see any further than their nose end'.

The snide, vindictive members of his class found chinks in his armour and bullied.

'I wonder if Nicky would have fared better with the gentle Miss Sugden?'

I'm sure he would have done, Ronnie. I think she was probably thinking of retiring by that time and nothing could be quite the same without Miss Sugden.

Fortunately, Nicky found faithful friends elsewhere and holiday times were enriched by tree-climbing, chasing and 'riving about', as Grandpa called it. Nicky was finding his own pathway, his own love of life....

My life was moving on apace and there was talk with Miss Brier of being entered for Verse Speaking Classes at Hull Musical Festival! Amazing! Mammy, which now had become 'Mummy' for some unknown reason, (interestingly, Daddy still referred to my 'Mammy' when I was thirty-five years old!) mentioned moving on to another School. I was almost eleven. The prospect of leaving my beloved Foxdale was intimidating and daunting to say the least. I was growing up and for so many reasons I didn't want to grow up....

Nicky entered Kirk Ella Primary School a year after I began my Secondary Education at Hull Convent in 1950.

'Quote Mammy: "She's going to be a Lady if it kills me!"

THE CANNONESSES OF ST. AUGUSTINE HULL CONVENT

1950-1955

'A convent is a place of retirement for women who wish for leisure to meditate upon the sin of idleness'

(Ambrose Gwinnet Bierce, American Civil War Soldier, wit and writer of War stories, who influenced Ernest Hemingway)

'That's something I might have said – well, if I'd been clever enough!'

My first impression of the Convent was one of gloom. The main building was set back from the road. Park Grove was a minor street sprouting from Spring Bank in Hull and backing on to Pearson Park. The School buildings occupied a large expanse of land. At the rear, the Nuns' residences, about three – dark and sombre if I remember correctly – sprawled on the other side of lawns and outbuildings.

A visit was arranged. I was to meet Mother Superior. My Parents parked the car near Pearson Park. Daddy was driving a very smart Humber Hawk at that time. The business must have been doing well.

'I thought you were going to say it was the new Riley!!'

The main Convent house was an imposing Victorian dwelling standing some distance from the kerb. I was nervous. It might be true to say that Mummy and Daddy were nervous. One doesn't encounter a Nun every day of the week...

Daddy tugged at the bell-pull. Several minutes passed. The door opened slowly to reveal a black-robed figure. A smiling, rosy and young face peeped out from a white bib. Her hands were enclosed within open sleeves of her habit and hanging from the waist was a long chain and crucifix.

'I suppose you found out what that was long afterwards...'

I was to find out about a lot of things, Ronnie. It was all a bit alarming.

The entrance hall stretched before us. It was furnished with antediluvian furniture and lit by a ceiling skylight high above the tiled floor. A redolent air filled the hollow space.

"Hello Susan. Would you care to come into the sitting-room. The Reverend Mother will be with you shortly". The voice was clear and youthful. Our guide opened a side door and we were piloted inside. As silently as she had appeared, our usher disappeared, closing the door behind her.

A piano dominated much of the room. Carpets were threadbare and ornaments placed upon the marble fireplace were crazed and chipped. I longed for Miss Sugden and the cosy fires of Foxdale!

'Poor little thing...I was about to crack a very old joke about dirty habits, but thought better of it!'

The door creaked open and another Nun crossed the threshold. She was tiny. I was nearly as tall as her. Daddy and Mummy, then me, rose to our feet. "Good afternoon, I am Reverend Mother. I am so pleased to meet you". She looked at me carefully and as she continued to speak, we were motioned to sit down while she explained in detail the workings of her School. All the while, her head nodded and turned jerkily; her piercing gaze left me feeling very uneasy. Her expression was not an unkind one, but it was direct. There was no mistaking her meaning or intention. She reminded me very much of a Sparrow, a little Cock Sparrow scratching or pecking the soil in search of an unsuspecting worm.

'How very complimentary!'

The Reverend Mother concluded our meeting. "I will be very pleased to welcome you, Susan, at the beginning of our Autumn Term". We were then accompanied to the front door and took our leave as it closed silently behind us. I seem to remember a "Phew!" from Daddy. My Parents were intrigued no doubt, but very satisfied that I was to be initiated into a beneficial, wholesome regime. I have a feeling that my Mother thought that being schooled within the confines of a Convent was really going to fashion me into a refined, genteel young woman: a person of culture, elegance and breeding.

'How come, then, that you became a gin-swilling Actress familiar with the coarse and vulgar – like me!'

Stranger things have happened, Ronnie...

~

Although apprehensive and somewhat jittery at first, I soon settled into my new School life. I liked my brand new uniform and had a full trying-on session where Nicky was anything but helpful. He seemed to find my yellow beret a source of great amusement. I had a navy blue tunic, white blouse, tie and lisle stockings which were almost as troublesome as my childhood gaiters had been. I gradually became accustomed to a suspender belt which was a necessary anchor for my wrinkly hose. To complement the whole ensemble was a pair of navy blue knickers, complete with pocket.

Not a word, Ronnie....!

I became used to a much longer journey to reach my destination. Often, Daddy would drive me to the Convent on his way to work, but, on other occasions at 4.00 p.m., I walked, via Cave Street, took the trolley-bus along the main Beverley Road to Paragon Station in Hull, where I could transfer to the East Yorkshire Anlaby charabanc.

On my opening School day, I was allocated to a first floor Classroom, C1. It was small and housed only a few pupils. The desks were single, heavy-lidded, wooden and cumbersome. There I met two friends who would become a loyal and trusted pair during my first year. Barbara Coletta and Betty Thompson were funny and mischievous. I remained close to them for some time – especially to Betty. We were both devoted to the Cinema and spent many happy hours together totally engrossed in the melodrama of the day, Pathe News, and Edgar Lusgarten's Crime which always made up the B Movie of the day before the main feature began.

The cloakrooms were on the ground floor and seemed to be supervised by a very youthful Nun by the name of Mother Mary de la Presentation. I remember her flawless skin colouring and brisk control of minutiae! After the morning Assembly, forms were marched to classrooms.

Parquet flooring covered all parts of the building and the solid oak, imposing staircase leading to classrooms, was polished and shiny. At Break, forms filed neatly and formally down the steps. On reaching the entrance vestibule, we would see Reverend Mother waiting – nodding, beady-eyed and expectant. Each girl, instructed to curtsey before her, would receive an astute, keen nod before being given the all clear to proceed. Reverend Mother occupied a small, ground floor office close to the front door; somewhere to keep clear of!

Mother Therese, surely French, oversaw the concoction of a particularly disagreeable and cloggy chocolate slab cake for Break snacks. This was washed down with the mandatory milk.

'Ugh....!'

Mother Therese was strict. She did teach, but I saw her infrequently which was something of a relief. She, too, was diminutive but could certainly pack a punch if she was on the warpath for misbehaviour or dereliction of duty. I always thought she should have had 'beware' tattooed upon her forehead. "Susanne Ubble!" she would rasp whenever I was nailed for talking, which was many a time and oft. Sometimes, small persons can be more menacing than giants.

Mother Cecilia was my very favourite Nun. She was elderly and bustled about. Her Scripture lessons were captivating, enthralling. Classes were all the more memorable because she enacted each Bible Story on the raised platform at the front of the classroom. I was utterly spellbound....

The Raising of Lazarus was particularly inventive. As for the Crucifixion, well, that was a tour de force. Each character was instantly recognisable. The weeping of Mother Mary as she gazed in agony moved us all to tears. There were times when one could observe, at close quarters, the magic of Mother Cecilia. Most of us collected Holy Pictures and tucked them into our Bibles. Mother Cecilia had a remarkable hoard and we could approach her at the Teachers' desk to choose. She had one of the loveliest faces I had ever seen. Her skin was translucent; her mouth always curving to smile, but it was her clear, shining eyes which gently gathered one in to her very soul. I was not a Roman Catholic and I was not coerced into becoming one, nor were my companions, if I remember correctly. The creed was unimportant. Truth, meaning and substance stood us in good stead. It was enough.

Mother Cecilia taught as I imagine Jesus would have taught. That was all I needed and I have never forgotten those lessons. My faith deepened and became strong all those years ago.

'Chosen people are sent to us....when there is something lasting that we need to learn...'

Mother Cecilia presided over the Stationery store. This cupboard was a shadowy repository at the top of a winding flight of first floor stairs. It also housed the Clock mechanism! The Convent Clock had a noble, grandiose chime which reverberated and echoed throughout the building; a varying repertoire of sounds would emanate on the hour, a quarter past the hour and on the half hour: booms, tolls, jingles, clangs and dongs.

Girls would queue on the steps waiting a turn to request exercise books and texts. There was much chatter and overall ado. Mother Cecilia sat at the summit, rather like a Buddha, ready to serve each customer.

At various intervals, the innards of the Clock would prepare for a Strike. Strange whirrings and clanking of gears deafened all within close proximity. Poor Mother Cecilia would halt mid-sentence, gesticulating in annoyance and teetering precariously on her rickety stool. She recovered unscathed but the whole caper left us weak with mirth. It was high jinks that we all looked forward to with glee.

'Susanne Ubble!!'

Rank and file Teachers from the outside world made up the Staff: Miss French who threw chalk, Mrs. Arithmetic who handled Mathematics and rather ham-fistedly handled me. Maths was not my strong suit, although I had mastered it well at the beloved Foxdale. Mrs. Arithmetic, gowned and reeking of tobacco, was forbidding. So much so, that

I was terrified of her and very loath to put up my hand. She must have been particularly irritated on one occasion. I found myself on the receiving end of a splenetic invective: "It's like teaching the dead, teaching you Maths, Susan!"

'Nowadays, she'd have been pinned to the School gates by an irate Parent!'

I was crushed. I did not recover and developed an intrinsic fear of numbers in any shape or form. That tirade left me mathematically-marked for the rest of my life.

Miss Geography, was, in comparison, a gift to all children. Glad, jolly anticipation filled the classroom and her easy acceptance of fidgeting, vexatious and wayward adolescents, made for relaxation and untroubled learning. She did, however, quite unconsciously, lay herself wide open to some good-natured ridicule.

Miss Geography was tall, angular and in possession of a row of protruding teeth. Now this did not draw undue attention, but the fact that she had a bosom of lavish scale and size, did invite some girlish ribaldry. More so, Miss Geography did not wear a brassiere! Consequently, much bouncing went on. Imagine our delight when we were learning about South America's Lake Titicaca!

'Dear God, can it get any more racy!!'

Now.... Miss Gym was my bete noire.

'Was she a Wolf in Nun's clothing?'

It is difficult to suss where she came from. Perhaps there was a local works, or plant, where the likes of Miss Gym were moulded, cast and foisted on to unsuspecting scholastic seminaries. She was a force to be reckoned with.

Miss Gym was feared. She may, on the quiet, have been a most personable individual, but to the quaking teenager, she was the devil incarnate. Her status within the school was perplexing to pinpoint. She certainly assumed a notable presence. Nevertheless, it is not beyond the bounds of rationale to define her role as despot, martinet, drill sergeant....

'Arthur or Martha?'

That may well have been a dilemma, Ronnie – looking back, I venture to add that that may well have been a distinct disparity!

Miss Gym was a somewhat dumpy figure. Her hair was straight and basin-cut. I often wondered if her hairdresser was vindictive! One thing for sure, it hung in lacklustre strands and framed dour, aquiline features.

'Poor bugger...'

One redeeming factor was her proficiency as a Physical Education teacher.

Miss Gym reigned supreme over one of the best features of the School. The ground level Gym was a large, parquet-floored, high-arched area. It was suitably equipped with vaulting horses, climbing frames which could be pulled out from the walls and ropes which hung ominously from hooks in the ceiling. Miss Gym, as taskmaster, took great delight in commanding her pubescent charges to haul widespread puppy fat to the top.

'Oh, those navy-blue knickers'.

All the while, much instruction was punctuated by Miss Gym's whistle signals. This shrill pipe seemed to be glued between her lips. She would blow vigorously, exhorting intractable momentum. Then silence, while the whistle remained in position. Only her lips shifted to keep a grip. In the hush that followed, the gimlet-eyes would rove over her captives.

'Perhaps her real moniker was 'Jim'!

The most favourite piece of equipment was the Giant Stride.

'Not a Nun's party-piece?!'

This was a centre-of-the-roof moveable, rotating fixture on which were tethered six long ropes. On the end of the ropes were two rings. The idea was that girls, once having taken hold, would run around the Gym perimeter gathering impetus and propulsion. Once enough power and thrust was reached, feet could leave the floor and swing high above the ground, only touching down when further push was needed. I guess it could have been dangerous. It was, however, the highlight of the Gymnastics lesson and must have produced elephantine thigh muscles.

So, Miss Gym has been faithfully recorded in my Convent chronicles and certainly occupies a fateful, portentous place in my memory.

~

Time moved on and largely due to an excellent Academic Report – top of the class in all subjects (even Maths!) – I was promoted to Form C2. There, I met Beryl Wright who became my trusted companion for many years after.

Convent, Canonesses of St. Augustine, Park Grove, Hull Gymnasium

Convent, Canonesses of St. Augustine, Park Grove, Hull

Convent, Canonesses of St. Augustine, Park Grove, Hull
The School from the grounds

I was twelve and approaching a momentous time in my young life. Again, such a milestone was not mentioned at home. I'm talking about the onset of Menstruation.

'Oh dear, out of my depth, love....'

I'll explain...

'Must you...!'

The first I knew about it was when my friend, June, told me of her horror story. She thought she was bleeding to death! Frantic, I regaled Mummy with the story. I met with "Well, you know all about it, don't you?" But I didn't know all about it. I assume that she thought periods had been widely discussed within my School circle. When it was obvious that I was totally ignorant of this procedure, Mummy was sympathetic, but in no way forthcoming. She armed me with the necessary equipment, a brief explanation about how it operated, a hot water-bottle, told me to rest on the couch and said I was poorly; there followed no explanation, no reasons for this vital and significant growth and unfolding. My friends and I were left to muddle through as best we could.

'Well, I reckon the Nuns were a write-off and as for Miss Gym...need I say more...!'

Well, suffice it to say that Sex Education was non existent. We were cast adrift in what might have turned out to be troubled waters. At the same time, we grappled with inexplicable, although not unpleasant, feelings. Nowadays, such emotions are rightly assessed as hormonal change. In the Fifties we coped with 'growing pains'. I still do not know what sort of pains those may have been. Menstruation was referred to as 'the curse' or 'the time of the month'. My Mother constantly alluded to it as 'being poorly'. I noticed that it was a favourite topic of discussion when she was socialising with her friends. I suppose Sex was chattered about, but always in hushed tones and under a blanket of secrecy.

'Mam used to send me, with a note, to the Drapers in Hartlepool. The lady behind the counter would hand me a

brown paper parcel to take home. I often wondered what it was!'

Hormones stimulated organs into action, or near-action, when us Convent girls encountered the boys from Trinity House Naval Academy on the homeward bus.

'Little madams!'

The boys' uniforms were styled as those befitting Naval Officers, black and trimmed with silver braid. They wore black caps the tip of which was artfully perched over one eye. A carefully-timed wink would send this bevy of girls into giggling rapture. The whole throng escalated our amorous Schoolgirl fantasies into ecstatic, raunchy and stargazing reveries. This role play -

'I'm glad you didn't say foreplay!'

I'll ignore that Ronnie.

This role play was a daily communion which was executed on the top deck of the bus. There would be snatching of Convent berets and girlish voices raised in mock protest, before an irritated Conductor would shout up the stairs "Give over! I'll be up there in a minute!"

This evolution and its unravelling was a relished topic of conversation with my friends. Some Mothers were more unreserved and as a result, second-hand detail and information was passed on from one to the other. I remember finding out was not always to one's advantage and misinformation can lead to frightened, sleepless nights.

May Wellburn, a protuberant, generously-endowed member of C2, was in possession of some startling narrative and did not hesitate to blurb the low-down on numerous occasions. "Mummy's bought me my first Bra and it's all covered with coffee-coloured lace...!" bragged May.

'Baggage!'

Well, that's what Jessica must have thought and announced, "Well what do you want one for? No you can't". Perhaps because she didn't wear one as I found out in due course.

'Perhaps she thought you didn't have anything to put in it!'

Fortunately, she didn't say that, Ronnie, or it would have added insult to injury.

It was the coffee-coloured lace that was the biggest pull. I reckon Mrs. Wellburn thought it was an apt way of steering through the whole business of May's growing up. Perhaps she didn't visualise periods and brassieres to be anything other than a natural celebration of womankind; a preparation for the joy of a loving relationship and motherhood. Mummy didn't allow my growing up too soon. Perhaps she was afraid of it. It was all very strange.

This uncertainty coincided with Miss Brier introducing me to an extract from the play of 'The Diary of Anne Frank'. It was to be an Own Choice selection for a Guildhall Music & Drama Grade examination. It could not have come along at a more fortunate time. Here are Anne's words:

"There is one great change. A change in myself. I read somewhere that girls of my age don't feel quite certain of themselves. That they become quiet within and begin to think of the miracle that is taking place in their bodies. I think that what is happening to me is so wonderful – not only what can be seen, but what is taking place inside. Each time it has happened I have a feeling that I have a – sweet secret. And, in spite of my pain, I long for the time when I shall feel that secret within me again".

'Oh Sue, what a comfort that must have been....'

~

Over the next few years, I spent much devoted time to Speech and Drama. This, it may be said, was to the detriment of my School Academic performance. There, I rested on my laurels. I was clever but found much deviation in larking about.

At that time, my Parents were less diligent when it came to the discipline of study and the grind of programming homework. I escaped. I did request Parental help on occasion, but met with Mummy being busy doing other things and my Father, exhausted with work and long hours, lacking in patience. The prospect of appealing for help with Algebra and Geometry, was anathema to me. I could not face invective behaviour; being on the receiving end of an exercise book being hurled in temper across the table because I could not grasp the complexity of numbers.

'Oh, 'eck!'

So, all my energy was poured into studious, hard-work for the Musical Festivals in which Marjorie Brier was so eager in have me take part. Mummy was undoubtedly encouraging, reassuring and supportive.

Learning, practice and the repetition of Rehearsal was not a chore. I took pleasure in the joy of words and accomplishment of an impressive Technique.

I would practise my Pieces sitting on the apple-tree swing in the miniature orchard at the bottom of our garden; over and over, until memory, craft and knowledge were supreme.

I was twelve when Miss Brier entered me for my first Hull Musical Festival Verse Speaking Class: a test piece to be mastered with skill and artistry.

I won. So, another element was introduced: the component was Competition!

My life was full. Miss Brier concentrated on Musical Festivals in a big way. We were taken on excursions to Mexborough, Pontefract and a real favourite – Cleethorpes! Cleethorpes held a special place in our hearts for it was situated across the water! The River Humber! This meant a mode of travel to Lincolnshire in the days before the Bridge was built.

'How did you get there?'

The Ferry. It was called 'taking the Packet' in those days and involved a short river bound journey to Barton on the other side. Those exciting trips were a fillip from the daily routine of school. The Packet was a paddle-steamer. Accommodation was arranged over two decks; the lower one housed sitting areas for shelter in bad weather. We always hotfooted it to the top deck where we could watch the waves crashing under the paddles and wave to barges or River Pilots as they manoeuvred their passage through the swell. Also, we counted the hours until the journey home. After an arduous day competing and often armed with Certificates and trophies, we would clutch newspaper fish n' chips, race to the top deck and guzzle our well-earned reward!

'Tell me about it...a fish n' three-penn'orth would always be bribery and corruption for me!'

Cleethorpes had another major attraction – a Fun Fair which sported a Big Dipper!

'Dear God, dare I ask....?'

Miss Brier would only allow a ride after we had finished Rehearsing and before we needed to report to the Festival Venue. Now, when I think about it, she took a risk! All manner of misfortune could have overtaken us!

Miss Brier would rehearse Pieces in any available, appropriate place. Well, I say appropriate. On one occasion, she had me practise The Sermon on the Mount in a Ladies Public Convenience! We were coached and drilled until the last minute.

Classes were varied, testing and fiercely competitive: Bible Speaking, Verse Speaking, Duologues, Monologues,

Story-Telling, Mime and Movement. It was a motley, a diverse training which prepared us all for every eventuality.

Barbara and Valerie joined me on these adventures and we became very close friends. Barbara and I became particularly inseparable after being chosen as frequent participants for Play Scenes.

These day trips and expeditions led to several fortuitous meetings. Adjudicators were appointed for each Festival: Professors from Academies and Drama Schools situated in London. In our experience, we encountered important Tutors, Mentors, Dons and Lecturers from the Guildhall School of Music & Drama. I became acquainted with Rex Walters, Ambrose Marriott and Daniel Roberts, all of whom would play an integral part in my future career.

'Little did you know it at the time, darling.'

No, Ronnie, but Rex Walters certainly came to play a prominent part. It's fair to say that all Judges gave me many Awards and it was then, I think, that Jessica came to realise the importance of nurturing this ability and talent. She was always there to watch, to appreciate – and to push!

'Could easily have been why Academia was put on the back burner'.

~

Barbara and I were very successful as a partnership and our prowess attracted some attention from the Press. As a result, this publicity prompted an availability enquiry from the BBC. Huw Wheldon, responsible for 'All Your Own' – a topical programme for children which presented interesting achievements by young people in the North – approached us with an invitation to broadcast a reading of our most recent piece. This was to be an extract from 'Children in Uniform' by Christa Winsloe. The play had been first produced at the Duchess Theatre in London in 1932 starring Jessica Tandy and Cathleen Nesbitt.

'You're going back a bit now, love...how wonderful though. I remember Children's Hour and Uncle Mac.... were you going to be Stars?'

Well, Ronnie, at the age of about thirteen or fourteen it was, to us, beyond our wildest dreams but I'm talking about it for another reason. This opportunity brought about my first encounter with unforeseen guidance.

'More things in heaven and earth, sort of thing?'

Exactly. Barbara's Parents offered to mastermind the whole campaign. Her Father would drive Miss Brier, his Wife Lena and the two excited Performers over to Manchester BBC Studios. The morning Broadcast involved an early start, so a hotel was booked for an overnight stay. There, I faced another crippling dose of homesickness which rallied help from the caring Barbara.

'Poor little Susie...'

Soon, we were homeward bound. The Broadcast had been triumphant!

Mr. Wheldon was charming and the Studio transmission provided us with valuable insight into how Radio operated.

It was late afternoon and as the weather was fair, Mr. Bilton, Barbara's Father, decided to journey home over the Snake Pass. The Snake Pass winds its way high over the Pennines and has a treacherous reputation if the outlook is inclement. Mr. Bilton, a heroic and gritty trawler Skipper, was not likely to be thwarted or quail at the promise of an isolated shower. We set off.

'Fog! Was it fog?'

Yes Ronnie, it was fog – with a vengeance! Mr. Bilton was struggling to see the cat's eyes, in fact any discernable means of direction. Mrs. Bilton, vainly offering to help by getting out of the car and walking in front, was met with "No, Lena, you can't – it's a sheer drop on the other side – you could go over the edge!"

'It must have been terrifying...'

It was Ronnie. Even Miss Brier was holding our hands so tightly that circulation was impaired. Eventually, the car ground to a halt. It was impossible to move. We were stranded. Fear permeated the air and no sound could be heard.

A motor bike appeared; mute, noiseless, no echo or reverberation. Its rider could be seen as Mr. Bilton wound the window down. "Follow me slowly" called our deliverer. He moved ahead. We could not see his face and only the red tail lights of his bike were visible. Our Guardian Angel led us over the Pass until we could see town lights ahead – then - He disappeared.

'He didn't speak?'

No. We were safe.

He must have known the Snake Pass like no other. The fog that night was impenetrable.

Throughout my life, I have known helpers. They come, they go and they guide. I have never questioned. Only believed....

'There is a plan....'

~

I was now in my early teens. I was still riding but gradually Drama and all that it promised began to take precedence.

'So you gravitated to other things...'

Some puzzling developments were coming about on the home front. My Mother was focussing her attention on moving house!

'Not Charlie?'

That's difficult to say, but I came to realise that finance was becoming an issue at home. My Riding world must have been expensive, so I daresay it could have been a relief to my Father to have me gradually relinquish it.

Convent 1955
All girls together, Susan at front second left

Also, I noticed friction when the School Fees were due! My Father's face tightened and a cheque would come hurtling across the dresser...life was changing, the country was changing after the War and consequently, there was a possibility that proceeds from the Shop were changing. All things beyond my grasp....I was only the witness of change at home. So, Ronnie, when you ask if my Father wished to move, I cannot give you an answer.

Viewing visits were arranged to see a house in Beverley Road, Anlaby. This area was slightly more top-drawer than Lowfield Road. No.355 was imposing and detached. Originally owned by a timber merchant, it had been left empty for a while until building of interior features could be completed. As one may imagine, wood played an important part in fixtures. The floors were impressively parquet. The dining room was luxuriously oak-panelled; the staircase polished oak.

Needless to say, both Parents craved this four bed-roomed, tasteful and exceptional homestead. "Wouldn't you really love to live here, Susan?" said Jessica. So, unwittingly, I was involved in persuasive argument!

'Ah, so that was the way the wind was blowing...'

Well, Ronnie, who knows? I suppose I didn't need much persuading. The house was lovely. The rolling lawns, garden, and rear landscape overlooking the gracious grounds of Anlaby House, were lovely. Of course I would really love to live there.

I can recall that several friends of my Parents had moved to this allegedly de luxe neighbourhood and things were looking up. A standard of living was being observed; being able to afford that standard of living, was another matter....

We moved to 355 Beverley Road, Anlaby in the early Fifties. The house was spacious and my Mother's unusual, elegant and discerning taste played an important part in establishing its unique ambiance. Nicky and I rejoiced in the luxury of the house having four bedrooms: so, one each! The back bedroom sported twin beds. I remember that my Mother preferred to sleep there. Apparently, this was in preparation for Nicky having a Bronchial bout. He would need to have her near. It was odd. Therefore, my Father occupied the front bedroom. This arrangement seemed to bring about a noticeable change in atmosphere; an air of something not quite right.

'Beginning of the end?'

Nicky was unaffected and I did not question. I assumed that this was the plan for all Parents.

Nicky was growing up and approaching seven years or thereabouts. He was a happy child and photographs taken at the time, reveal a joyful, engaging little boy who revelled in a contented, happy environment. His illness no longer threatened repeated, insidious onslaughts and we lived in hope that he would grow out of it. Dr. Donaldson offered a likely explanation for Nicholas' problem. Could it be caused by stress? If so, then, in his opinion, Nicky may grow out of Bronchial Asthma at age seven, fourteen or after.

'Certainly a possibility, Sue. In view of what was going on... unforeseeable tension must have crept into Nicky's life too...children soak it up...'

The Burts lived further along Beverley Road. Edi and Harold Burt were within the same circle of friends as my Parents. Their home was set back from the road, detached and opulent. Harold had made something of a fortune assembling gaming tables, early models of fruit machines and the like. Most important of all – they owned a black miniature Poodle. Poodles were very rare then. Dominic was dazzlingly gorgeous!

'You wanted one!'

Oh, Ronnie, how did you guess!

'I knew...I knew because I love you...even though I didn't know you then...sometimes I think I've loved you for ever...'

Daddy knew. He also knew that my fifteenth Birthday was coming along. He chattered about how lovely it would be to have a Labrador or a Spaniel. "Poodles are sissy dogs. If you think I am walking down the road with a Poodle, you're mistaken". That was that.

On the day of my Birthday, after School, I opened the front door. I heard a unfamiliar yapping sound.

'Funny how I can always predict what would come along on your important Birthdays!'

Yes, Ronnie. There he was. He was a tiny bundle of apricot-coloured fluff.

'I hope you gave him a swanky name, pet...like Darcey...that's French you know!'

A Poodle puppy, Ronnie! I called him Simon and don't ask me why. I have no idea why. He was Simon. Everyone loved Simon. My Mother adored Simon and Daddy, well....who took Simon for his early morning walk when I caught the bus for School?

'Dear God....Charlie! How are the mighty fallen!'

So, Simon became a dearly loved member of our Family. He lived for fifteen years and when the time came for him to leave us, I thought I would never stop weeping.....

~

Life at the Convent was moving on apace. O Level examinations were approaching and I was ill prepared. I had wasted time; frittered it away. I had not been urged to be far-seeing. I had drifted. I was about to pay the price.

Speech and Drama, Festivals, Guildhall examinations were all advanced, all secure. My energy had been spent cultivating a peerless, priceless gift.

'So, my love, you learned the hard way...'

I did. At the age of sixteen, I obtained one O Level – Art. I suppose my Parents did not know what to do about it. Nor did I. But...I did know one thing. I wished to become an Actress!

'Not a fallen woman, I hasten to add!'

Well, I think Daddy must have had that in mind when he announced: "Well, if that's what you want, you'd better have a second string to your bow. You're going to the College of Commerce for a Secretarial Course. You'll have to earn your living somehow!"

HULL COLLEGE OF COMMERCE

1956

'The first thing a Secretary types is the boss'

(Donald Trump)

Hull College of Commerce was set back from a main thoroughfare which led into Hull City centre: Beverley High Road. The Secretarial classrooms were positioned towards the front of the building. The Typewriting rooms were much larger than those used for Shorthand, Book-keeping and the like. I hasten to add that with my track record of anything resembling figures and Maths, I steered well clear of Book-keeping in any shape or form!

'Mrs. Arithmetic would have been proud of you!'

I was in my seventeenth year when I began to conquer the rigors of Shorthand and Typing. I was initially enrolled for a one-year course, but it leaves little to the imagination when I say that it became increasingly obvious that I would need to enlist for a further period of study when that drew to a close.

'In other words, you'd be an indeterminate challenge to all those entrepreneurs in the cut-throat world of business.'

I approached this new venture with a somewhat flippant attitude which, although entertaining for all and sundry, did not hasten progress and brought about a reprimand from a Miss Pearson who was the Shorthand Supremo:

"Well Susan, I just hope that you never have to earn your living doing this!" A remark that put the kibosh on my Father's hopes and dreams! Nevertheless, I did enjoy the Course.

Typewriting skills, bashed out to the rhythm of a gramophone belting out 'Keep Right On to the End of the Road' and other tried and true Marches, were great fun. The goal was approximately sixty words per minute!

I made lifelong friends while studying, or rather struggling with office precision and etiquette. Much to my dismay, I discovered that the slightest Pitman's Shorthand error could lead to embarrassing gaffes.

I met Ann Kerr and Pat Johnson. We remained close for many years. Another newcomer in my life was Susan Harrison. Susan hailed from the West Riding. Her family home was in Newland Park, a crescent leading off the Cottingham Road and near to Hull University. Susan wished to become a Journalist and had all the attributes to become a successful one. Several years later, she astonished all by throwing the whole idea in the air and marrying the lovely John; she went on to produce three children and her future was clinched.

'So where did this gaggle of girls go in their spare time?'

Well, in those days Ronnie, Ballroom dancing was all the rage. That's where our Parents thought we were likely to be out of harm's way.

'Oh, the misguided impression that there was safety in groups! Ha!

My Verse Speaking crony, Valerie, introduced me to the Harry Butters Dancing School on Anlaby Common. This was a short distance from home and on a very reliable bus route. There, we learned to dance and came into contact with a hotchpotch of callow, untried youths. We did not recognise them as such and had our eye on one or the other. Valerie hit it off rapidly with a swain by the name of Albert.

'Don't tell me you were a wallflower?'

Certainly not, Ronnie. There was one fellow, Terry, who was handsome, very smartly dressed and polite.

'And....'

Well, he crossed the floor repeatedly to request the next dance. It was the custom for girls to occupy a row of chairs facing the dance floor. The boys would stand in quivering, abashed and sheepish groups trying to pluck up the courage to brave the obstacle race to reach a chosen girl.

'Not fortified with booze either, poor little sods...'

Of course, one could never refuse to dance, however unprepossessing the young man appeared to be. That would have been looked upon, particularly by Mr. Butters, as being grossly rude and unkind.

'Ugh....'

Well, yes, it could have been that sort of reaction, but one had to keep qualms or misgivings carefully under one's radar. So, it was in such circumstances that I found myself in the arms of the very good-looking, winning Terry. During the Last Waltz -

'Ah, yes, memories are made of this – Victor Sylvester on the Wireless...'

Terry suggested that he "see me home".

'I guess you said that your Father was meeting you off the ten o'clock bus!'

No I didn't Ronnie, because he wasn't. I was allowed to walk alone from the bus stop. So, as home was within walking range, I agreed to forgo the whole bus ride, walk and be escorted. Now, once within the periphery of 355 Beverley Road and shaded by a convenient group of trees, Terry decided to take the whole initiative a step further and kissed me goodnight.

All hell broke loose. My Father appeared in the driveway of 355. "Inside, now, young lady!" I fear I was rooted to the spot for a moment or two before turning frightened eyes on the ill-starred Terry. Without another moment's hesitation, I ran indoors. Jessica, framed in the doorway, hissed "You dirty little bitch!"

'No! Sue....'

I was transfixed, frantic. I burst into tears and blurted, "I'm sorry, I'll never do it again! I'm so sorry..." My Mother turned on her heel and walked away.

'For God's Sake, what did Charlie do?'

Nothing. Perhaps he didn't know what to do. All I can remember is being deeply, deeply shocked. I trembled from head to foot.

'I suppose you weren't knowledgeable enough to know what it was to be a dirty little bitch!'

Darling Ronnie, always so full of common sense. I suppose that incident could have disturbed or deranged me for the rest of my life. It didn't. Nonetheless, it was a long time before I recovered enough to be able to dismiss it from my mind.

My Mother didn't utter a word to me for several days and when she did speak, it was to say, in front of my Father: "Did you know his Mother is a Charwoman"!

~

At the end of my first year at the College, my speeds in Shorthand and Typing were improving and by the time the vacation came around, I was sufficiently qualified to look for a Secretarial holiday job.

'Wow! Wow!.... they croak with monotonous regularity these days!'

Yes, Miss Pearson was full of praise and put me on to a 'situation vacant' advertisement for a Typing pool at

Reckitt & Colman in Hull. This firm supplied cleaning materials, Reckitt's Blue, starch and other essentials for a spotless kitchen!

'Another Wow! What more can a girl want?'

Brace yourself Ronnie...I got the job. The hours were horrific, almost as horrific as first sight of the Typing Pool. Pool was the operative word: a massive room containing approximately a dozen or more Typing positions.

'One two, one two, type a word – or two,
Arrow left, arrow right -
Keep those fingers nice and tight'.

Where did that come from Ronnie?

'Don't know...I was inspired!'

I was to begin work at 8.30 a.m. and finish at 5.30 p.m. with one hour for lunch. So, the alarm was set for 6.00 a.m. and by 7.00 a.m. I would be walking to catch the Anlaby Road bus. In Hull, I boarded another bus which travelled via Holderness Road and into Dansom Lane where Reckitts was located.

The work was soul destroying: forms, orders, sheets of products and lists.

I did, however, come through victorious. The incessant tapping of umpteen typewriters operated by innumerable female automatons was enough to drive one insane.

'Never mind, love, you were earning some money...'

My weekly wage was somewhere in the region of £5. I was proud of it. It went towards paying for my lesson with Miss Brier. I was less involved with Musical Festivals and concentrating more on my Grade Examinations. I was still mulling over a Theatrical career. I intended applying for a Guildhall School of Music & Drama Performers' Course when I was eighteen.

Meantime, I did not wish to rely on my Father for financing Examination fees and expenses. I knew I had War Savings. These Savings Stamps had accumulated over time and would now be most useful for expenditure needed to foster my proposed ambition. My Parents didn't raise any objections and I was delighted to realise my independence. It was very important to take charge.

'Well done, kidda...'

A highlight of my sojourn at Reckitts was a lunch time visit to Daddy's shop on Porter Street. It did involve a bus and trolley-bus trudge but it was well worth it when I saw how thrilled Auntie Elsie and Auntie Annie were to see me. There was only enough time for a ham sandwich, but time enough to absorb part of a very taxing, wearying way of life: hard work of a different calibre.

'You didn't have one of those Auntie Elsie Pork Pies then? I'd have found time for that!'

Of course you would, darling.

I valued the Secretarial experience that Reckitts had afforded me. I found myself rejuvenated when I began my second year at the College and forged ahead in an attempt to charge up my speeds even more. Thoughts of my ultimate aim were uppermost and I knew that my Father had been right. He had been prudent. I was about to find out how politic and perceptive his advice had been. In the Autumn of 1957, I applied to Audition at the Guildhall School of Music & Drama, in London. If accepted for the proposed Performers' Course, I would begin studies there the following September. Rex Walters, who had kept in regular touch with Miss Brier and me, was in full support. He remembered my work and achievements in Musical Festivals and gave great encouragement.

'Did you go alone to the Audition?'

I seem to remember that Marjorie came along, Ronnie. I hardly think I would have been allowed an unaccompanied venture to the Smoke!

The Guildhall School, in John Carpenter Street was reached from the Victoria Embankment. The entrance was imposing, but more so was the oak staircase and entrance hall. I had been asked to perform two selections: one Shakespearian extract and a choice from a Modern play. I was well prepared. I kept company with several other hopeful candidates and waited. I could hear sounds of violin, piano and song. Passing students, colourful and unconventionally-dressed, moved up and down the stairs. All atmosphere was new, animated and infectious in its motivation.

'You mean 'arty'!'

Oh yes, Ronnie. You would have loved it. I passed the Audition and within a few days, I knew I had been awarded a place! Everyone was thrilled: Miss Brier, Mr. Walters (who was to be my Professor) and of course my Parents.

'There was to be a shock, wasn't there?'

Yes, my darling. A massive shock.

I applied to the Hull Education Authority for a Grant. I was told in no uncertain terms that a Performers' Course at Guildhall was not to be financed. It seems that the Authority could not expect to be reimbursed in future years by an Actress! My only option would be to enrol for a Teachers' Course.

'You're right – it must have been a massive shock. What the hell did you do?'

I had no choice. I was not going to be defeated, although any idea of my being a Teacher seemed ludicrous. Me? A member of such a dignified profession?

'Ah, well, the Lord works in mysterious ways his wonders to perform!'

The next numbing shock was that Guildhall, although willing to place me on the Teachers' Course, could not do so unless I produce five O Levels and one A.

I was left to rue every hair of my head for wasting my time at the Convent.

A decision had to be made.

'What did you do, petal?'

I still had a further year at the College of Commerce. I resolved to study at night for the required qualifications. It was going to take me longer, but I would do it. I did possess one blessed O Level – the solitary Art! So, four or five more to go! I signed on for English Language at Evening Class and approached dear Mother Cecilia to coach me for Scripture – which had graduated to Religious Knowledge by then.

My interview with the wonderful Mother Cecilia was somewhat hilarious! After I had done all my explaining to her and outlined the proposal for Teaching she said: "Oh no, Susan dear, you were such a naughty girl"!

'Bless!'

Rex Walters was very disappointed. He was, however, completely reassuring and sympathetic. He guaranteed that my place would be held open until I was ready to accept it. It was hard slog for the next couple of years.

In spite of myself, I enjoyed the extra study. There were times when I became disillusioned and wondered if it was all worth it, but I didn't give up. My friends shored me up and I was a frequent visitor to their homes, the Cottingham Tennis Club and of course the pictures! During College vacations, I took holiday jobs.

'Dear God. I suppose thereby hung a tale!'

How did you guess Ronnie? At Christmas 1957 I worked on the Post! The money was fantastic. I pocketed £14 for the whole week. Granted, I did have to start at 6.00 a.m. but could be finished at lunchtime.

'You say "could be"?'

Well yes...er...one day I did forget my parcels and it took me until 3.00 p.m. to deliver them all. On bitterly cold mornings, I was clad in my hooded duffle coat. Consequently, my hair would be out of sight. Admittedly, it was the last straw when some irate householder yelled, "Come on, Sonny, get a move on!"

'You should then have revealed your golden curls – a bit like Rapunzel!'

The Easter holiday of 1958 took me to work at an Opticians. I was to be Receptionist at a Mr.Pizzey's Consulting Rooms on the Anlaby Road.

'Was that his real name? You did meet some strange people!'

It turned out to be a strange job. It was convenient although rather lonely. There was just a desk, filing cabinet and typewriter; no other human distraction. While wiling away the time between typing up Patients' records and meeting them for appointments, I had little to do with Mr. Pizzey – a somewhat taciturn, unforthcoming figure – and could catch up on my swotting for O Levels. I was to take two exams in the Summer. So, a couple of weeks with Mr.Pizzey were useful.

The College's Summer Term was busy. Now, wait for it Ronnie – I did well in the Pitman's tests and graduated with 80 Words Per Minute in Shorthand and 60 Words Per Minute in Typing!! No one was more surprised than me and the valiant Miss Pearson. She sent me off with the following advice and tongue in her cheek:

"There is basic equipment required: a headset, a Dictaphone to play the tapes that must be transcribed and – patience. You need a willingness to become a human conduit as the words of others enter through one's ears, course through one's veins and drop out unseen through fast-moving finger tips".

'That smacks of a well rehearsed, gregarious quote from The Secretary's Guide Book!'

Another feather in my cap was obtaining a good English Language O Level and with Mother Cecilia's gracious help, another O in Religious Knowledge!!

'Darling, you were on your way!'

Well, Ronnie, there was still a long trail to follow. Two more O Levels and an A were needed. I knew it would take me another couple of years at night school.

'Hell's teeth....'

Most important, I needed to work. Summer of 1958 brought a golden opportunity. A fitting vacancy came up at the Royal Station Hotel in Hull.

A member of staff was taking leave and a Receptionist for the main entrance desk was required. Dressed for the part, I applied, was triumphant and became their Number 2 or, well, it may have been their Number 3 or 4, amenable bidder and greeter of guests!

My short stopover at the Hotel was, in the main, uneventful. Only one incident remains locked in my memory. An African Prince and his entourage took up most of the First Floor for two or three days. Various flunkeys came to the desk with assorted requests. Most enquiries were easily dealt with and without aggravation. Imagine my consternation when, at 8.30 p.m. one evening as I was finishing my shift, the Prince leaned heavily towards me over the counter and murmured, "You come to my Room, now, I have drinks!" Fortunately, a senior Receptionist was hovering and about to relieve me – relieve being the operative word – and in courteous, cordial fashion gave him his marching orders. I made my getaway through the Hotel's main revolving door...

'Like a bat out of hell! Ah well, petal, all good practice for Theatre life!'

~

'What was happening to Nicky while all this was going on?'

Nicky was about to begin Secondary Education. He was eleven. I mentioned earlier that he had had much time away from school when he was ill. My Parents must have thought that he needed some help and a Home Tutor was engaged. In due course, Nicky was to begin his studies at Pitman's College, a private Academy in Hull. The Tutor, Alan, came along weekly to coach. I was detailed to serve tea halfway through the session.

'Oh yes....'

Alan was relatively good-looking; dark-haired and tall. I suppose he was about twenty-seven. He was fairly quick to involve me in small talk as I put the tray down and eventually I learned that he, too, owned a Poodle.

'Ah, common ground is always useful....'

Eventually, he took to walking Sooty – pronounced "Soo-ti" –

'Must have been a black Poodle! And was Alan from the West Riding?!

– over to our house – to meet Simon, if you please...

Things moved on apace. The ardent, earnest Alan asked me out! Of course my Mother knew him, approved – he was a teacher after all – and, I was eighteen, for goodness sake!

Our first outing – now called 'date' of course – was to the Priory Cinema. Nothing stirring happened and it was a pleasant jaunt.

'You don't sound very impressed.'

No, Ronnie, I wasn't. Our next 'date' was a trip to Bridlington for an afternoon. Entertaining enough, but amorous Alan decided to try his luck at kissing. Although inexperienced, I must have gone along with it and tried my best to respond. I met with, "Do you always kiss like that?"

'Cheeky bugger! I reckon one wouldn't know how to set about it if one had been called a "dirty little bitch" for doing it!'

Well, that was it as far as I was concerned. To make matters worse, on the way home, he ran over an injured rabbit on the road.

'Dear God – must have been an accident'.

The car in front had hit the poor creature and Alan excused himself by announcing "I thought I'd better kill it". In all fairness, it could have been the kindest course of action, but I was very distressed and couldn't wait to get home. Funny isn't it how some things disgust you. I dismissed Alan from my life. I had no wish to see him again.

'And – I hope that in future he went without his tea!'

I offered no explanation to my Mother – in fact, I don't think I ever told anyone. How could I, when Alan was entrusted to Nicky's care. He was an affable, agreeable man and I was pleased when I heard that he had married a teaching colleague who had yearned, lusted and thirsted after him for some time.

'I 'd like to bet you had her worried!'

I came to realise it was all part of life's rich pattern, Ronnie, but – at the same time, resolved to learn how to kiss properly! Thankfully, I did discover, however, that when real chemistry is around proper kissing doesn't enter into it. You just feel right and it happens. Nevertheless, I was vulnerable and the Fifties was an age of grievous double standards. The young were left to trial and experiment, but woe betide them if mistakes were made. They were judged, condemned and left to pay the penalty if things went wrong. The normality of Sex and healthy, normal functions of the human body was subjected to smut and whispered shame behind the bicycle sheds.

'Fear ruled...fear of pregnancy, fear of being pilloried... of being stigmatized...now, change the subject...all this talk of Sex... What were Gran and Grandpa doing all this time?'

Oh they were lovely, Ronnie. I visited them every Sunday morning and walked from home with a bag of goodies from Daddy's shop. I know they were very pleased and it was one of my favourite times. I could confide in Gran and Grandpa. Of course, they were always coming to the house and Birthdays and Christmas were Gran and Grandpa days as well. I was thinking, I don't remember them ever coming along to see me in the Musical Festivals...in fact, no one came. Only Mummy came...she was there always – ready to praise and encourage. Jessica was my champion and it may be true to say, lived her life through mine.

By the Autumn of that year, I was happily settled in a new, permanent Secretarial post, enrolled into Evening Classes and on the brink of my first romantic and serious relationship.

HARLANDS

1958

'Happy is the man with a wife to tell him what to do and a Secretary to do it'

(Benjamin Mancroft, 3rd Baron,
Peer & Politician)

The Land of Green Ginger in the Old Town of Hull was home to Harlands the Printers. The neighbourhood consisted of winding streets; some cobbled and narrow. Fine architecture could be seen and Holy Trinity Church was a visitor's paradise. The Pier and River Humber were in walking distance and one could spot the statue of King Billy near the Old Corn Exchange. Daddy would take enormous pleasure in regaling us with a story of how the King would dismount from his charger at midnight and go into the nearby Pub for a pint.

Harlands posted an advertisement in the Hull Daily Mail for a Shorthand-Typist.

My holiday job at the Hotel was about to draw to a close, so I took advantage of this timely possibility and applied for Interview. Miraculously, The College had given me good references. Lo and behold – I got the job! I was installed in the Sales Department.

My desk was one of four. The room was poky and separated from the main Department by a very flimsy wall partition. On the other side, the Sales Manager – Mr. Cayley – resided along with other participants in what appeared to be a thriving unit or subdivision of the firm.

My office companions were: Mrs. Robinson, a lady in her Forties who presided over all with wisdom, superiority and grace; Maureen, who complained off and on about inconsequential things and Belinda who was of a similar age to me. Belinda was a comely, engaging blonde. She dressed with immaculate taste – fitted jumpers and full tight-waisted skirts both anchored by fashionable leather belts – and was walking out, so the well-informed Mrs. Robinson told me, with The Boss! The Boss being Son of the Director and owner of the Firm.

As I remember, this young Gentleman was somewhat eccentric and while stripped to the waist, was given to mowing a minute expanse of grass at the façade of the building in the pouring rain!

'Now, how did you get on with the Typing and how many wastepaper baskets did you fill with mistakes!'

Since you mention it, Ronnie, quite a lot. Belinda was not really a good role model. All at once, we would hear "Belinda, letters!" being hollered from the main office. "Coming Mr. Cayley!" she would yell in reply. We would then hear her heels tapping on the lino as she made her way to the clamour of next door. A short interval would pass and Belinda would reappear groaning under an armful of correspondence. Several letters and errors later, her basket would be overflowing with paper. Belinda had a most impressive ripping action when removing it from the typewriter; paper torn from its moorings was crumpled and hurled into the rubbish bin. More often than not, it would miss and the floor then be littered with what looked to be a ream by the end of the day.

'So you took a leaf out of her book?'

A Mr. Newham also occupied a place in the other office. His letters, or memos, were short and uncomplicated and to begin with, it fell to me to take dictation and type them up. He was a man of few words, but I coped fairly well, albeit with shaking hands. He seemed pleased. At intervals, I was able to glance across to where Mr. Cayley would be tied up in frenzied telephone conversation with customers.

'What was he like?'

He would be about thirty, I deduced. He had a mop of curly hair which kept falling over his eyes and hands which were constantly on the move.

Gran would have said he had pianist's fingers; they were long, slender and expressive.

'I used to bite my nails you know – until I met you....'

His conversations were loud and punctuated with rousing, convulsions of laughter. His chair would swivel round and round as the exchange became more lively and buoyant. He was a popular, humorous and intriguing man.

At this time, I came to know Bill Semple. Bill, or Billy as he was affectionately known, was a young Junior Clerk and in the early stages of learning how Sales operated. Billy was a Scot and easily thrown off kilter. Billy would blush. I reckon blushing was infectious, for I found myself flushing in embarrassment whenever attention was drawn to my typing faux pas and clangers. I did try so hard, but they seemed to appear with monotonous regularity; everyone was very patient. So Billy and I were partners in crime when it came to the effort of hiding our blushes.

The journey to and from Harlands was a lengthy one. I took the bus along Anlaby Road into the City station and then had a strenuous, taxing trek into the old Town.

'Wearing high heels?'

Oh yes, Ronnie. At least three inches high! It was engrossing and the shops of Whitefriargate were awash with gear and glad rags. This Street led directly into the Marketplace which became a hub of activity at weekends, largely because of Carvers. Carvers was regarded as the most delectable fish n' chip stall in the vicinity and attracted many from far and wide. Its only rival was The Gainsborough which was a Fish Restaurant and lodged next door to Goldstones near the City Centre; soft furnishing specialists frequented by Jessica when she was scouting for carpets and curtains. Mr. Rutter....

'Now tell me more about the fish n' chips....

Well, both these establishments were renowned for praiseworthy meals. The Gainsborough reached for the sky and occupied numerous floors, nooks and crannies. After a stiff climb, one could grab a corner table and wait for a long-suffering Waitress.

'I bet it was worth it.'

Now, as I was saying, Mr. Rutter presided over the first floor of Goldstones. His pattern of speech fascinated me whenever he visited 355 Beverley Road –

Oh, I forgot to mention earlier that our house was called Cerne Abbas; it was quite some time before anyone knew the origin of its name – to take measurements.

'I hope you didn't stare!'

Well, I couldn't help it. Mr. Rutter was a large man. His bulk even taxed the confines of our Breakfast Room. There was never enough leeway for him. He had very fleshy lips...

'Your portrayals are most unkind. Poor bugger....'

... and when he spoke, it sounded as if he had a mouthful of potato.

'Now you're digressing. What else was happening?'

Belinda was called to Secretarial action several times for the Boss. It became necessary for her to be transferred from Mr. Cayley's beck and call.

'Don't tell me you were to be promoted? Your waste paper basket was already full!'

I was very nervous, but yes, the call came "Susan, letters!"

'Susanne Ubble!'

I'll have you know that I managed very well and Mr. Cayley was fun. He was heard to groan several times but he was full of praise when I got it right!

Belinda lived at Brough. This village was just beyond Anlaby. So, now and again, Belinda would offer me a lift home. This was a spree of sheer luxury for she was allowed to borrow the Boss's car – a Mercedes Benz Sports model no less!

'Did he know what he was doing?'

I did wonder, Ronnie, but in truth neither of us cared! It was bliss to scoot along the Anlaby Road; the roof down and the sun burning.... the only alarming thing was that Belinda insisted on driving with bare feet!

'Don't tell me more...I'm feeling sick...'

When I drew Belinda's attention to this potentially dangerous, quirky practice, she remarked gaily "Oh don't Sue, we'll be OK. We'll have to be – this bloody car's his pride and joy! He thinks I'm wicked already!"

'The pair of you sound like Thelma and Louise!'

I had enrolled at Evening Classes for my next two O Levels. It was hard work. I was known to flag but determination and the blessings of youthful energy spurred me on. Some social gatherings softened the edges of toil and my friends were a salvation.

Susan Harrison introduced me to a new fling, a new exploit. She suggested that all us girls try out the University Saturday evening dances.

'Jessica quote: "Your Father will come and collect you! When does it finish?"'

'How did you guess, Ronnie! You've hit the nail on the head. Daddy did come and collect this risqué band of gels at the stroke of midnight when the dancing ended!

'I hope you didn't leave your slipper on the pavement!'

Fortunately, the Fathers did take turns to ferry their offspring every Saturday, so poor Daddy wasn't on duty for every occasion. It was quite a palaver getting everyone in the car. We were all wearing abundant, profuse Fifties skirts with equally exuberant tulle petticoats. Even the bus conductors on the outward ride shouted, "You'll 'ave t' go upstairs – I can't do with that lot down 'ere!"

'Quite!'

It was a joyous, laughter-filled time. We did not know fear. Our Parents did, of course. Mothers and Fathers intent on being over protective; ever vigilant, ever watchful and yes, ever possessive eyes. Yet, not once did my Parents unfold or disclose the reasons for their uneasiness. Did they realise or acknowledge that under our civilised veneer we are all primitive. Our animal heritage is a force that drives and will not be denied…no doubt that's why they were fearful!

'We had to learn coping tactics but few of us were taught how to'.

That was the Fifties bane. Fear of consequence was uppermost in our uncertainty. To be fair, I doubt that my poor Mother was in any way sophisticated or in the know. Nevertheless, shame played an important part in this quandary. What if one's friends knew of offspring 'getting into trouble'. That would be mortification indeed; far worse than Daughter or Son's suffering or disgrace. As for contraception – well, don't get me going on that Ronnie! Now I am ancient and have plenty of time to think on these things, I am convinced that my Mother was a most effective mode of contraception in those days!

'Oh you mean she frightened you to death!'

I had no knowledge of such things until I was well into my Twenties and then facts were sketchy. In any case, an

Agenda was fixed: Marriage and leaving home came first. Couples married so that they could sleep together. Now, many of those same couples are divorced.

Time moves on; the jinx is lifted and secrets are exposed. The emancipated young are not hindered by dogma and old wives tales. Their love is wholesome; they are footloose, fancy free and unfettered.

Pal Susan and I were great fans of Traditional Jazz.

'You're not going to tell me that you were Groupies!'

We did trail round the Concerts and Chris Barber and his Band often came along to play at Hull's City Hall. It was bliss listening to Ottalie Patterson and as for Monty Sunshine's Clarinet playing – well that was...

'Something else?'

Lonnie Donegan was another favourite and I must admit my Parents and little Nicky were very tolerant when the house was filled with 'Rock Island Line' and 'The Cumberland Gap'....

'Saints preserve us Alice!'

Mummy was determined to make sure that I had all the appropriate clothes for these teenage airings. I know she was not financially flush at this time. She did not work and I suspect that Daddy was not overly liberal with the housekeeping.

'Not tight, surely?'

I have a feeling that there was a suggestion of living beyond means. Mummy was generous and hell-bent on her daughter being turned out in artistic, aesthetically pleasing...

'Schmutter?'

Just the word I was looking for, Ronnie! I think Jessica had eventually got her head around the fact that she couldn't bring my growing to a halt and decided that she would launch it in the most spectacular way that she could.

'Bless her….'

So, the laudable Mrs. Sizer was hustled into service once more. Remnants of material were transformed into visions of delight. Mummy had original, novel ideas and her innovative notions drew gasps of appreciation on more than one occasion.

Edi Burt became a further source of extravaganzas. Edi and Harold Burt had a daughter, Hilary. "our 'ilary" as she was referred to…

'You are wicked!'

As it happened, "our 'ilary" was away at College – the Guildhall School of Music & Drama in London, no less – studying Music…

'What a coincidence..'

Wasn't it just….well, 'lary it seems had a considerable wardrobe of London clothes and wanted to get rid of a few…

'I bet the lovely Jessica stepped in and said "Oh, our Susan would love that".

Ronnie, you're a mind reader. In due course, Edi would pass on a whole suitcase of fabulous Model, as it was called then, creations: Susan Small, Horrockses Cottons and Pringle sweaters! Mummy – and me – were ecstatic!

So, every now and again, another suitcase would arrive and Mummy and I would rummage delightedly through mounds of booty! Presumably, Mum and Edi came to some financial arrangement. I know that my Mother would insist upon recompense. She was very proud and I learned from her fine example.

'No wonder you didn't mind when I kitted you out in stuff from the Nearly New shop!'

"our 'ilary" later went on to marry a Ship's Doctor she had met on a voyage to Ceylon. She was to visit the home of an Indian College friend. That really set the tongues wagging in Kirk Ella and every Mother was on the lookout for other eligible Doctors for their Daughters to hitch themselves to! Jessica announced: "Oh that's lovely – lovely to marry a Doctor a good bit older than yourself, who would look after you like one of the children!"

'Extraordinary! She wouldn't have had me in the running then! Sounds as though she was looking for the ultimate in protection for her little girl...'

My Mother was competitive and ambitious. She aspired to greater things. She was ingenious, spirited and keen....

'For you, certainly....'

At the time, all those years ago, I found it demanding and taxing. I was trying to mature into my own person but often found myself striving to fit into someone else's shoes. Perhaps I did need to be driven!

'I'll quote Jessica again: "I want the best for Susan. I don't want her to suffer. I can see the pitfalls I want her to avoid. She could go far – she is talented"...she loved you Sue and wanted a glowing future for you.'

That's probably why, one day, she said to me "Oh, there's more to life than having children". Yet is that not what most young women yearn for one day...

Fortunately, my Mother did have interests of her own. She was a very eager member of the Kirk Ella Amateur Dramatic Society. There again, her rival for the leading parts, a Joan Dennett, was dismissed as a somewhat pushy, contentious individual who got under Jessica's skin when Auditions were taking place!

'What fun!'

While all this was going on, my Father was attending his Masonic Hall meetings. That was all rather mystifying but seemed to be the done thing for Hull's businessmen.

Also, my Parents did have a wide circle of friends: a mixed bunch consisting of Lena and Eric Wright (Eric was an Optician and Lena was a regular telephone communicator, much to the apparent irritation of my Mother who invariably, in hushed tones, murmured "tell her I'm out" or "I've got the Insurance Man here"). En passant, Insurance agents collected premiums at the house in those days. Also, the Vernons intermediary man would call for completed Football Pools coupons. My Mother filled these in religiously every week, but didn't let on!

Several friends were Fish Merchants – Mr. & Mrs. Crack –

'I don't believe it!'

– and other folk engaged in Commerce or Trade.

'Oo...er...shades of the pretentious, snotty Miss Jefferson!'

Auntie Anne and Uncle Erbie, tried and true, were always regular callers.

They came over to play cards. Jessica was a dab hand at Poker. By the bye, Uncle Erbie's barnet seemed to have recovered from my infantile ministrations!

So, Ronnie, all this diversion enabled me to get on with the very elaborate, concentrated arranging of Saturday night Hops at the University with Susan Harrison and cronies.

~

The main Students' Union Building at the University of Hull in 1958, was set back far from the main Cottingham Road and approached by an exceptionally long driveway. Once through the Entrance Archway, Students and Visitors had a choice of two dancing areas. The predominant space housed a dance band.

'Victor Sylvester style?'

Yes, Ronnie. All the musicians were formally dressed. You know, white jackets and bow ties. My Harry Butters' shindig days had been worth their weight in gold, for the prospect of wrestling with Waltzes, Foxtrots and Quicksteps held no dismay.

The second Venue was across the walkway where the Jazz and Rock n' Roll jiving took place. This was probably a Study area during the day, but on Saturday evenings it was smoke-filled, hot and dim. Elbow room was in short supply and thumping, throbbing Bill Hayley and Elvis could puncture the average ear drum.

'No booze, I presume?'

There was a Bar on the first floor. Now Jessica would have raised Cain about that, but she didn't know, so it didn't matter. Drink was a no-go area for ladies in the Fifties, Ronnie. It would not have occurred to me to partake of anything other than orange juice.

'You must have been a barrel of fun! You certainly made up for it later!'

As for going into a Pub alone, unaccompanied by a Gentleman, well, you may as well have been a lady of ill repute...I think the Student likely lads hobnobbed in 'The Railway' on Cottingham Road before fraternizing with this vista of femininity, but they never appeared to be the worse for wear.

This maidenly ritualistic celebration all began on Saturday afternoons when I would commandeer the Bathroom for doing hair, face and everything else that needed doing. Then it would be time to meet the girls, take the bus, giggle and so appear primed and ready in the Ballroom.

We were never short of partners. The Ballroom strategy did not waver; men in a group and women in a group. Eyes were roving over each and girls were just as choosy as boys. From afar, one could size up the options and sit, hoping against hope that the selected quarry would pick on you and have the nerve to cover the distance across the Ballroom to ask for a dance. If one hit the jackpot and glances were exchanged provocatively, then it was time to look away with chaste blush and wait in suspense.

'Of course, he might have been looking at the girl beside you!'

Quite, Ronnie. That was indeed disappointing and more so if, instead, his mate, who was not overly dishy, had you in his sights. That would be time to shuffle along to the Ladies Lavatory!

'How deceitful!'

That's as maybe, Ronnie, but ballroom dancing is a very intimate, intense affair. One is held very close. One is aware of bodies touching in a heightened and odd way. One can feel another's breath in your ear!

'Oh, give over!'

Imagine a small person like me, no more than 5'2", being clutched by a 6'0" giant! Only a chest would be visible. Dancing with the wrong person could be an excruciating pursuit.

We were faced with a conglomeration of multinational Students. It was exciting and different. I remember so clearly a chivalrous black Student by the name of Nat – I guess short for Nathanial, wouldn't you say Ronnie?

'Sounds like it, pet....!'

Nat would make a bee-line for me. Quick-steps were his favourite and I would be utterly zonked by the time the band played the final strains and I was released from a vice like grip. Nat could cover the floor at a forcible rate of knots. He was a courteous, courtly Gentleman and it was a pleasure to know him.

Pal Susan also made a jiving conquest. Benca Coca, as he was known, was also a black fellow. Benca Coca had something of a reputation.

'Go on, don't stop there!'

He was a stunning, sensational dancer. Benca spent most of the evening in the Jazz quarter and believe me, was never in search of a partner or an audience. I reckon many of his chums must have been green with envy. The story goes that he was of Royal blood and certainly not short of cash. He had a following. Not surprising, for most of us were mesmerized by his jaw-dropping gyrating. His was an embarrassment of riches, for... he was also hypnotically handsome.

'Oh God, what next?'

Well, he became enamoured of Pal Susan. Susan was a very fetching blonde with a beguiling bearing...

'And....'

Susan could also dance. So, she was taken to the floor, repeatedly.

'Not literally I hope?'

Certainly not, Ronnie, but Susan did allow him to see her home which of course was very near to the University. Unbeknown to Susan, her Mother, a formidable lady with a very exacting code of behaviour, was at an upstairs window.

'All this sounds vaguely familiar....!'

Susan told me later that she had quizzed Benca about where he was going after. His reply was a trifle enigmatic – "You really do not want to know that, Susan"! Of course this cryptic comment conjured up a flight of fancy; we imagined a multiplicity of disreputable, honky-tonk dives in the City Centre.

'What about Mother Harrison?'

Ah, well, her opening gambit was "Don't you dare come home with that black youth again!"

'God, 50's racism as well...'

Yes Ronnie, it did not auger well. Hers was an unjust presumption, for Benca treated Susan with utmost gallantry and respect. Like Nat, he was a cultivated, mannerly Gentleman; always remembered as a jiving genius who happened to weave a magnetic, seductive spell on the dance floor.

~

'Now, come on, you said earlier that you were on the verge of a love affair. When did that happen?'

In the Autumn of 1958, I met Tom Downey. He was a Geography student at the University. As usual, I had gone along with the girls to the Saturday dance. I was wearing a dress which had been passed on from my Mother.

'Stylish?'

Oh, yes Ronnie. She had been a guest at "our 'ilary's" September Wedding. Mrs. Sizer had really come up trumps with her dress. Mum had chosen a cream fine wool sheath pattern and accessorised it with silver grey shoes, hat and handbag. It had generated compliments all round. This dress had been hanging in the wardrobe ever since. When my Birthday came round in October, I had the gaggle of girls round for a pre-Saturday-night-Dance supper Party. Mum seemed to think that her dress was being wasted so suggested, very generously, that I give it an airing. Again, it met with huge approval from my friends and I felt very sophisticated wearing a fitted number instead of the black taffeta skirt and flounces so fashionable at the time.

My Mother was an accomplished, nimble Hostess. There was much moaning went on before guests arrived, but her preparations were detailed and careful. She went to enormous trouble to think of everything. The oak-panelled Dining Room with its crackling fire in the grate was the ideal space for entertaining; the table sparkled with polished cutlery and glass. This time, the walls rang with the sound of girlish chatter.

'Did Charlie and Grandpa beat a hasty retreat on such occasions?'

Gran was there to help and Daddy would be on Midnight Taxi Duty.

'I expect that took the poor bugger some time if he had several girls to deliver to the far reaches of Kirk Ella'.

He didn't seem to mind, Ronnie; he was always jokey and good-tempered. My friends loved Daddy. Invariably, he would have a supply of daft stories to tell them. As he reached the punch-line, Daddy would burst into uncontrollable laughter and give the whole thing away.

The main University Ballroom was full that night. Nat appeared as usual and piloted me around the floor. As we sped by, I caught sight of someone I hadn't seen there before. He was looking at me rather intently. I caught his gaze and found myself smiling. The Quickstep finished and Nat dutifully steered me back towards the rest of the girls.

A Waltz was the next on the list. I felt a tap on my shoulder and turned. Before me was a white-jacketed young man. I recognised him immediately. He had been watching me.

'Don't stop there – I'm on the edge of my seat!'

He was of medium height, broad-shouldered and very dark-haired. His eyes twinkled. His face was striking as opposed to handsome, but as he grinned I noticed the even, white teeth and generous mouth.

There was instant charisma. How do you explain such appeal, such magnetism, such force of personality? It was all there in that brief, passing moment. "D' y' want t' dance?" said he. I nodded....

'Go on...you always stop at a crucial moment...!'

Well, I was about to say that his accent was very strange. I had not heard it ever before. The speech was thick and sounds seem to originate at the back of his throat. That didn't seem to matter in the least, for neither of us spoke again. I was being moved very skilfully about the floor. More importantly, I don't think there was an inch between us! We danced every dance together after that and when the strains of the Last Waltz wafted through the air, we danced cheek-to-cheek....

'It seems that Jessica's dress had done the trick! I bet the rest of those girls were agog – you were obviously away with the fairies!'

All I could think of was that I was behaving in an incredibly fast way. I mean to say, cheek-to-cheek! I had only met this boy a couple of hours ago!

'Now come on, I want to know all about him!'

Well...the reason that his accent seemed so strange, was that he came from Liverpool. At that time, I hadn't a clue about Liverpool. He might have said he came from the Moon! He called me "Mate" quite frequently and spoke of being a "Scouser". He was astonished when I asked him what a Scouser was! Tom was of Irish descent. I now realise that his black curly hair was such a typical characteristic of his ancestry. Also his disarming, irresistible and persuasive conversation totally threw me.

'You were hooked!'

I was Ronnie. He laughed uproariously when I told him that my Daddy was collecting me from the Dance, but asked very politely if he could walk me to the main road where the car would be waiting. The girls were tittering in the background and having a whale of a time at my expense.

I was on cloud nine and oblivious. As we got nearer to Daddy and my coach, Tom asked how he could meet me again. Feeling very forward and fast once more, I gave him my telephone number!

'Hussy!'

All was revealed to my Parents, well…nearly all! They seemed fully satisfied that this was a normal course of events and I didn't receive any negative feed-back. I did say, "You'll have to meet Tom soon". That didn't arouse any suspicious glances, so it seemed I had been given the go-ahead!

Our first date was somewhat hilarious. Tom met me from the bus and we went over the road to Hull's Regal cinema.

'Don't tell me you sat on the back row?'

We certainly did Ronnie, but, I hasten to add, we didn't see much of 'Gunfight at the OK Corral' which was the film showing at the time. We were surrounded by kissing couples, cigarette smoke and the prying eye of an Usherette!

The opportunities to meet were infrequent. My job at Harlands consumed my days and Night School occupied a couple of evenings. Towards the end of each week, up to Tom's Christmas vacation, the phone would ring and the Tom voice would enquire "Are y' goin' t' the Dance?" We would dance the whole night through.

Eventually, Tom was introduced to my Parents. Daddy, bless him, broke all ice by saying "Now, Tom, I hear you're fond of a pint. We'll go to the Red Lion some time". Jessica -

'Bless her…'

– invited Tom to a meal now and again. She summed him up thus: "Well, I like Tom, but I can't understand what he's saying!"

Once Tom had found his way by bus to 355 Beverley Road, our date nights increased. Tom was living in digs at that time. Ironically, his Landlady lived in Cottingham where most of the University Students were berthed. Many were staying in Student Halls of Residence. He caught the same bus route as Grandpa and I had done all those years ago in the riding days.

Our keeping company or wooing took place on long country walks during cold Autumn nights. Poor Tom came very ill-prepared for a hike and would often exclaim, "Look, mate, I'm bloody freezin'!" I suppose it was a measure of how much he cared for me that he put up with the drop in temperature. It puzzles me now, when I remember. Why on earth didn't we stay at home? There would have been plenty of room for a courting couple!

'Perhaps going out was freezin' but private – romantic....'

I still remember so clearly following behind Tom as he forged ahead, singing 'Danny Boy'! The black curly hair, the un-weatherproof white jacket and the call "Cum on, mate, 'urry up!" To this day, they are treasured memories....you don't mind, do you Ronnie?

'How could I? He was a man after my own heart! Besides, I could see that he loved you, perhaps before you ever knew how much...'

Soon, Tom left for the Christmas vacation – back to Exeter Road, Bootle, where he lived with his Mother. As far as I knew she was a single Parent. Tom did speak of an Uncle who went to sea, but -

'There were a lot of Uncles around in those days!

Soon, the letters came – "Heard 'Wake up, little Susie' by the Everley Brothers. Seemed appropriate somehow. Missing you a helluva lot!"

I discovered that I was missing Tom a helluva lot too! We saw a great deal of each other over the coming weeks and soon Easter 1959 was approaching.

Tom moved into Needler, a Hall of Residence in Cottingham. I came to realise that he was quite a street-wise guy.

'In what way?'

Well, I suppose I didn't really cotton on to the fact that Tom did waste a lot of study time. That didn't really affect me. I was very attached to him, blind, oblivious and – young; nothing else really mattered.

'What are you trying to tell me?'

I heard the word 'Poker' bandied about quite often and it seems Poker schools at Needler were happening very frequently, so often in fact that they became lucrative and students could supplement grants very profitably with winnings. Tom was winning. Hence, were lectures being cut?

'Ah..'

As Spring turned into Summer that year, we realised we were in love. The relationship, although a pure one, had moved to a different level. Our feelings for each other were deep, profound; our meetings were more frequent.

Visitors, girl-friends mostly, I suppose, were allowed at Needler Hall on Sunday evenings. I asked my Parents if I could meet Tom there for a couple of hours.

'Did they put the mockers on that?'

No, Ronnie. Much to my amazement, they didn't. My Mother's sole comment was, "Well, I don't know. That's where they sleep, isn't it?"

'Bless again....'

Tom and I savoured those private moments. I had learned to kiss properly by then.

'Eureka!'

In those days, Ronnie, everything stopped there. I was a virgin, Tom was a Roman Catholic and for both reasons Sex before marriage was a noli me tangere situation: no touching. Both of us knew our love would be honourable and true until the right time.

'He did love you, pet....'

One such kissing moment is locked in memory of those far off days. The Radio was playing in the background, lights were dimmed and Sunday night's 'Sing Something Simple' struck up a rousing chorus of 'Toreador'! "Bloody 'ell!" exclaimed Tom, "Well, mate, that sure is an antidote for temptation!"

Tom was in for a bitter disappointment. He failed his Finals. How well I knew what had happened. I had been down that road too. Like me, he picked up the pieces, made his way home to Liverpool and enrolled at the De La Salle College there to acquire Teaching qualifications. We were to be separated.

The parting did not lessen our love. We lived for the letters dropping on to the doormat. I indulged and wallowed in writing to Tom. He wrote long, fascinating letters about his work, his home and his life. We planned to meet in the Summer when he had a break from studying. He spoke proudly of staying at the New York Hotel in Hull and taking me to the Dinner Dance there.

'What were Jessica and Charlie making of all this?'

I was about to mention that, Ronnie. The crunch came when my Mother cornered me in the Breakfast Room. "Is this serious, this with you and Tom?" she fired. I found myself stammering, not really knowing how to answer. I said, thinking she would be relieved to hear that all was above board, "Well, yes, but in the nicest possible way". Her retort devastated me: "After all that's been done for you! Well, you'll have a lot of children if you marry Tom! Oh, but if he's your choice!"

'Meaning he wouldn't be hers! Mmn, difficult to take, love....'

Yes, Ronnie, it was. There was no explanation. No reasons were given. I was just condemned to disappointment, disapproval and displeasure. Silence between us reigned for days.

'Dear God...'

I defied her, Ronnie. I continued to write to Tom. I did have to offer some reasoning to him and he was saddened. Although Marriage had not been discussed, I am sure that is what Tom had in mind. He was a lovely man. "One day, I will prove how much I love you", he said simply.

'I think you really loved him, didn't you?'

I did, Ronnie.

In spite of this disturbing upset, I continued with my studies – continued until Tom and I could meet once more. In the Summer of 1959, I obtained two more precious O Levels: English Literature and Geography.

'Presumably, by then you knew something about Lake TITIcaca!'

Tom did take me to dance at the New York Hotel. He stayed in his old Cottingham digs for a Summer weekend. We met again on Sunday and took the bus for an afternoon in Beverley. I recall Auntie Anne and Uncle Erbie visited that weekend. I sensed that they had been let in on what appeared to my Parents to be a grievous, destructive debacle. There was something of a frost!

'What a dreadful shame...'

I spent some very lonely hours over the coming weeks. There was no discussion, no sympathy or understanding. I had stepped out of line; I had been disobedient and so was subjected to reproach and disapproval. I stuck it out for as long as I could, but the feeling of isolation, criticism and blame was overwhelming.

'Perhaps if you had had some clarification...perhaps if your Parents had discussed Tom's religion and its

implications with you, or hopes for your future and why they were disgruntled, it might have made some sense...'

Yes, Ronnie, but there was nothing, only emptiness. It wore me down eventually and Tom seemed to drift further and further away. It was easier to comply, to give in....I seem to have spent much of my life doing that –

'Until you met me!'

If only I could say how sorry I am. Say how much I loved Tom. I was unhappy, utterly miserable and sorry; I would wish him to know that. I treated Tom very unkindly because I knew that was expected of me. I was required to turn my back on a good, loving young man who could have made me very happy. Throughout my life, Tom never left my thoughts. From time to time, I remembered our innocence, our happiness and our joy. He was my first real love and has remained so, in my heart, forever.

'Oh darling....how very sad...'

There is some irony to this tale, Ronnie. My Father's Sister, the pampered mollycoddled Laura, was married to a Roman Catholic and had converted to the religion herself. Not a word passed any lips.

'I'm surprised that Gran and Grandpa didn't have some say in all this...'

Yes, it was strange and yet, when I was visiting one day, I remember Gran saying "Is he black, this boy?" I was shocked, but couldn't see any point in further discussion. There was an obvious bias going on..."No, he's just an Irish Catholic, that's all..." I said.

'Was Tom completely over after that?'

No, Ronnie. He came back into my life some time later, much later...

From time to time, I received postcards from Tom. There was a link that neither of us could bear to break. He never faded from my life. A message from Italy read:

"Mark's Square and the Basilica – one dream did come true..."

~

Reality returned to a familiar round. Harlands was fun and I looked forward to work. My friends, knowing of my sadness and Tom, did their best to cheer me up. My 20th Birthday was in October and another foray to the University Saturday dances was fixed up. Those evenings, for several weeks, seemed very alien and remote without Tom. I could see him around every corner.

'How did you feel about meeting someone else?'

Well, I wasn't looking. Life, however, plays strange tricks. It moves along and often the unexpected happens.

'Who was the unexpected one this time?'

A bearded Chemistry student by the name of John Hooker. He was engaging; an appealing young man. I suppose one could say that his credentials would fit in very well with my Mother's predisposed formula for Admirer.

'Oh Eck!'

John was a very kind, jolly man. I was attracted to him and our liaison grew stronger. The driving force was his acceptability. He was suitable; satisfactory and appealing to my Mother. He was approved.

'Church of England, petal?'

Goes without saying, Ronnie. Physical attraction plays such an important part in youthful fascination. Tom had it in spades. In those days, our salad days, we could be blinded by it. The code demanded that we observe the rules. What a pity we couldn't have slept with our lovers; so to bypass, circumvent and dilute the sexual anticipation.

'Then get down to the important business of sharing four walls, you mean?'

I reckon many did just that, but it was all covert, veiled and sly. I was too scared to push the boat out. I did, however, progress somewhat and my kissing must have been more up to scratch.

'You've got a thing about kissing...just forget that tactless remark of the insensitive Tutor Alan and remember what Ingrid Bergman said:

"I do not know how to kiss, or I would kiss you. Where do the noses go?" '

Brilliant Ronnie!

So, I saw John frequently in the months to come. He had known Tom for both had lived at Needler Hall. John, a year below, was once heard to mention "the charm of Tom"; how well I knew what he meant.

Life was busy, my studies were busy and the hours were long. I thought of Tom a great deal.

'Out of sight, out of mind?'

No, Ronnie, not really. Our lives had drifted apart and distance played its role in separating us. The young can be very fickle, rash or unthinking. Someone once said to me "Life's tragedy is that we get old too soon and wise too late"!

'In a nutshell...'

~

John graduated in the Summer of 1960. His family came up to Yorkshire to attend the Ceremony. I was introduced and invited to join the Hookers for lunch. I liked them enormously. They hailed from the tiny village of Yalding in Kent.

Rose Hooker, John's Mother, was a most welcoming woman and her stories of apple-picking and country life were entertaining and warm.

John's Father drove an aging Morris and very generously allowed John to take me for a spin. John's only Brother, Clive, was a good-looking teenager who seemed to like me. John had already told me that another member of the clan, Auntie Billie, kept house while the family was away.

Before the Hookers left for the South, I was offered many invitations to holiday with them. There were to be significant developments, however, before I was able to accept.

~

That Summer, my future at Guildhall hung in the balance. If all boded well, I would be able to take up my place in September of that year. Much to my dismay, I failed my A Level English Literature. The long, tiring hours of work during the day and study at night, had taken its toll; I was bedevilled. Or, so I thought....

'You contacted Rex Walters?'

Yes, darling, I did. He said, "Don't worry, I'll move everything to get you here – I'm sure the A Level won't carry too much weight".

He was right Ronnie. Guildhall accepted me and it was to be all systems go for the beginning of my Teachers' Course in September 1960.

In the meantime, Harlands was moving its premises lock, stock and barrel to Springfield Way, Anlaby...

'Darling, you were already there!'

It was July. John invited me to take a week's holiday from the Office and visit Kent. I was excited and my Parents didn't seem to block the idea. After, I would be hell-bent on preparation for Guildhall.

John met me from the train at King's Cross. That station was to play a precious, prized part in my life for years to come....

'Yes, my darling, how well I remember….'

I had not travelled by Tube before. Can you imagine? Escalators terrified me and I was relieved to be in John's care. Then, we took another train to Maidstone and from there on to Yalding. 'Kenwyn', a bungalow on Vicarage Road was home to the Hooker family. I was given a momentous, homely welcome.

'Did you like the village?'

Oh I did, Ronnie. It was an old Medieval Village and its lanes wound close to the River Medway. At the heart of this untroubled, tranquil retreat and hideaway, was The Walnut Tree Pub. The weather that week was hot and balmy. John and I spent leisurely hours strolling along the river bank and stopping now and again to give way to more than the average bout of kissing. My sexual edification took a leap forward that week!

'Now then…!'

Interestingly, no member of the Hooker family raised eyebrows when I returned with grass in my hair! I was at ease that week. I was cosseted in the glow of a country existence where no pressure bore down upon me. I was free…

John and I borrowed the old Morris on more than one occasion to visit Hastings and Folkstone. Anlaby seemed a long way away…

'Then you were woken with a start!'

How did you know that, Ronnie? Yes, there came a phone call…. "Sue", said Rose, "your Father has called. Will you ring back?"

'Oh hell…'

Daddy explained that they had been concerned because I had not telephoned since leaving home. I was reminded that I would be going away to College soon, so it had been thoughtless not to realise that that would upset my Mother enough, without not hearing from me when on holiday.

'Bugger...your peace shattered once more...'

To be fair, I had been inconsiderate. I was young, I was happy and I was carefree. In a single moment, however, I felt nothing other than guilt... self-reproach and blame. I felt the apron strings tighten once more.

~

I returned to work and began to make plans for Guildhall. At that time, I had no idea where on earth I was going to live when in London. The College did not offer an accommodation list. I didn't have a clue.

Now, nearly a lifetime later, I am full of admiration for Parents who guide their children to face an independent life away from home. I see cars, laden with belongings, bound for unfamiliar destinations. I see them vetting Halls of Residence and Cities, intent on safety and security. I cannot recall any Parental assistance when I was contemplating life in such an estranged, untried environment.

I had given my notice at Harlands and when August approached, I was still wondering...

'Was panic setting in?'

Well, it was Ronnie. Then, out of the blue, a Guardian Angel materialised. Betty Lovell, while staying with friends in Hull, was working for three weeks as a temporary Typist at Harlands. It transpired that Betty was a Music student at the Central School in London. She was earning pocket money before returning to her home in Southall, Middlesex.

"Sue, why don't you come and stay with me, until you find somewhere to live? I'm sure my Mum and Dad would be pleased to have you..."

'Your Saviour!'

Meantime, Hull Education Authority reviewed my case and awarded a Grant for Fees and Maintenance. Added to that, I won a David Holt Scholarship for my studies – worth £100!

My parting from Harlands was sad. I was quite overcome by the good wishes and hopes for my future. Mrs. Robinson, the complaining Maureen and dear Belinda who was soon to be married to her Boss, David Morrison, were all tearful. When the time came for me to say Goodbye to Billy, I too was in floods of tears! He pressed the following Poem into my hands, blushed and whispered: "Good Luck, dear Sue!"

To Sue
Let the birds in the morning greet you,
Let the golden sunshine meet you,
Let the bells of Heaven peal,
Let the Queen come down and kneel.

~

Let all the men that know you,
Love you,
For those ignorant of your presence
Have lost the treasure of Life.

'Did you know he was in love with you, Sue?'

I had no idea. Now, so many years later, wherever Billy may be, I would wish him to know how much I have cherished his winsome, exquisite words. His touching, matchless emotion has brought much comfort when I have needed it most.

~

A friend in need, once more, was dear John. He came to Beverley Road a couple of days before my Term started. He was to drive me to Southhall, Middlesex, London.

'Sue, he was a diamond…'

I met many diamonds in my time, Ronnie.

I'm sure my departure was very painful for my Parents and young Nicky. He was then fourteen years old. I was to celebrate my 21st Birthday in October, so perhaps the wrench was to be short-lived. They would look forward to my brief weekend return in a couple of weeks.

"If you don't like the look of it, don't leave her there!" called my Mother. What on earth she thought John was going to do if he didn't "like the look of it", beats me. She was laying all responsibility on to him, poor dear.

'Surely your Father could have left the Shop to Annie for the day and taken you himself!'

Quite, Ronnie.

THE GUILDHALL SCHOOL OF MUSIC & DRAMA

1960/1963

'You have Witchcraft in your lips...'
(Henry V – William Shakespeare)

Betty's terraced home was in the heart of London's suburbia. Row upon row of houses stretched as far as the eye could see. At intervals, the random parades of shops interrupted streets and banks of dwellings. Neat, fenced front gardens revealed spruce hedges, compact lawns and late Summer flowers.

John brought the Morris to a halt as dusk was falling. "Well....here we are", he said and took my hand.

'Well, did he like the look of it?'

There was little we could do about it then, Ronnie. Night was drawing in and John had yet to cross London and make his way home to Yalding. He had a job to go to on Monday, the following day. He was working in Dartford, for ICI.

Mr. and Mrs. Lovell were most welcoming; jollied on by Betty's animation and vitality. She was a chatterbox!

Soon, it was time to bid farewell to John. As I waved and watched the old Morris disappear, I felt vulnerable, exposed and weak with homesickness.

I was frightened. I was trapped. Why was I in this place? Why had I turned my happy, safe life around? I didn't want to be here. There was no remedy, only some force driving me on. I couldn't cry, I couldn't let anyone see....I just wanted to go home.

My room was tiny, trim and consoling in its privacy. I remember two water colour paintings which dominated the walls. They were baby pictures; one baby with a blue cover and one with a pink cover!

'Astonishing the things we can see in our mind's eye – so many years later...poor love. I wish I had been there to give you a hug!'

Perhaps you were, Ronnie, in a funny kind of way... somebody was, for I spent a wretched night and hardly slept. All the house noises were odd, bizarre and peculiar. The smells were not Anlaby smells! Dawn broke and after broken sleep, I realised where I was...

'Now, come on, let's talk about important things... what did you wear for your first Guildhall day?'

A lovely chocolate brown, linen dress. My hair was long then and I wore it in a French pleat. It was very conservative, Ronnie...very Jessica!

Betty was due at Central School by mid-morning, so she had plenty of time to shepherd this Yorkshire novice on her first harrowing plunge into the unknown! I was utterly adrift! I had my sight, but was blind...each step forward was tentative, unwonted and un-trodden. Betty's brisk, spry control of the situation was most supportive and refreshing.

We took the Bus to our first Tube Station – Park Royal. At 8.30 a.m. it was bustling and crowded. "We go as far as Hammersmith on the Piccadilly but then I'll have to leave you, Sue, to change to another line. You need the District Line via the Embankment to Blackfriars. That's the Green one".

'Fuck!'

If I had been in the habit of using the F word in those days Ronnie, that's the word I'd have chosen. I was paralysed at the thought of being abandoned.

"Now, Sue", announced the faithful, confident Betty, "I doubt you'll be at Guildhall for the whole day, your first day – probably be finished by 4.00 p.m., so I'll meet you at Hammersmith Station about 5.00 o'clock to take you home." With that, Betty disappeared into a dense commuter crowd.

'Now, Susanne Ubble, screw your courage to the sticking place!'

Ronnie, I had no choice. I suppose with wide eyes and trembling frame, I asked a very approachable, ordinary middle-aged woman if I was about to board the District Line. "Yes, duck, City or Heathrow?"

'Another Fuck!'

"Blackfriars", I spluttered. "You're OK, duck", said she.

I managed to get a seat in what turned out to be a very packed train. All passengers seemed to be immersed in newspapers, books or an imaginary dream world judging by the vacant expressions. One young, trendy and modish girl spent an age massaging hand lotion into her fingers while she stared stonily ahead. All the while, my eyes never left the station map above the opposite row of seats: Embankment, Temple – and then…Blackfriars!

'Good girl, at least you weren't sick!'

My thoughts had moved rapidly from one thing to another, all the time trying to ward off panic. I thought of home. I thought of my Mother, Father and Nicky. My Mother had steered me towards a disparate life, a Theatre life, but had not focused or prepared me for its hardships. I had not been trained to be self-sufficient or independent.

Conversely, I had been trained to be reliant, needy and sensitive. I did not possess any of the tools. I was not autonomous. When childhood invitations came along, perhaps a sleep-over as it is now called, I would be eager to accept, only to be met with "Oh, you don't want to go, do you?" This was a frequent quandary, a predicament. I learned from an early age that only maternal approval governed consent and called the shots.

'Those apron strings kept tweaking, didn't they?'

Never mind, Ronnie. Perhaps if I had had a Mother who was slipshod, lax or remiss, I wouldn't have achieved half as much; nor would I have met you!

'Oh, I'd have found you, pet!'

The walk from Blackfriars, along the Embankment, has remained etched in memory. That first September morning was bathed in sunshine and the River glistened and dazzled. Then, I knew that I would grow to love London. The Temple and its lofty Inns of Court were beginning to hurry with black gowned figures and soon John Carpenter Street was before me.

'Now I can feel your knees knocking!'

The Reception Area was manned by a kindly Commissionaire. I was directed to the oak staircase and informed that I would find a queue of new Students on the first floor. Sure enough, about half a dozen young men and women were waiting. I took my place. The girl next to me introduced herself: "I'm Movita Allen from Northampton and here is my friend Mike". Mike was very tall. He seemed to find the whole event very comical and interspersed each comment with gales of laughter. I was so relieved to find some chatty companions and warmed to them both at once.

The queue moved along and in due course we were directed to various areas and departments in the School. I was allotted to my individual Professor, Rex Walters. Mo – as she preferred to be called – was to study with Dorothy Dayus.

We learned that Classes would be arranged: A Mr.Rolla would be in charge of Dance & Movement, Miss Wildeblood was to be tutor for Period Movement and a Miss Leonard responsible for the Art of Stage Make-up. Added to the Curriculum, would be classes in Improvisation with Rex Walters and Mime with Ambrose Marriott.

'Sue, this was so exciting! I would have loved Drama School!'

I know darling. I did realise how fortunate I was. This was what I had worked so hard for. I was on the brink of a whole new experience. I had to dig deep for courage, but....I was helped along every inch of the way.

That first day overflowed with activity of one sort or another. First, we needed to find our way around the building. Soon, we became a foursome when we encountered Freda, an outgoing, friendly Cockney girl. From that day on, Freda became Fred....

'You have remained close to Fred for the whole of your life, haven't you?

I have Ronnie. It's a paradox. We never met again after our studies were finished. We took diverse, assorted paths, but the ties that bind cemented our friendship and glued us together for the rest of our lives.

The main Dressing Room, we discovered, was in the basement. This seemed to be the congregating area; a thronging rendezvous where Students could be found in various stages of undress, applying make-up or just passing the time before class. I found it daunting. In these cosmopolitan, blasé surroundings, there seemed to be no shortage of confidence and sophistication.

'Did you feel that you were 'up from country'!'

I experienced that feeling for some time, Ronnie. Fortunately, my new found friends were also experiencing the same instinctive attitude. The gist of this was going to take a while to get used to. In the meantime, we feigned an element of self-assurance and sang-froid; we came to the conclusion that there was safety in numbers…

'In accord, pet – of one mind…'

We laughed together. Humour created a very close bond from day one.

The environment was rich, colourful and unconventional. Our bourgeois, staid mouths were dropping open with disbelief. We came from traditional, orthodox backgrounds. At the time, we failed to realise how valuable our native perception, understanding and insight would be.

'You were in awe. Had it occurred to you that those who appeared to be so blatant, obvious or even brash, were as nervous as you? We hide our instability in so many different ways…'

No Ronnie, it hadn't. It all felt very strange, insecure and intimidating. Never mind, I knew that dear John would listen and comfort. He phoned me every evening at Betty's….usually after I had phoned home!

'Dear diamond John…'

Mo told me that she was looking for a Flat, but meantime would commute from Northampton. As she spoke, I was thinking how bold and advanced she appeared to be. A Flat! To live there all alone! The whole idea left me aghast! How brave she was!

'How grown-up!'

Now you're teasing me…

"I'm going to see a Flat in Streatham this afternoon, Sue. You can come along with me if you like. Help me to decide…" said Mo.

'Good. I hope you agreed'

Yes, Ronnie, I did. We had finished for the afternoon when this was suggested. I was somewhat apprehensive and explained that I was to meet my friend later at Hammersmith. The resolute Mo reassured me saying, "Oh, you've loads of time!".

Streatham seemed to be miles away and I began to feel very on edge. Eventually, we found this rather rundown, dreary Flat. My Mother would have despaired. To be honest, so did I. "No good," concluded Mo, "I can't afford the rent". So, that was that. The time was now approaching 4.15 p.m. and I was beginning to feel a trifle frantic.

Much to my relief, we managed to catch the next train to Elephant & Castle. There, it was a mad dash to pick up the Bakerloo which would take me to the District Line at Embankment. All this took the form of garbled instruction from Mo. She was bound for Euston.

'Guardian Angel – come quick!'

Quite Ronnie. Somehow, by some means or other, I made it on to the Tube bound for Hammersmith. By then, it was 5.30 p.m. and I was still travelling. I was certain Betty would have given up and left. What would I do? I was in agony and a frenzy of hopelessness.

'Now come on, pull yourself together petal'.

"Mind the gap! Mind the gap!" What gap? What bloody gap? Oh, that gap...relief washed over me. Hammersmith! Now how do I get to Park Royal? Where do I go from there? I couldn't even remember Betty's address!

'Dear God...'

"Sue, Sue!" the familiar voice called. And there was Betty! She had waited...she had waited for over an hour. I could have sobbed with relief.

My only thought as we climbed on the bus at Park Royal was...

'Oh Fuck, I've got to do all this again tomorrow!'

Why do you always hit the nail on the head Ronnie? I was not, however, going to think about that then. I would think about that tomorrow.

After all, "Tomorrow is another day" said Scarlett.

The following few days were frenetic. Betty was not always available for protection and I had to master the intricacies of travel alone. In spite of missing my Blackfriars stop on one occasion and ending up at Mansion House, I triumphed with only clammy palms to tell the tale.

My first week at Guildhall was heaving with activity. I had my introductory lesson with Rex Walters. Much to my chagrin, there was something about him that I didn't like...

'Oh dear, that was unfortunate – you were to be saddled with him for some time to come'.

I had had little real contact with him at Musical Festivals. He had always praised my work and had been most enthusiastic about me becoming a Student at Guildhall, but....when face to face with him over a desk, I felt uneasy. I was no longer a child ready to recite a piece of Poetry. I was a young woman and felt unnerved. I had already taken Examinations up to Grade 8 with Miss Brier, so was very well qualified to begin my Course.

But... I had been spoon-fed. I realised that very soon when Mr. Walters put the wind up me by requesting two selections for my next session – one Poetry and the other a Shakespearian scene of my own choice.

'Am I led to believe that Marjorie Brier had chosen all your pieces?'

Yes...exactly, Ronnie.

'Ah, you were growing up in more ways than one! I hope you tried to ignore your misgivings – perhaps he had his eye on you!'

Least said about that at the moment, Ronnie.

Movita was a huge help. We seemed to agree on our general summing up of people and events. We had much in common and Cockney Fred made hilarious contributions to character study. We were quick to see through artifice and affectation. There were many who seemed to thrive on the synthetic or phoney. It was interesting to notice how many Staff members seemed to fall for this contrived, spurious and bogus panoply...

'Don't tell me Rex Walters was one of them?'

You're a mind reader, Ronnie. Mr. Walters conducted the Improvisation Classes. To be honest, the word Improvisation scared the pants off us.

I had not encountered it before. Miss Brier had always worked with scripts, leaving naught to chance. The idea of inventing dialogue for a given situation, was terrifying. No Rehearsal, no safety net, just one's own resources...on the spur of the moment with nowhere to hide....

'Dear God, the exposure! Don't tell me, there were some little shits who absolutely revelled in all that posing...'

Consequently, we found ourselves sitting on the back row. Mr. Walters, aware of our reticence, drew attention to it, while praising those who had been bold enough to strut their stuff. There was no real encouragement, just short-sighted, ill-considered remarks which sent fervid shakes through all.

'You didn't forget that, did you my darling.'

Never Ronnie. I vowed that no one, especially the sensitive, would ever suffer that humiliation at my hand. I didn't like him!

~

We met Mr. Rolla. Kitted out in leotard, tights and ballet shoes, we reported for our first Movement lesson. Fred spent the whole time drawing attention to her widening girth and well-upholstered legs! We came to the conclusion that this was largely because a vision of lithe, lissom and lustrous elegance mutated into the shape of a certain Jacqui Hogan.

We were all green with envy. Jacqui became the apple of Mr. Rolla's eye. No wonder – her leg extension was something to behold. Those legs were the embodiment of perfection. "Shit!" said Fred and pulled her leotard further down.

Mr. Rolla...

'I can hardly wait...was he a Greek God?'

...Well, he thought he was! He sported an enviable tan. I think it must have been genuine for spray ones hadn't really been invented then. He was....

'Camp?'

Oh certainly Ronnie – certainly Camp, although I wouldn't have been familiar with the word then. Daddy might have referred to him as a 'pansy'.

'Nuff said, darling, I get the idea...'

Nevertheless, Mr. Rolla knew his stuff and although clad in a disgustingly brief pair of shorts and equally brief vest, he put us through our paces in a very professional – bearing in mind the physical shortcomings of some of his charges – and sympathetic manner.

These were absorbing sessions. Most of the time, our lumbering bodies responded to unbridled contortion and we repaired to the Restaurant, groaning, but bathed in the self-satisfied conviction that the thrall and thrash was doing us good.

~

Ambrose Marriott was a dear; a plump Jewish gentleman of unkempt appearance and kind heart. He offered absorbing, arresting escapism into the silent world of Mime. His lessons were an oasis of calm and mindfulness. He was also a fount of wisdom. Many months later, when I was worried, astray and anxious, probably about an Exam, he took me to one side, said: "Now, tell me all about this predicament of yours". By the time I had outpoured and shared all, Mr. Marriott determined: "Now, I'm sure you have decided what to do. By the time one has voiced all, you know the answer yourself. You don't need anyone to advise".

'A very wise man....'

Miss Leonard, an accomplished and thorough Make-up Artist, enlightened and to some extent, enhanced her sundry flock. She referred time and again to the perfect oval face which would provide a flawless canvas for any Stage Make-up; consequently, many hours were spent in studious scrutiny. Those who gazed to the nth degree before their reflection, revealed in minute detail by unforgiving naked light bulbs, were hell-bent on receiving their answer to: ".....who is the Fairest of them all?"

Miss Leonard examined each Make-up box. This had been listed as an essential item of our equipment. Mine was a small, black tin one. It had two trays; the first was divided into sections for Greasepaint Sticks. As she outlined the purpose of these, she imbued in us valuable tips about how to care for our complexions, how to cleanse and how to apply. "Do not touch your face repeatedly. Very damaging. Apply and leave alone! The skin is delicate. Treat it with respect!" The mainstay of our collection was Leichener Removing Cream, Stick No. 5 followed by Stick No.9 for Foundation. Max Factor supplied Mascara in the shape of small blue oblong boxes, complete with minute brush...

'A modicum of spit was required before scraping the brush on the black stuff!'

Absolutely Ronnie. Miss Leonard had amassed a wealth of knowledge when working in the Professional Theatre. She became our guru and our pundit.

As the weeks progressed, we were to meet other Professors: Daniel Roberts, the grand old man of Theatre and Christobel Burniston, a vivacious blonde who specialised in Speech and Voice. Mo gave a detailed, rollicking imitation of her Professor, Dorothy Dayus, who, in ritzy plummy tones, announced time and again: "Star quality, dear. That's all that matters! You've either got it, or you haven't...yes...STAR QUALITY!"

As the end of my fledgling week at Guildhall, Diamond John drove over to London to whisk me off to Yalding for the weekend. In the meantime, he had acquired an impressive Sports car! Driving through the twisting, serpentine lanes of Kent by such a grand, powerful mode of transport was the epitome of pomp and circumstance! I was so looking forward to the warm, convivial hospitality of Rose Hooker and her family.

Life at the Lovells's had been heartening. Betty's Parents opened their home to me and I was immensely grateful. My homesickness had diminished, but very spasmodically. I was still rent with tears – in private, but oftentimes they breached all and I fought to stem the flow. As the Autumn nights began to draw in and gloom fell all around, I found myself yearning for the beckoning flames of Mammy's roaring fire. All this gut sensibility was secret and concealed. It was my skeleton in the cupboard and certainly my Achilles heel.

Gradually, I settled. This was largely because I knew I was going home for my 21st Birthday! John managed to take leave from work and we sped up to Yorkshire in Sports-car style. In those far off days, one's 21st was celebrated as the coming-of-age. Now, at eighteen, one is supposed to be ready for the fray.

It was wonderful to be home once more and a wrench to leave. This time, it was exciting to impart news of College and the people I had met there.

My Mother, on the quiet to me and never failing to astonish, remarked : "I thought that perhaps you and John were going to get engaged!!"

'What!!'

This speculation was accompanied, not by joyous exclamations of hope, but rather by the unspoken words: "You'd be making a mistake – I thought you were going to be an Actress!" So, needless to say, I imagined the dissatisfaction and eyebrows being raised; in my Mother's considered opinion, I knew a serious liaison with John was not written in her stars.

'ere we go again.... sounds as if she just wanted to know what the chances were...'

She certainly had the knack of nipping things in the bud! I was facing displeasure yet again. Nevertheless, I soldiered on – John was a kind, generous man.

'He loved you, Sue....'

Diamond John lifted me out of the gloom in the following weeks. When he was not around, Mo, Mike and Fred filled in the gaps with audacious mockery and mickey-taking. It sustained us.

I did not look forward to my sessions with Rex Walters. Certainly, he was a handsome man. He sported a row of gleaming white teeth, which he bared with alarming regularity; the smile, however, was not reflected in his eyes. They glittered. Perhaps I irritated him. I was nervous and he didn't seem to have much truck with those whom he deemed to be feeble or ineffective, judging by his attitude in Improvisation classes. I was shy. As I waited outside his door, I felt nervous, frail and inadequate. Needless to say, it affected my performance and most of the time his steely gaze made me feel like a rabbit caught in the headlights.

'Didn't you tell me he had acquired a nickname – 'Sexy Rexy', wasn't it? Perhaps the sensed you weren't interested?'

No, I wasn't. Besides, he was the Professor, not a potential Suitor. My antennae bristled in his company! He knew that I was contemplating a career in Theatre, so perhaps thought I needed toughening up.

'I always thought you were a hard nut to crack!'

Thank you Ronnie. By the way, Mo found out that he was married to one of his previous students. All hearsay, of course...just gossip. Ah well, each to his own!

'Her own, it seems....'

It was useful blurb. I learned from then on that all of us thrive on encouragement, not put-downs, nepotism and preferential treatment.

One does not snub the less bold. Rex Walters had several favourites: "Wee Jeannie" was a prime example, but the poor buggers who sat quivering on the back row were considered a write-off!

'They don't always come up with the goods, darling. Remember, you can't teach STAR QUALITY! Dorothy D. was really talking about charisma: she was right, you've either got it or you 'aven't!'

~

The friendship between Mo and I was growing. Mo had boundless common sense; she was canny and a wide-acre. Needless to say, she was not one of Mr. Walters' favourites. She had summed him up and he knew it. As I was Mo's Chum, it could explain much of his behaviour towards me. I often think I also raised his dander.

'Well, there's no answer to that...!'

There was some leisure time and Mo and I often took off to explore the likes of Harrods and Galleries Lafayette. Needless to say, we had nothing to spend and our shopping was purely of the window variety, but for me all was learning; a heightening of sophistication and insight.

Each weekend, I was rescued by the Hooker family. These intervals gave time to draw breath, time to be peaceful away from the hurly burly of Guildhall life. On Mondays, after John had deposited me at the station in Dartford, I was rejuvenated and ready for the next augmentation.

'What the hell was that? Why can't you just say 'development'!'

OK! I sensed the possibility that the Lovells were hoping to have the house to themselves very soon. They had been most hospitable; it was obvious that although I was still in the throes of adjusting to London life, their kindness couldn't go on forever and it was time to think of moving on. The Christmas vacation was looming and once again, the prospect of being homeless afterwards was becoming apparent. Via the grapevine, I had heard of a London Hostel 'for young ladies'.

'Dear God...!'

Well, Ronnie, it was worth a try. I made some enquiries and sure enough the Bourne & Hollingsworth Hostel, Warwickshire House, was located in Gower Street a few doors down from RADA (Royal Academy of Dramatic Art)...

'Well of course, even I know that....'

It turned out that this accommodation was really intended for young, or old for that matter, single ladies who worked for the Store. They could be Assistants, Secretaries or -

'Not working girls...!!'

For goodness sake, Ronnie. This was a very respectable establishment and one needed referees when applying for a place. You had to be vetted by The Warden.

'The what...sounds like déjà vu to me – you know, the moustachioed Miss Gym...'

Well, I thought it would do no harm to approach Warwickshire House. My letter received a very promising reply, but unfortunately at that time there were no Vacancies. So that was that.... I was, however, encouraged to re-apply at the beginning of 1961. "You'll just have to come and stay with us in the meantime" said Diamond John, "Mum would love to have you". I hoped that Rose may agree, but it was a lot to ask. My stay was bound to involve some upheaval; the Hooker's bungalow was not massive. Much shuffling around of sleeping arrangements would ensue. It was a generous offer and one which I did not deserve when I think of how the future transpired.

'You're going to tell me, I hope....'

The end of my first Term at Guildhall was coming to a close. I had made progress and was relieved to secure a further Grade exam in spite of the somewhat cool recognition from Mr. Walters. He seemed to think that the examiner's comments on Theory were disappointing.

'Well, you always shelved that side of study with Marjorie Brier'.

True, Ronnie. It bored me, but I did make an effort. I had to or the comeback would have been failure. I found facing Mr. Walters over the desk most unnerving. Those glinting, gleaming eyes seemed to bore right through me; subsequently, I avoided looking, was struck dumb and stared ahead, out of the window, hoping he would presume that I was searching for some overwhelmingly compelling Academic answer. I couldn't think of a thing and there was silence. Obviously, he thought I was an utter duffer. He did not know how to bring the best out of me.

I hated waiting in the corridor before a session. My stomach churned. I did notice, however, that students due to leave before my lesson would be waved off with much joyous banter – "Bye Bye Judy, lovely to see you again.... lovely work".

'Did you have the urge to tell him to piss off?'

Bide your time, Ronnie – bide your time....

~

I took the Pullman train from King's Cross at the end of the Autumn Term.

The journey to Hull was nearly five hours in those days. The stops were few, but the wait at Doncaster was interminable – a whole hour. I managed to get a vacant seat on the same table as a family of three.

'Table?'

The Pullman was grand Ronnie. Plush seats were arranged around small tables set for Dinner. A small lamp gave off warm tones and the cutlery was polished and shiny. Stewards in full uniform took orders and needless to say, dining was expensive; far too dear for a ravenous Drama Student! I had plenty to read. It was tricky averting one's eyes from the luscious spread which appeared before my travelling companions.

'What about a packet of crisps?'

Somehow, I didn't have the cheek to wolf down a crumb of anything!

"My dear, I wonder if you would care to join us for coffee?" said the matronly lady. "Please do..."

'How lovely – perhaps she had noticed the corners of your mouth dribbling...'

I thought it a most friendly, warm-hearted gesture and spent the rest of the journey in animated conversation.

They were very interested in Drama Schools, my career as an Actress and "was it really such hard work in an overcrowded profession?"

'Just the comment a fledging Actor wants to hear!'

We parted company at Doncaster. As we came to the home straight for this homebody and the train puffed its way beside the River Humber, I breathed a sigh of relief. I was home. I could just about catch the niff of fish wafting through the carriage air vents.

'Yes, my darling, home is where the heart is....'

John was to spend Christmas with us. I think my Parents thought the invitation for him to visit would, in some way, show appreciation for the goodwill and favour that the Hooker family had shown to me and indeed were proposing to do after the holiday. I was to stay in Yalding for several weeks of my Spring Term 1961 until alternative arrangements could be made.

I received a bolt from the blue. Tom phoned just before Christmas!

'Oh eck!' Cleft stick time.'

Ronnie, I can't believe that I actually said that John was planning to come for Christmas!

'Sue!'

I know...I was so taken aback and spoke without thinking. There was a silence before I heard Tom say, "Oh well, Happy Christmas, Mate! Give my regards to that boozy Hooker!" He rang off....

When my Mother asked who had phoned, I blurted out what had been said. "Well, that wasn't very nice of you. It was unkind!"

'What?'

Tom, the mediocre....the person who wasn't good enough for me...the boy she wanted to dismiss forever....

So, I spent most of the Christmastide thinking of Tom and his sadness. How I must have hurt him...would I ever stop searching my soul in a distressing, heart-rending attempt to please my Mother...

'If only you had known then that one day you would.... in the meantime, life's lessons have to be learned and the price paid....

The wounds, Ronnie, take some time to heal.

~

The New Year brought fresh thoughts and a new start. Guildhall beckoned once more and I was looking forward. Fear was banished, for within the bosom of the Hooker family I had found a home-from-home. Safety and comfort played an important part in my adjusting to Guildhall once more. The travelling still gave me the collywobbles but I was becoming more used to the difference between North and South; of England I mean!

'What exactly do you mean?'

Well, Southerners appeared to be self-contained; purposeful and dynamic. Northerners, as we both well know, are cautious, chary; perhaps a little too ready to be on the defensive.

'Anything specific in mind?'

Guildhall was determined to rid one of Regional Accent. I suppose judgement or exposition was geared to the precision, nicety and exactitude of BBC Television Newsreaders, the likes of Mary Malcolm and Sylvia Peters. Many, many years later, I overheard a Director say that he could detect RADA Students a mile off for they all spoke in an identical way.

'I say, it was a good job that Albert Finney and Tom Courtenay appeared on the horizon!'

It was certainly one in the eye for Rex Walters – he was intent on stamping out rich Northern vowels. In time, I came to the conclusion that 'posh' was just as much a dialect as any other and treated it as such when called upon to play upper crust characters! When Albert and Tom created 'Billy Liar' on the West End stage, all records were broken and pretension thrown to the winds. In the early Sixties, 'kitchen sink' Drama had arrived! So, my confidence began to blossom!

~

Life in Yalding, particularly at weekends, was leisurely and without strife.

John took great pains in teaching me to drive. This was most good-humoured of him: that Sports-car was burnished gold. He was an admirable Tutor who possessed boundless patience. His principles of good driving, motorcar maintenance and rules of the road remained with me for most of my life.

I was happy with John. I was regarded as a member of his Family. I was settled....

'But...'

I was torn, torn with indecision and yearning.

'Something happened?'

I couldn't stay in Yalding indefinitely. I applied to Warwickshire House once more.

'The home for graceful, well-bred young ladies!'

The same, Ronnie. This time there was a vacancy. It would coincide with the middle of my Spring Term. From a practical point of view, it was sensible to follow up. I hoped that at some time I would take part in plays at Guildhall. Plainly, I couldn't commute to Yalding when Rehearsals were in full flow. I explained to John. It was some time later, that he confided to me that Rose had observed "Once Sue is in London, she will be completely preoccupied".

'How true was that?'

All this tallied with news from Tom. He knew I was at Drama School and wrote to me at Guildhall. He was to attend London University for a couple of days as part of his Teaching qualification.

'You saw him, didn't you?'

I did Ronnie. I behaved in a very deceitful manner. I told John that I would be needed at Guildhall on the Saturday that Tom was to be in London. I spent the day with Tom.

'Did it prove anything?'

I think it proved more to Tom than to me. He noticed the change in me.

Some of my naivety, inexperience and ingenuousness had diminished. I was innocent, yes, but force of necessity had me become more knowing, more urbane. One thing was certain – the bond had not broken…for either of us….

~

'Sue, I'm curious to know why you have not spoken of Gran & Grandpa for some time. I know they were very important….'

They always were, Ronnie. I think they were keen to take a back seat when it came to teenage advice, preferring to remain on the periphery of my evolvement. After all, there had been enough clashes beforehand with my Mother; they were content for her to be in the driving seat.

It was a painful blow when Gran died in March 1959. She had been ill for some time. I remember her last hours spent at Beverley Road. There was nothing I could do but gaze at her sleeping face before she quietly slipped away. I hold most dear and precious the memory of her cool skin when she comforted me; her entrancing story-telling.

"Charlie", said Grandpa, "you said I could come here to live when anything happened". So, Grandpa lived out the rest of his years, protected and cherished by his family.

'Not any easy path for Jessica…generous of Charlie….'

~

I received word from The Warden at Warwickshire House. An appointment had been made for me. I named Marjorie Brier and Rex Walters as referees.

'Bit of a cheek when you didn't really worship the ground he walked on!'

Actually, Ronnie, he was very obliging. Largely because he saw the common sense of living in London and not the backwoods of Kent. The journey from Guildhall to Warwickshire House was an absolute doddle after the complications of Betty's route and the trek to Yalding.

The main entrance was huge. This opened on to a large Reception area, where Secretaries and a uniformed Doorkeeper were posted and a large central, circular seat dominated the floor space. I was shown into the main Office where the Warden greeted me. She was a friendly woman and left no stone unturned when giving me the low-down on Hostel layout and arrangements. She was very keen to point out that male visitors were not admitted beyond the Ground Floor.

'I hope she was reassured by your modest, virtuous demeanour!!'

There was, however, a very spacious Lounge to the rear of the main area. Gentleman callers could dally there until the Lady of their choice appeared.

'Armed, presumably, with a clunky and unwieldy corsage!'

I was not given a tour of the actual rooms. Apparently, there were several floors which housed shared living quarters. A fully equipped Dining Hall, situated in the basement, provided a simple, snack Menu. Kitchen facilities existed for those wishing to cook for themselves.

'Sounds pretty good, Sue...'

It was, Ronnie. I was delighted when the Warden seemed to pass me fit for merit. I was given a place and permission to move in within the week!

'Good for you, darling, but how were the Hookers and John going to take it?'

Thereby, came the heartbreak, Ronnie. I say that because it was very upsetting. John asked me to marry him....

'Oh darling...what a decision....'

I was in complete turmoil, Ronnie. Yet....I said no.

'You loved him, though, didn't you?'

Yes, but it couldn't have been enough, for I was unshaken. I was training for a career. I was sensible enough to see that. I would be expected to relinquish all. Also, my Mother's reaction to such a Proposal was uppermost in my mind....

'Ah....the cords that bind...'

Saying Goodbye to Rose and the Hooker family was very upsetting. I was distracted; all seemed disordered, untidy and chaotic. I was giving up my home again; my solace, shelter and unconditional love of Diamond John. I was forcing myself, yet again, into an uncharted, unplumbed tract.

'Was the break total, outright?'

Yes, Ronnie. It was final, savage...destructive for John.

John left me at Warwickshire House on a Sunday afternoon. It was in the middle of my Spring Term. I found the change quite overpowering. The first days in my new home were filled with activity. This, in many ways, was profitable. I had no time to think...think about John's unhappiness, his tender-heartedness and solidarity.

'Knowing you...I would imagine your sorrow monopolized much of what was going *on...'*

It did Ronnie.

My room was on the third floor. It was a basic abode. Two single beds and a couple of high-backed chairs were the only ostensible fittings or effects. A washbasin adorned one corner and floor-to-ceiling cupboards occupied most of the fourth wall. A double sash window overlooked Gower Street far below.

I was to share with Fiona Williams, a Stage Management Student who was studying at RADA nearby. Fiona was quite charming: softly, but precisely spoken, somewhat shy and very welcoming. She seemed enthusiastic and keen to have a room-mate, especially a Drama Student. Fiona explained, in minute detail, the rules and regulations: where the Telephones were, how the Lift operated and a road map for Bathrooms and Lavatories!

She was an only child who hailed from Guildford. Her Father, I came to know, was an influential, prestigious figure in Philips Radio.

I decided to travel home to Yorkshire that first weekend. I was very, very taken up and upset about the parting with John. My Parents had been told and must have been aware of my heartache and regret.

'You were grieving....full of self-reproach...'

My Mother said, "Well, if you're so upset and crying, perhaps you shouldn't have given him up..."

I didn't know how to answer her. There was no answer...just mourning.

At Guildhall, a letter awaited me. Tom had written asking me to meet him from the train at Euston. I had not received the letter....

'You were in Yorkshire...'

He must have looked for me. I wasn't there. I would have been there had I known. Of course I would have been there on the platform, longing to see him.

'Oh Sue, what a twist of fate...'

I sent word immediately but it was all too late...too late.

~

Fiona and I became very close friends. We were different...

'But compatible?'

Yes, Ronnie. I can still visualise Fiona at 7.30 a.m. extricating vast, monster rollers from her hair. Then, armed with towel and a bountiful array of toiletries, she would make her way along the corridor to the bathroom. Fiona was a gentle girl. Her Mother ran an impressive Secretarial business; I surmised she was a formidable woman who looked upon her daughter as a cosseted Juvenile. In fact, that is the impression that Fiona seemed to have of herself. I would hear of invitations to dinner, usually from older men. "I always order milk", Fiona announced, "I think Waiters look upon us as Father and Daughter".

'Reminiscent of Nanny in the Nursery'.

Absolutely, Ronnie. Consequently, whenever I expressed myself in a rather risqué fashion, it would be met with "Oh Sue!!" as if I had broken some sacrosanct rule of etiquette. The difference between us, however, prompted much gaiety and glee. This manifested itself when food parcels arrived from our respective Mothers. Fiona's parcel arrived by special delivery from Fortnum and Mason; mine arrived care of Jessica.

'Bless!'

Fiona, brimming with excitement, would insist on opening mine. Dear Mum would have packed everyday essentials: sweeties, toothpaste, a tin of salmon, soap and maybe ten Woodbines!

'When did you take up smoking? I'm aghast!'

You can blame Grandpa for that! He initiated my

smoking! I suppose I was curious and he shared the odd puff with me...

'Now you know how I feel about 'puffs' !'

Ronnie, I didn't know about the other kind until much later on! Anyway, we didn't give much credence to the dangers of smoking in those days. I recall that Mo also smoked – Du Maurier ones in a very opulent orange packet.

Fiona's food parcel was a much more elegant affair. Delicacies of every description would be bursting from cellophane and sophisticated wrapping.

'Did she let you open it?'

Oh yes, Ronnie, she was most generous. A lasting memory was of Droste chocolate pennies: some milk, some a mixture of milk and plain and some orange-flavoured chocolate. Now, so many years later, whenever I see a tube of Droste chocolate pennies displayed in some swish Confectioners' trimmings or trappings, I think of Fiona's Fortnum baskets.

These goodies would be secreted in our cupboards and used as treats for visiting guests. There were times when I would wake in the middle of the night, unable to sleep and feeling hungry. The thoughtful Fiona took this on board and got me hooked on Chocolate Digestives. I would find a store placed by my beside table with the message "For Night Starvation"!

'It all sounds like the Fourth Form at Malory Towers!'

Got it in one, Ronnie! Once, the staunch, stalwart and steadfast Jessica sent a roast Chicken by post!

'God, I can't take any more of this – I'm of a nervous disposition!'

Fiona and I were delighted. Anxious that the bird would go off if left in the close confines of our Room, we devised the plan of securing it on the outside window sill. It did seem a good idea at the time, but unfortunately a breeze got up from nowhere and blew the chicken down to the pavement below!

'I hate to say this, but you were four floors up!'

Quite. We slammed the sash window up and peered down. A person was retrieving the Chicken from the road! I daren't look! Much to our consternation, the same person then went through the main entrance of Warwickshire House! Panic, shock and horror!

'Did you lie low, waiting for a Warden visit?'

We resolved to be in total denial. When the dust had settled, I made an urgent phone call to my Mother – just Woodbines in future, please.

~

My Mother wrote letters to me every day. I tried to reply as often as possible, but the work load from Guildhall was beginning to be heavy and it was an added task to an overloaded day. The letters were disturbing. There was a constant flow of disappointment and self-pity from my Mother. This took the form of dissatisfaction and complaint; the blame levelled, painfully, at Daddy. I was utterly powerless to assuage Mum's accusations and protest. I found myself being persuaded to sympathise, to...

'Take sides....?'

Yes, Ronnie. It was easier. Added to that, I didn't receive news from my Father, or little Nicky. Communication was via my Mother; I did not sense any real balance between my Parents. I never really knew how much interest Daddy was showing in my college life. I suppose he was content to let Mum oversee and command. Perhaps it was easier for him. Daddy always seemed proud of me, glad to see me....I have no doubt that he loved me very much. Instinctively, I knew both Parents loved me but neither put it in words;

my sixth sense played its part. Demonstrative love seemed vague, elusive. 'Love' appeared on Birthday and Good Luck cards but I don't remember the word being spoken. It was almost as if self-consciousness was uppermost.

'I wonder what was going on behind the scenes? Perhaps the shop took Charlie's attention?'

I didn't expect word from Nicky. He was fourteen by then and absorbed, no doubt, with school. What fourteen-year-old bothers about the doings of his twenty-one-year-old Sister?

One is inclined to think that others do not notice elements of unrest. Fiona was aware of my constant letter-writing and remarked on it. "Sue, you seem very troubled by all this....is there anything I can do to help?"

I did reveal some detail. She, in her unassuming manner, suggested that there should be fewer letters from my end. Surprisingly, the outspoken Mo put the matter into perspective: "Sue, your Mother should not be writing to you like this...it's an unnecessary onus, especially as it's a problem that you cannot solve".

This was consoling, but I could not banish the image of my lonely Mother. I tried my best to help her, but the urge to show compassion and condolence made for many sleepless hours as I wrestled with constant worry and a welter of unanswered questions.

I journeyed home for the Easter break. Needless to say, I was overjoyed to see everyone once more. Grandpa, it seems, had been giving poor Mum a run for her money. It's possible that he was coping with the early stages of Dementia; this was unveiling its own mammoth hurdles and hazards.

'Poor Jessica. I seem to remember that he had told his pals in the village that his money was being confiscated by your Mother..'

True Ronnie. I was very sympathetic, but couldn't come up with a solution.

'Darling, you couldn't...you could not solve an insurmountable dilemma'.

There was another component in the mix. My Mother was resorting to drowning her sorrows most evenings, but not until approximately nine o'clock. Then, she would also have a couple of cigarettes in addition to several Sherries. This extraordinary exposé was blamed on Wartime air raids.

'To dull the fear, I reckon. Old habits die hard....'

I did not attach undue importance to this. I understood. I did not realise at the time, however, that I was being encouraged to join in. My Mother needed the conviviality and rapport of a partner in crime. I didn't object. I enjoyed my Mother's company and her obvious immersion in Theatre, Guildhall and my Acting future.

'One drink can lead to another....did you think of the danger...did your Mother?'

I very much doubt it, Ronnie. I was, although unaware of it at the time, fulfilling my Mother's need....

~

At the onset of Guildhall's Summer Term, a posting for a forthcoming Student Production was advertised. Angela Lavers, a studious and capable girl was taking on the Direction of 'The Tudor Wench' by Elsweth Thane. It was to be presented in October 1961 by the Students Repertory Club.

'Did you prick your ears up?'

I did, Ronnie. I was familiar with the Play for Marjorie had introduced me to extracts from it as Festival Own Choice pieces. It was an intriguing tale. The action centred around the young Queen Elizabeth I and her association with Sir Thomas Seymour while living in Catherine Parr's dower-house at Chelsea during the year immediately following the death of Henry VIII.

'Come on, petal, I hope you Auditioned!'

Unlike me, Ronnie, I was very secretive about it. I put my name down and then studied the Play once more, very carefully, with a view to choosing the excerpt that would carry the most weight and show off some versatility....

'Wow...you little bugger...on the hunt for STAR QUALITY, eh!'

You bet, Ronnie!

I was quizzed closely by Mo and Co. about the Auditions and my choice of character. I evaded any temptation to disclose details. That was the first time I had ever been so reticent. Mo and the others didn't wish to Audition, so I didn't feel as though I was harbouring a guilty secret!

'No harm in playing your cards close to your chest... incidentally, what did you Audition for?'

Nosey Parker! I went all out for Elizabeth!

'Darling, you had the je ne sais quoi – that indefinable something!'

How do you know, Ronnie?

'Well, you had it many years later, when I met you! I told you often enough!'

Darling Ronnie – thank you so much. I suppose I never really believed you, but somebody did all those years ago....I GOT THE PART!!

'Well, that was sticking out a mile, he noted smugly...'

I met with gasps when the Cast list went up – some of admiration, but there was a marked, conspicuous silence in particular quarters. Mo, Fred, Mike and the sincere, unaffected and guileless members of our group were overjoyed; tickled pink, I think, that the favourites for the lead had fallen by the wayside this time.

The male starring part, Sir Thomas Seymour, was to be played by Michael James. Michael was an exceptionally talented Student. He was attractive, very masculine and ruggedly good-looking. Caps were set at him repeatedly.

'Oh, how well I know that feeling! Yes...then what?'

I began to feel very insecure. How the blazes was I going to cope in Rehearsals with this blitz of virile, strapping and macho energy?

'For God's sake, kidda, you were hardly as plain as a pikestaff!'

Angela Lavers, a competent Director, seemed I sensed, to be very enamoured of the craggy, vigorous and robust Mike. He was, however, more aware of the Stage Manager, Lynn Farleigh.

'Oh, wheels within wheels, eh? What fun!'

On that auspicious, triumphant evening, I returned to Warwickshire House and the loyal Fiona on cloud nine.

'Did she crack open another box of Drostes?'

Don't be facetious Ronnie! Us girls had a riotous evening on numerous cups of tea! Fiona was ecstatic! My phone call home that night was met with uproar, colossal pride and much loving congratulation. Mum was exhilarated... in raptures...as I knew she would be....

'Her hopes were being realised....but were yours? We shall see....'

~

The remainder of the Summer Term involved preparation for the end of Term Examinations. My relationship with Rex Walters jogged along in a fairly productive way. He seemed impressed that I had been chosen for Elizabeth – I sensed a flash of surprise.

'Mmn – I never talk about flashes!'

Of course you wouldn't, Ronnie! Now, I was accustomed to choosing my own selections and there was a favourable response, but the uneasiness prevailed. I considered myself fortunate that he did not intervene with any suggestions for the love scenes in 'Tudor Wench'!

Rehearsals had not progressed in great detail. There had been a first Read-over which I had found nerve-wracking. Michael sat next to me, smiled and was very ready to make a connection. He certainly put me at ease.

'I bet he could sense your nervousness. So, my love, he would be very eager to engender something of a relationship if you were to work so closely together....'

Mo was very supportive. She and Fred armed me with some caustic comment should the going get rough! At least I did have the Summer vacation to psyche myself up for the following September, when Rehearsals were planned to take off in earnest.

I could hardly believe that I had almost completed my first year at Guildhall. Successful Exam results put the seal on achievement.

'You had come a long way, pet....'

Yes, Ronnie. I had put down some roots at Warwickshire House and established a measure of domestic routine. I felt that there was some order in my life and a grain of independence. There had been adjustments, unhappiness and loneliness, but I felt the transition. Life had become a whole new ball game. Dare I say, I was growing up? London had played its part in this medley, this melange... once it had been a terrifying entity, but now, step by step, I had made myself ready for its complexity and rich diversity. I was home....

Soon, I would be travelling to my other home. There, arrangements must be made to engage in work of another kind. I had managed my Grant allowances admirably; now it was time to supplement...to take up the cudgels and buoy up the Bank balance!

'I'll hazard a guess on Harlands....!'

I'd sent a hopeful message to Mr. Cayley asking if there were any vacancies for Typists at Springfield Way. It was good news! His Secretary was taking leave and could I help out over my holiday? I say help out but knew my speeds would have dropped a few notches!

'I have a feeling that they just wanted to welcome you back!'

It was so wonderful to meet old friends once more. Billy had moved on up the ladder, but I did see him from time to time and he was so eager to hear all the news of Guildhall. Mrs. Robinson had left and a voluptuous, amiable lady called Sylvia had taken her place. Belinda, now married to the Boss, was otherwise engaged! Her Husband, it seems, still mowed the front lawn of the Printing factory in the pouring rain!

'Were you summoned by "Sue, letters!...." again?'

Of course. I felt as if I'd never been away!

Life at 355 Beverley Road moved along at customary pace. Mum was elated to have me back. There was much animated discussion and exchange of news which prevailed well into the evenings.

'With sherry-prompting?'

Yes, Ronnie. There was no change...it had not abated....

Grandpa seemed to be constantly in a cloud of vapour. He took up a sitting position behind the sofa where he could watch the television from a distance. He kept his "smokes", or Woodbines, close at hand. Anyone taking up position on the sofa, found themselves peering through an impenetrable haze, a fog exhaled at regular intervals by the intrepid Grandpa!

'No wonder poor Jessica was hitting the sherry bottle!'

Yes, I was able during that Summer to appreciate how very trying life must have been for my Mother.

The fourteen-year-old Nicky was full of beans. I'm sure he was pleased to see me again, but naturally the age-gap left us with little in common. He seemed to be thriving at Pitman's College, but now it was time off and away days; everything else in his world was left to chance.

Daddy was very much on the perimeter of my life at that time. I sensed protracted distance between my Parents. Both were drowning...

'You couldn't save them both, Sue...'

No. Now, as I look back, through the mists of time, I know I erred on the side of my Mother. I misjudged. I was persuaded to judge. My confusion, in that transient, ephemeral Summer holiday, helped to put the stamp on my Mother's determination to shut my Father out. He became a stranger.

'They were just two lonely people living together...'

My Mother was disaffected because my Father had spoken of retiring early. He was sickened of the Shop and its relentless responsibilities. My Auntie Annie had married and therefore wished to begin another life. Charlie, I reasoned, wanted to move on. I suspect financial strain was taking a hold. The Supermarket trend was becoming more and more predominant and future for the small businessman was uncertain.

'Sounds as if all was uncertain at that time...but, petal, not your problem..'

True, Ronnie, but it hung around my neck like the Sword of Damocles.

'Bit dramatic, pet. Now come on....what was going on at Harlands?'

Mr. Cayley and I were hitting it off very well. There was a definite bond between us; an affinity cemented by constant laughter. I looked forward to working each day, knowing there would be something to drive the energy along. I was also becoming fractionally worried about my celeb Elizabeth role.

'I hope you had started looking at the lines! I always needed to start months before out of sheer fear!'

Well, Ronnie, I knew I would manage the part, but...I was getting the breeze up about the love scenes!

'For God's sake, Sue....not the kissing again!'

Yes, the kissing again. I have no doubt that Michael James would know what he was doing, but would he know that I didn't...well, not in public! I think I had got better at it in private!

'Sue, darling, you've just got to go for it! Michael James will do the rest, mark my words! Remember, you are Elizabeth, not 'Susanne Ubble' and everything will be *just right!'*

The Autumn Term of 1961 at Guildhall was soon to begin. My debut on stage was imminent! It was time to say another farewell to Harlands.

"Sue, I'm coming to London on business, middle of September. Any chance of taking you out to dinner while I'm there? I know Students don't get enough to eat!" announced Mr. Cayley.

'Should I be encouraging this?'

Perhaps not Ronnie. It was all above board, I'm sure – said she, not really believing it was!

'Only one way to find out, darling....just make sure he says "Sue, letters!" and nothing else...!'

Either way, Ronnie, it would be great fun...

'Well, I suppose, either way...I'll be here to pick up the pieces!!'

The first day of a new Term at Guildhall was reminiscent of the first day back at school, minus the clutter of unsullied exercise books, pencils and uniform. After a couple of months at home, engaged in a totally different pursuit, it took a while to acclimatise.

'I'm dying to hear about Rehearsals...'

The schedule was time-consuming Ronnie. I was unnerved and flustered. I have always found the scrutiny of other Cast members, supposedly detached and lolling about on the Rehearsal room fringe, very uncomfortable. One is laid bare, open to the elements and on trial while striving to find a key to the character.

'The buggers are willing a hole to appear so that you can drop yourself into it!'

I knew what I was doing; a noticeable silence pervaded when I was working. Director's notes were few and supporting players were gracious.

'Now then, I hope you didn't blot your copy-book with the love scenes!'

No, darling, I didn't. Mike was a tower of strength.

'Literally?'

Absolutely. I suppose as the young, gullible and trusting Elizabeth, I could get away with being tremulous and quivering with...

'Sexual anticipation?'

Incidentally, the main love interest for Elizabeth was Fernando Aubrey, a page-boy in Elizabeth's household at Chelsea. He was handsome and she was not indifferent to his admiration.

'So you were fighting off the advances of both!'

Of course Michael James was the main inducement for feminine hearts to flutter; I was aware of my umpteen rivals' ripple of covetous desire when the bodies of Thomas and Elizabeth were entwined.

Michael was a compelling actor. He governed the stage. I found myself watching, half amused and half fascinated, as he moved about. He walked as if he was going out to bat! It was a distinctive, powerful walk, displayed with just a shade of arrogance. Many, many years later, I would recognise that walk on the stage of the Royal Shakespeare Company, in Stratford. Who could mistake that walk! Of course, by then Michael James had become Michael Jayston and star of the film 'Nicholas and Alexandra'. He was a lovely man and a giving, accomplished Performer.

'Did Mr. Cayley follow up his invitations to dinner while all this was going on?'

Oh yes Ronnie, he did. I had been back in London a little while when I received a phone call. Mr. Cayley was in Town!

'Was Jessica aware of the fact that her Daughter was to meet her ex-Boss and a married man?'

She was, Ronnie, and did not broach any opposition!

'Do you think she perceived an element of safety? After all, he was spoken for. Therefore, as she saw it, presented no foreseeable danger. There was unlikely to be any further development? How naïve was your Mother?'

That did not occur to me at the time. Later, however, much later, it came to my notice that Mr. Cayley had contacted my Mother. Apparently, he had mentioned coming to London and "was there anything she would like him to bring to Town for Sue?"

'Talk about encouragement?'

I came to enjoy my meetings with Mr. Cayley, so I was pleased that there seemed to be such agreement. It made a pleasant change.

Mr. Cayley collected me from Warwickshire House before whisking me away for dinner at various notable, sumptuous eateries. He drove down from Anlaby and resided in some very expensive hotels while on business for the firm.

Fiona and I spent much time deciding on what I was to wear for such auspicious, rosy occasions.

'Now here is where my services would have been invaluable!'

I know, darling, but my love for you was to happen many years later. How I wish I had known that such happiness was to come my way...

'Hope is the only constant...unfolding and progression cannot be hurried...'

I had a little black dress. Everyone in those days had a little black dress. Mine was a sheath dress and at the waist was a fine belt anchored by a diamante buckle. It was teamed with black stilettos and a clutch evening bag. I hasten to add that this little black dress appeared on every London occasion. Mr. Cayley never commented except to say that I looked lovely!

Mr. Cayley was always 'Mr. Cayley'. I did know of his Christian name, but 'Mr. Cayley' was apropos, fitting and apt.

'You sweet, old-fashioned thing! By the by, I was given to understand that you were a Convent pupil – 'Susanne Ubble' what were you doing?! A married man indeed!'

Mr. Cayley found the Warwickshire House Reception area to be an unsuspected dangerous place, a death-trap for slippery shoes. Without fail, on seeing me, he would rise at speed from the central seat and slide, precariously, to a juddering halt somewhere near where I was standing. All the while, his curly hair, characteristically out of control as usual, would drop over a winking eye as we made a relatively unsteady exit through the revolving door and out into the dusk of Gower Street.

Mr. Cayley would stay at Brown's Hotel in Dover Street where the Afternoon Teas were quite splendid; there, one could experience a dash of Olde Worlde English elegance. My evening treats were supreme and unsurpassed.

'Don't stop there....!'

I was wined and dined at a Polynesian Restaurant deep within the basement of the Mayfair Hotel. Tables were arranged around a fully operating lagoon, complete with sound effects and music from Hawaii.

'But you didn't have a grass skirt!'

Mr. Cayley turned out to be a polished dancer and I was whirled around the floor with marked and salient skill. All at once, much to Mr. Cayley's trepidation and amid a final twirl, we found ourselves face to face with a Senior Management official from Harlands!

'Bugger! Found out!'

It could have been crimson faces all around, but Mr. Cayley carried the whole thing off with august aplomb. His colleague was greeted with silver-tongued comradeship and I was introduced as his Guildhall Student guest and former Harlands employee!

Mr. Cayley frequented many memorable Restaurants. At that time, Wheelers was a renowned Oyster Bar; there, I partook of some delicious food – far beyond the expense account of Drama Students. Another adventure was a table at Kettners, a French Restaurant in Soho.

'Pure luxury!'

On return from these excursions, Fiona would be regaled with events, chapter and verse. Excitement and girlish giggles would carry us through until the small hours.

After each and every Mr. Cayley meeting, a parcel would be delivered to me at Warwickshire House Reception. The contents revealed a wooden chocolate box from Floris; a chic, traditional packaging for their delectable confectionary. The accompanying card read "Thank you for a wonderful evening – Stay Young! – Mr. Cayley".

'I suppose he was some years older than you?'

Yes, Ronnie. I would think about ten years. I was cosseted and spoiled by Mr. Cayley. I kept those wooden boxes for many years as remembrance of a timeless token and keepsake...

'Do you think he came to love you?'

Who knows? I think I was special to him. We had much in common and our relationship had a unique, like-minded understanding. Our meetings were many and Mr. Cayley's visits to London were marked with anticipation and happiness.

'Presumably all good things come to an end?'

There came a time when it was no longer acceptable for us to enjoy each other's company or dance to the strains of Mancini's 'Moon River'.

'You were getting too close?'

Yes. It was saddening, but correct. I have often wondered about Mr.Cayley over the years. I have tried to "Stay Young"! It would be tribute to a dear friend and to the gaiety and gladness of those far off times.

~

The First Night of 'Tudor Wench' was nigh. The play had caused excitement above and below stairs...

'Below stairs?'

In the main Dressing Room. Students were thronging and it seemed that I was generating more interest than I had ever deemed possible! De facto or, in effect and all honesty, the curiosity was more in my connection with Mike James!

I had lost a considerable amount of weight and at only 5'2" was a diminutive partner for the burly Mike. Brian

Hughes, who was playing the youthful Fernando, was more of equal dimensions to myself.

Mo found a remarkable potion for colouring my hair. "You've got to do something..." she announced, "Elizabeth had red hair". She then went on to produce a suspicious-looking vermillion or claret glinting powder, which was puffed on to the head in substantial dollops. At first, the effect was a trifle uneven but after replay, redo and re-run, the resulting tinge was promising and met with sharp intakes of breath from Fred and Mo. This was not a permanent dye which was just as well, for I ended up, on first attempts, with very roseate, blooming ears and nose.

'Hell's teeth! I hope you warned the valorous and valiant Mike that he could be in danger, when passion was running amok, of turning rubicund when running his fingers through your hair!'

I received Good Luck telegrams from Mummy and Daddy, Nicky and even two members of Staff at Daddy's shop – Archie and Frances. Surprisingly, none from the Aunties or Cousins. Mo's card read "You're certain to be Great Like Bach, Brahms and Beethoven! What I mean is, DON'T WORRY! We all have our off days!!" Cards came from unexpected people, people whom I had regarded as contenders or adversaries....

'Perhaps they thought you'd put in a good word with Mr. James!'

Ronnie, you are so cynical! Smacks of truth though!

My Mother was coming down to see her Elizabeth. I seem to remember Marjorie Brier and her new Husband Arthur were to make the journey by car. Mum was invited to join them. I recall Mum saying, some time later, that as the curtain went up she had exclaimed: "Oh God, she's so thin and she's dyed her hair!"

'Bless Jessica. She must have been proud!'

She was Ronnie. I did not have much opportunity to talk after that First Night. Marjorie was anxious to set off. They were driving back to Yorkshire through the night! I remember Mum saying "Never again, it was sheer Hell. Arthur lost the way over and over!" Poor Mum...

I do wonder, to this day, why arrangements couldn't have been made for my whole family to come down and stay overnight.

'One of life's mysteries, petal. Perhaps the shop took precedence. Perhaps your Father and Nick were just not interested...who knows?'

~

In the New Year of 1962, I was in Rehearsal for another play. 'The Curious Savage' was an unusual piece, but my Part in it was nowhere near as challenging as Elizabeth. The experience, however, was very useful.

Miss Wilhelmina, a warm, generous Care Home Nurse, was albeit, ordinary to say the least. Nevertheless, the venture prompted a witty telegram from Nicky: "Who could be more Curious?!"

'That may well have been a caption thought up by me!'

Mr. Walters had little to say about this second foray. He'd said enough about my Elizabeth love scenes – "Well, just like High School clinches!"

'As your Mentor, was that the best he could come up with?'

Well, my confidence took a bit of a dip, but, thanks to Mike James, it rose once more and with a great deal of gratitude.

'Bless...'

Yes, Ronnie, he took notable pains to congratulate me on my Performance and also to seek me out when we were both taking a breather in the Dressing Room.

'Were you observed by his posse of admirers?'

We were Ronnie and it wasn't long before I was usurped by the relentless few!

I could hardly believe that my second year at Guildhall was coming to a close. At the conclusion of the Summer Term I would be taking Final examinations in order to qualify as an AGSM -Associate of the Guildhall School of Music & Drama! The tests would include Performance but most of all, the dreaded Theory: questions which would revolve around: Classification of Vowels and Consonants, Modulation & Inflection, Structure and Speaking of Blank Verse, Suspensive and Metrical Pauses, Diaphragmatic Breathing and Control, Resonance and Projection, Literature and Improvisation.

'Don't – I can't begin to imagine the fear!'

Well, Ronnie, put it this way – much work needed to be done! There was, however, a lot of water to go under the bridge before then...

'I'm on the edge of my seat!'

Well, brace yourself! I had a showdown, face-off, clash and moment of truth with Rex Walters!

'No!'

Yes, Ronnie. I'd had enough.

'Well, don't stop there – you always stop at the crucial moment!'

On the afternoon in question, I attended for my usual Session. I was on time and kept waiting in the corridor for ages. Judy, the student before me, left Rex's den awash with effusive comment – "Bye-bye, love, so good to see you again...wonderful work as usual...."!

'Bloody Blah....'

Much to my astonishment, he greeted me with "You're late!" I lost my temper. The upshot and conclusion of the confrontation was: "That's it! I will be asking to be transferred to another Professor!"

'No!'

Yes, Ronnie. I was moved and without any objection from the powers that be. I wonder, was I one of many complainants?

'We are left with the conundrum – why be so unreasonable and unkind?'

That is a teaser I will never be able to solve, Ronnie. I've tried. In due course, I was taken under the wing of the gentle, gifted Mr. Daniel Roberts. He nursed me through....

'Did you go from strength to strength?'

I trusted Mr. Roberts and the belief in myself; my talents flourished.

'Again....you had come home...'

Mr. Walters was a prudent, sagacious Tutor. Unfortunately, he and I were the victims of a personality clash. I suppose it needled us both. Student and Teacher had set out with great expectations. Mr. Walters, an experienced Actor and Theatre buff, had much knowledge to impart. I am sure that for some he was a sympathetic, encouraging ace. I have no doubt that I proved to be a disappointment to him.

We were, nevertheless, to meet again many, many years later .....

'When you became the successful Teacher that he never thought you could be?'

Just so, Ronnie.

~

The countdown to my Final Examinations was nigh. I was in the thick of revising but still the letters from my Mother prevailed; her discontent and unhappiness was prevalent. I decided on a course of action which, in the end, made not an ounce of difference.

'Now what?'

I wrote to Daddy. As a rule, I did not have any direct word from him while I was away. I have no doubt that my Mother passed on any news from London.

'What did you say?'

I spoke of my worry. I spoke of my upset and fear. I spoke of my wish that all could be harmonious between my Parents. Incredibly, I remember expressing a wish for my Daddy to "save his marriage". Now, I can hardly believe that I was so unequivocal and candid in that letter. I did not receive a reply. I did not receive a single word of acknowledgement...

'Silence?'

Complete. Nothing was ever mentioned. Not a word passed between us. My plea met a quiescent void.

'Nothing could be done, darling....remember, it was not your Marriage....'

~

Tom came into my life again. This time, he came with a different purpose.

We met at Euston and spent a happy day together. Hardly anything had changed. We were as one again...

'But?'

Yes Ronnie. There was a but. Tom had met someone else.

'Oh darling....so much had happened since you were together....'

As I reflect, I think Tom came to London one last time to make up his mind. He told me that he had known Geraldine for some time. At the close of that last day, we were sitting in the lamplight Lounge of Warwickshire House. Tom's disclosures came as a total shock.

'Did you have any right to be shocked?'

No, Ronnie, I didn't. I had deceived, hoodwinked and kept Tom on an emotional hook for a long time. Of course I didn't perceive it like that then. This was a bombshell and a rude awakening. All at once, I was looking at Tom as I must have done when first we met. I saw the twinkling eyes, the curly hair and the oh-so-Irish countenance. Now, they would be seen by someone else...

'Did you ever really lose him?'

No, Ronnie. He remained in thought all my life.

'Darling, I understand completely...heart and soul'.

I watched Tom move away and down to the street below. He turned to wave. The inexplicable happened. I ran down the steps, kissed his cheek and simply said "I love you, Tom" before fleeing. He did not follow me.

I don't remember how I returned to my room. Fiona was away for the weekend. All I can recollect is the isolation, the desperation and the loneliness of that night. Now, I was to grieve as Tom had grieved for me so many times before. I had left it too late....

'Did time heal?'

Eventually. Some months later, I received a letter from Tom. He explained that he had had a profound and searching return journey to Liverpool on the night of our final meeting. I got the impression that there had been much conflict of thought. He had, however, made his decision and intended to be married to Geraldine within the year.

'That was that?'

Oh yes Ronnie. That was that. I wrote congratulating Tom and wished him every happiness. My footnote was that he would have a place in my heart forever.

'And he did?'

Yes, he did Ronnie. Whenever his University friend Roger McGough was in my area giving readings of his Poetry, I would attend and find an opportunity to enquire about Tom. I learned that he had had four children. All became Doctors and Lawyers. It sounded good....

'Do you reckon he taught them how to play Poker?'

~

My sojourn at Guildhall and Warwickshire House was coming to an end.

Fiona was accepting Secretarial jobs outside London and so would be upping sticks. Everything in my life was beginning to take a different turn, but I knew that my friendship with Fiona was an enduring one.

The AGSM examinations were tough. I worked tirelessly on Technique and Theory, so when the results came through, I had done well. The first half of my qualification was complete.

Mo and Fred were also successful; together, we were bound for the Final Year of our course which was to be at Trent Park Teachers' Training College in Hertfordshire. Interestingly, our first two years at Guildhall had been equivalent to a Performer's Course, so we were well prepared for whatever may follow. Guildhall did not specialise in Teacher Training for State School Education.

'I gather that Warwickshire House was too far away to commute?'

Yes, Ronnie. Over time, Mo and I had met Carole, another Student in our year. Carole had a Music Teacher boyfriend by the name of Paul. Over numerous cups of coffee, we arranged to house-share when studying at Trent. Joy, a somewhat eccentric mate of Carole's, whom Mo and I did not know, agreed to make up the company. Rent, split five ways could be handy. Paul seemed to be very savvy about accommodation, so we left it to him. He secured a pleasant house for rent in Cockfosters, a stone's throw from Trent Park.

Saying goodbye to my familiar life in London was strange. I had become so used to it. The City was now an old friend. Packing was done and tearful farewells were made to Fiona and Warwickshire House. Life was returning briefly to Anlaby, my family and the Summer holidays. Soon, I was to embark on the next stage…

A stint in a Newsagents was to be my Summer vacation job!

'Was it sweet shop? Did it sell bullets!'

TRENT PARK TRAINING COLLEGE

1962/1963

'Educating the mind without educating the heart is no education at all'

(Aristotle)

Mo and I were to spend most of the next year living at No. 20 Ashhurst Road which was a Thirties house in the residential suburb of Cockfosters. The doughty Paul had found a comfortable lodging which suited us well. Mo and I agreed to share a back bedroom. This gave us ample room and provided much scope to gossip about our fellow inmates! Indeed, there was much to chatter about. We discovered that Carole was pregnant! Now that was a ticklish problem that we had not bargained for or been given the chance to discuss...

'How developed was this development? I mean, was she likely to give birth on the kitchen floor at any given moment?'

Not exactly Ronnie, but as you can imagine, it would have been helpful to know. Mo, never caught on the back foot, tackled the sheepish Carole about it. Carole often reminded me of the wispy Jackie Kennedy. She spoke in faint, breathy and carefully modulated tones while peering through luxuriant eyelashes. I think she irritated Mo beyond measure. It transpired that the Mother-to-be had some time to go, so we breathed a sigh of relief, but little knowing that, later in the Academic year, we would be faced with vexation but, mercifully, not the promise of early delivery!

'All I can say is – fuck!'

If I had been in the habit of saying that at the time, Ronnie, I'm sure both Mo and I would have said it.

'What about the other girl, Joy? I hope she was hale and hearty...'

Yes, she was Ronnie, but....well...what can I say about Joy? Er, she was a trifle uncommunicative, rather dull and very lazy.

'Dear God, you do pick 'em, don't you?'

The poor girl was devoid of animation and her face nearly always betrayed an expression of total disinterest. On one occasion, we were discussing the likelihood of being accosted or chatted up on the Tube train and what action we would take. Poor Joy announced: "Well, that's never happened to me..." Mo's face was a study. She remarked: "Astonishing Joy – I can't think why!"

We took up residence at Ashhurst Road the day before Term began. There was much domestic preparation and sorting. It turned out that Paul, the Father-to-be, was a capable cook, so it was left to him to assemble paraphernalia and the like in the kitchen. Mo and I were only too pleased to leave him to it. Neither of us were hell-bent on rustling up anything more than the odd sandwich...

'Presumably the precocious Paul had a Teaching job in the area?'

Oh yes, Ronnie. That came to our notice, largely because he brought it to our notice. One of his commissions was being duty bound for the making of canes! Corporal punishment was still rife in those days.

'So did he sit of an evening whittling away at a piece of willow, or whatever the bloody things were made of?'

Well, yes, in-between ceaseless, long-winded snippets of tedious, insipid accounts of his Academic day. The breathy Carole nodded in wonder...

Mo and I went out in search of the nearest fish-n-chip shop! I'll tell you more about life at No.20 a bit later on...

'I can't wait!'

~

Trent Park College loomed at the end of a very long driveway. The building sprawled over immaculate grounds. We discovered that once trapped within its boundaries, we were isolated and disconnected from the society and sophistication of Cockfosters – such as it was! The route march back to the main road was not to be undertaken lightly!

For me, however, the Lectures were absorbing. Sessions included Class Management, Student Discipline and Lesson Preparation. Mr. E.J.Burton was the Tutor in charge of Education; before, he had had custody of Speech Work and Drama at Latymer School, Edmonton. He was an impressive man. His aim for Education was the full and healthy development of personality within a community. He believed that discipline should be largely imposed by pupils on themselves during Drama; a necessity for fuller expression within their society.

'Now wait a minute – did this man bring about a sea change?'

He did, Ronnie. Much to my surprise, I was hooked from day one. Here was I, quite sure that all this would never be of interest to me – all I wished for was the Stage. I had not predicted being engrossed in something else – something, supposedly, so adverse to my ambition.

His energy was infectious. He was interested in every Child as an individual – the whole Child. He wanted to work towards producing well-balanced, emotionally-stable members of society; the School society and that of the outside world. This was Educational Drama in the classroom; a training for life and not a training for the Stage.

During that first Autumn Term we were occupied entirely with School organisation and management for Secondary level Education; pupils would range in age from eleven to approximately eighteen or nineteen. As the final weeks drew to a close, we were informed in minute detail of our Spring Term commitment.

'Teaching Practice?'

Yes, Ronnie. I was absolutely terrified. Mr. Burton was to be my Tutor. He would supervise my work and be present in all classes. We were to undertake two practices. My first, lasting for a fortnight, would be in a Girls' school in Tottenham, London. The second, in the Summer Term, would take me to a large mixed Boys' and Girls' Comprehensive in Potters Bar.

'Mixed in more ways than one, I'll bet...'

Now, shall I digress while I take you back to life at Ashhurst Road?

'Oh, do! I'm sure it'll make for a scintillating account!'

It transpired that the whispery Carol had a driving licence. In due course, a car appeared. I have to admit that this was an inestimable indulgence, especially as the weather turned out to be disagreeable towards the end of Term. Frost and some snow prevailed. On foot, The Trent drive could prove to be a formidable test of endurance – but – a motoring handicap made itself known which prevented us from adapting to a life of Riley, or, should I say a ride of Riley.

'Puts me in mind of Foxdale's irrepressible Brenda and the new Riley!'

The bugger wouldn't start of a morning.

'I hope the pregnant Carole was not called upon to push at this juncture!'

If the intrepid, valiant Paul was around, it made the whole process a little easier. If absent, much graft, toil and travail befell the rest of us. Fortunately, Ashhurst Road was on a gentle slope, so our truculent vehicle was fairly quick to respond. The languorous Carole whipped up some energy and with the help of clutch, accelerator and a tad of urgency, coaxed the engine into life. By then, Mo, Joy and I were almost hors de combat…

'I trust you clambered aboard before the triumphant Carole made off without you'.

Well, much muttering went on while she, window down, blew kisses to the redoubtable Paul.

The Ashhurst Road Cleaning Rota proved to be problematic.

'The what?'

By mutual consent, our gathering resolved to keep the house moderately clean. It was decreed that this cycle should operate weekly and sections of the pad be allocated to each individual. These areas were to be followed in sequence. Thence, some variety came about. This was where we ran into some opposition; Joy flatly refused to clean the lavatory. In the finish, I was obliged to point out a home truth. I stated that if Joy wished to use the lavatory, then she should fall in with the general consensus and clean it.

'I hope you provided Marigolds for the green and unworldly…'

Well, Joy coped once Mo had given her root and branch of toilet cleaning technique.

While all this was going on and just before we were due to sit the end-of- Term exams, I developed excruciating pain in my jaw, visited a Dentist and learned that I had an abscess within the lower mandible; thus, a large tooth would have to be extracted.

'Ugh! Your mandible, love....'

After considerable tussling, the Dentist concluded that the tooth was too large to come out in one fell swoop. Thus, he took half of it out one night and the next half the following evening. I was in agony. No antibiotics then and I remember being plied with large dollops of Hooch at home, thanks to Mo, which provided some relief. I did, however, report for my first Examination with a cheek swollen to twice its size. It was all very dramatic and the Invigilator kept hovering over my desk.

'Did he have smelling salts?'

I rather think he was casting about for a stretcher – just in case.

Mo was very critical of Carole and Paul and did not curb venting her spleen loudly during our bedroom conversations. I have no doubt that both overheard and were not pleased.

'Mmn...awkward...'

Well, yes Ronnie. It was. Especially as Mo took off to her home and Boyfriend in Northampton every weekend, leaving me alone to hold the fort. I must mention that Carole and Paul had been very solicitous about my welfare and had often included me when they had taken weekends away to stay with relatives. I really appreciated that.

'Mmn...kind...'

So, those thoughtful gestures came to an end and I was left to spend Saturdays and Sundays rattling around in an empty house.

'Oh darling...'

Well, Carole and Paul's attitude was quite understandable and I should have told Mo to pipe down, even though I knew her fault-finding could, at times, be justified.

'It seemed that Mo was adept at stirring up trouble and then walking away and leaving it...'

Perceptive old Ronnie. The inscrutable Joy also buggered off to Town every Friday night. So, Ronnie... I was on my tod. I was, however, facing a state of affairs which was very new to me. I had never been left home alone before. I called upon every scrap and vestige of courage. Unfortunately, my grant would not stretch to repeated rail fares to Anlaby, so fait accompli ruled. Providentially, having mustered some strength from somewhere, I did not disclose any of these circumstances to my Mother. She would have been frantic, I know; probably, sending the fare on immediately. Come what may, I needed to learn. I needed to acquire self-sufficiency. It was only one of the requisites required for autonomy. Nevertheless, it was a lonely and unforgiving time.

'Character building is no fun sometimes, is it darling...'

The house was comfortable enough. A coal fire was the only mode of heating. Consequently, the bedrooms froze. Alone I may have been, but I was not fazed. Well versed in my Mother's method of "laying the fire", I soon had flames blasting up the chimney and Jessica would have been proud. I also recalled the lovely Fiona's tried and true comfort remedy – a Fullers Chocolate Cake!

'Dear God!'

Oh yes, Ronnie. These were very substantial cakes, usually supplied by Fiona's generous Mum, via Fortnums. On special occasions, they would appear at Warwickshire House in the form of luxuriously-wrapped parcels: an accompaniment to the regular Hamper. Lo and behold, I found one in a Cockfosters Patisserie!

'Bet they didn't have Mille-feuille, Alice! Remember that! My favourite!'

Thus fortified, I applied myself to Study. This enforced solitude gave me a worthwhile opportunity to absorb all that I had learned so far. I began to look ahead to my Teaching Practice debut. The Tottenham Girls' School had a rugged, tough reputation, if rumour was to be believed!

I planned lessons. Mr. Burton, in his lectures, had outlined lesson note procedure. Each session needed to be prepared meticulously with an Introduction –

'I suppose that meant the Aim of the lesson?'

Right Ronnie. Then followed the Development and Conclusion. These sections should explain how the activity would proceed, how it would be organised and finally a Deduction and Summary. In plain words, had the object of the exercise been achieved; had it been successful? These notes were to be scrutinised by Mr. Burton. It was disconcerting.

'So darling, the time alone turned out to be in your favour. There is only one way to deal with fear and that is to face it head on'.

Over the coming years, I found myself saying that time and again in class to insecure, frightened boys and girls. I had also been afraid....

My first lesson at Tottenham was a baptism of fire. My shaking knees had a mind of their own as I turned the classroom door-handle and faced approximately thirty thirteen-year-old girls. They eyed me suspiciously.

'What were you wearing?'

One of "our 'ilary's" smart suits paired with equally smart high-heeled shoes.

The theme was simple: small Plays centred on one incident or happening. The children were to work in pairs on familiar or typical situations: A quarrel. An excuse.

A plot. All were within the Students' own experience. Everyone should be able to relate to the task. After Rehearsal and Preparation, these could be performed for the rest of the class. Only, however, if Students wished to enact. No Child should feel obliged to do so. Watching and listening could be just as important. Class discussion would end the lesson.

'How did it go?'

I was thrilled, Ronnie. All Children were engaged, happy and produced some very interesting and realistic Scenes. Enthusiastic debate rounded off an exciting lesson. Guess what, Ronnie? Mr. Burton congratulated me on an excellent first attempt!

'Life presents some wonderful rewards, love'.

My next few days at Tottenham were dogged by – Fog! It was my first encounter with a London pea-souper! The school was closed for a couple of days which gave me welcome breathing space to prepare more lessons for the remaining time. But Ronnie – wait for it – at the end of my spell at Tottenham, the school offered me a job! The place would be waiting for whenever I chose to accept!

'And you had been such a naughty girl! Did it ever occur to you that somebody could be pulling the strings of your life?'

It certainly crossed my mind many years later, Ronnie.

Potters Bar Comprehensive School was a massive force to be reckoned with. The complex covered several acres and was divided into blocks of Study: the Art Block, the Science Block and so on. Schooling was Co-Educational. I found that very refreshing and -

'Normal?'

Yes, Ronnie. It made for some varied, provocative and challenging Drama. Here, one was contemplating thirty-plus teenage Children of varying ability, so pondering the test of captivating all by stimulating imagination and expertise was daunting. It was, however, exhilarating to see youngsters who had been labelled 'less able academically' take an equal place beside their cleverer peers. Everyone is good at something; all thrive on encouragement. Everyone can be clever in a Drama class. It was thrilling to witness the escalation of confidence in those who, like myself at times, had taken a back seat.

'You loved it, didn't you? Go on, I think I know what you are going to say next....!'

I was offered a post of Drama Specialist at Potters Bar Comprehensive!

Towards the end of the Summer Term I took my Final Examinations for the Teachers' Certificate, University of London.

Ronnie, you will never believe what I am going to tell you. I passed with Distinction! In his glowing Testimonial of my work, Mr. Burton went on to say that I was the outstanding Student of my group and would be a credit to any Teaching Staff.

'Darling...you must have been facing a huge crossroads in your life...what on earth did you decide to do?'

I was very undecided. I was still yearning to be an Actress. So, I did not accept either Post. Once more, it was time to think and plan.

'Were you very good at planning then?'

Since you mention it, Ronnie, I wasn't. I drifted once more.

Mo, Joy and the Parents-to-be, Carol and Paul, were moving on. Mo had failed the Exams and was returning to Northampton. Joy, relieved not to be on lavatory-duty any more, made her way back to where she came from. The lovely Fred did well Academically and went on to teach Drama and English in a variety of schools. We took different paths....

A comment from Mr. Walters came my way. Apparently, he had been heard to say, "Susan Uebel will never become a Teacher – she has no confidence in herself; how may she inspire it in others".

'I'd love to have been a fly on the wall when word of your Distinction reached him!'

As the years passed, my confidence grew. It grew in my Teaching of needy, shy and sensitive Children. Those who also lacked the magic ingredient. Through teaching Drama, I found a way to instil courage; to trust, believe and become assured. Together, we learned to be bold, to be self-reliant and to be sure.

'How long did it take you to follow the path you had been shown?'

A long time Ronnie...I took several wrong turnings...

~

As I floundered, the thoughtful Fiona suggested that I return to Warwickshire House in the Summer of 1963. "Just come to London for a week or two, Sue. I could recommend you for a Temp. Secretarial job. It may help you to come to some conclusion."

'The lovely Fiona....'

Fiona was as good as her word. She knew of a Doctor at a London Hospital who needed a Typist. It was all arranged and Warwickshire House beckoned once more. At least, there was some sort of plan looming.

I returned to Anlaby and became rooted once more in home. The wrench to leave, even for a short time, was great. Also, I was afraid again. Afraid of London and afraid of being alone.

'Oh Sue, darling....'

Surprisingly, Mum was eager to push me out of the nest.

'Had she a Theatre job in mind then, he said with a hint of sarcasm...'

“Think of this few weeks as a holiday” said she. So I did just that, stayed a week and came back in loneliness and despair. The engaging Doctor whom I did manage to work for while away, concluded thus: “Well, I expect you’ll just go home and marry a Farmer!”

‘Perhaps he thought you may have married him!’

My Mother’s comforting, welcoming deduction when I returned to the fold was: “Well, I did think you’d have gone round all the Agents...well, you’ll have to get a job if you stay here....”

‘Just as she had done, one would presume?’

The following day, I contacted Hull Education Authority. I was told that there were no vacancies for Drama Specialists in any Hull School.

‘Now what?’

It was extraordinary, Ronnie. Within a couple of days, I received further word from the Authority. Would I take up a Post at the School for Educationally Subnormal Children, in Northumberland Avenue, Hull?

‘The School for what? What an objectionable title... some things were ghastly in the early Sixties...’

When I spluttered: “Oh, I don’t think I could possibly teach there! I’m not qualified!” , the robust reply was: “Well, Miss Uebel, if you can teach there, you can teach anywhere”!!

‘So you were signed, sealed and – dare I say it – delivered!’

Deliverance was the operative word, Ronnie. There began some of the most rewarding, dearest weeks of my Teaching career!

‘Now I wonder who could have been in the driving seat!’

NORTHUMBERLAND AVENUE SCHOOL FOR EDUCATIONALLY SUBNORMAL CHILDREN

1963/1964

'Everybody is a genius. If you judge a fish by its ability to climb a tree, it will live its whole life believing it is stupid. Not every disability is visible'

(Einstein)

"I know that fella! He 'as a shop on Porter Street. Me Mam buys her chitterlins from there!" I was standing by the boot of my Father's car as he helped me unload various bags for School. "Are you comin' 'ere, Miss?"

Daddy, grinning, almost caved in. I replied, "Well, as a matter of fact, I am coming in to school. Thank you for recognising my Father. You're right, he does have a shop on Porter Street. It was good that you knew him." She beamed and said, "I'm Pat Edwards. I bet you'll remember me"!

'How's that for an introduction, Alice!'

So began my first day at Northumberland Avenue. As I made my way inside, I noticed how austere the School seemed to be. Everywhere was in shadow, gloomy and unprepossessing. A kindly Secretary escorted me along a narrow corridor towards the Staff Room where I was introduced to Kath, who was to be a Form Teaching colleague and – Mr. Knowles. He then squired me across the untidy room to where Mr. Sallis, the Headmaster, was chatting to another group of Teachers.

'Were you nerve-wracked, love?'

Oh, I was Ronnie. My palms had gone very clammy and cold, so I felt acutely embarrassed at having to take Mr. Sallis' outstretched hand in greeting. He didn't seem to notice, or, he was far to polite to acknowledge my nervousness.

"You'll be teaching a small class of fifteen-year-old girls, Miss Uebel," he announced. "Perhaps I don't need to remind you that they have the Educational ability of very young Children. Our teaching here is geared to their disadvantage. That very handicap can be a great hindrance in their capacity to learn. You will discover your own level of communication in no time!"

'Am I right in thinking that that was that'.

Well, it would have been Ronnie, but for Kath and Mr. Knowles, who proved to be towers of strength, expertise and humour. Mr. Knowles seemed very canny, very shrewd and very discriminating. He obviously knew Mr. Sallis very well indeed. "He's a dab hand at Country Dancing, Sue… if you follow me!"

'I'm sure you got the message….sounds as if Mr. Knowles, as opposed to Mr. Sallis, was used to working on the chalk face!'

He proved to be a very wise man, Ronnie, who possessed a wealth of understanding where those children were concerned.

I was directed to the Classroom where I would teach my Class from 9.00 a.m. until 4.00 p.m.

'What? Non-Stop!'

Non-stop, Ronnie. I was expected to cover every Subject. Wait for it!

Maths...

'Dear God, Mrs. Arithmetic, come back – all is forgiven!'

English, History, Geography, Art, and – Needlework!! My respite once a week was – brace yourself Ronnie – Country Dancing!

Guardian Angel Mr. Knowles put me wise to a very important consideration. "Remember Sue, these Girls are only lacking in Educational grip. This is largely because they haven't had the Family background or chances that kids should have. To survive, many of them have had to be street wise and crafty. Don't underestimate them. Just love 'em....I do."

'What a lovely man...'

He was a jewel, Ronnie. I have never forgotten Mr.Knowles and his beloved Spaniel, Fanny. Mr. Knowles lived out of town, in a village. He drove to work every day accompanied by his faithful companion. Fanny went on to deliver her puppies some weeks after my arrival – in the one-and-only Staff Room armchair! That door was always left open and the children could wander in and out at leisure. The Staff were forever available and Fanny's offspring proved to be an added attraction. It was Teaching at its very best; a Professional experience and inestimable gift, an endowment bequeathed to a beginner such as myself. Those days helped to form the foundation of my understanding and expertise.

The noise was deafening as I opened the Classroom door. I made my way to the front where the Teacher's Desk presided over all. A partial silence ensued. "Shurrup! It's 'er I told you about!"

'Pat Edwards!'

Pat Edwards indeed, Ronnie.

"Tell 'em te be quiet and sit in the desks, Miss"! Pat suggested helpfully. I took her advice and said just that, whereupon most of the class opened the lids and got in! Uproar followed and I laughed. I laughed because it was all so funny. They laughed. I laughed. The ice was broken.

From then on, I did not encounter any problems. I had an idea. I taught every single subject through Drama. At the end of each day, I was exhausted, completely spent.

At that time, one could allow children to visit shops at lunchtime. In an effort to master money-reckoning, I had one or the other of my little band shopping for ten Woodbines or a small Hovis. I supplied the cash and they were obliged to return with the correct change. Spot on. I attempted to put the equivalent amount on the blackboard in Pounds, Shillings and Pence and all were stumped...

Needlework was a stumbling block for all of us. The Craft Room, however, was purloined and we imagined making Scenery for a Play. Glue and paper was everywhere – everywhere except where it should be – but, the children were absorbed and – quiet!

Mischief abounded. Violet, an extremely fat girl, was something of a butt for jokes. Violet was so overweight that if she fell – one would hope by accident and not foul-play – she was quite unable to get up. She remained vulnerable, exposed and feeble, rather like an expiring chicken who was kicking its legs in the air. This misfortune occurred repeatedly in Country Dancing! It took the combined effort of Mr. Knowles, Kath and myself to shift and reassure the sweating Violet, while the class shrieked in mirth! Meantime, the record player continued its relentless pursuit of "Take your Partners and Do-si-Do!"

My days were filled with incident, joy and laughter. My collaborators, companions and comrades – Kath and Mr. Knowles – were indispensable. Their support, friendliness and humour buoyed me up; each day held an embarrass de richesses, a treasury of knowledge and advice. Without realising it at the time, I was learning; indeed, soaking up a wealth of Teaching proficiency, a facility which would see me through whatever may come to pass.

Out of the blue, I received a phone call from Hull Education Authority.

'It's always the unexpected that happens...sudden and startling?'

You could call it that, Ronnie. By now, you will have realised how settled and happy my life was...

'Ah yes, Alice, but your strings were being pulled again...'

"Miss Uebel, I have been contacted by the Headmaster of Kelvin Hall High School, Mr. William Pattinson. His Drama Specialist is leaving and he is looking for a replacement. He is very impressed with your qualifications and hopes you may be interested. He has asked for permission to phone you as soon as possible. Will this be in order?"

'Knowing you, I expect you were thrown into disorder and panicked! Change always upset the apple-cart if I remember correctly!'

You're absolutely right, Ronnie. I ran straight to Mr. Knowles....

"Sue, my dearest," said he, "you can't spend the rest of your life here. Now, listen to me...I know of Bill Pattinson. He was an H.M.I."

'Did you know the significance of that at the time?'

No Ronnie. Hadn't a clue.

"Her Majesty's Inspector of Schools. Apparently, he was tough..." Mr. Knowles went on: "He came in for a lot of stick when the Authority appointed him. This High School, now called the Pattinson Palace by those who applied and were passed over, is a new build on Bricknell Avenue in Hull. It's the apple of Bill's eye. He is very forward-thinking and you can bet your bottom dollar that his Drama Department Specialist Post will be a jewel in the crown. Go for it, Sue. You have got to think of your Career...go with our blessing, love."

'Oh Sue, what a wrench...those strings must have nearly broken...'

"Miss Uebel? Bill Pattinson here...I do hope we can meet. Perhaps you would care to see our School and find out what we do here. I suggest some time soon...."

On a grey November morning so long ago, I had my first glimpse of Kelvin Hall School. The building, very wide and narrow, was set back from Bricknell Avenue. The gardens and grounds, well kept and spacious, were spread out before what appeared to be a very modern structure of its time. I was tentative.

'Why, darling – after all, you were being head-hunted!'

True, Ronnie. I was being steered, but didn't know whether I wanted to go in that direction. I was wearing "our 'ilary's" smart two-piece once more and high heels, so, trying to muster some joie de vivre, savoir-faire, poise or whatever attribute springs to mind, I forged ahead towards the entrance. To summon up grit, nerve and resolution, I attempted to recall the tributes paid by my Teaching Practice ventures, but in spite of all, felt myself teetering, alarmingly, on the brink...

"Good Morning, Miss Uebel. Welcome to Kelvin Hall. I am so pleased to meet you".

'Well, don't stop there...what was he like? Did you fancy him?'

I hasten to remind you, my darling, that 'fancy' was not a word one used in those days!

Bill Pattinson was not what I expected. He was very, very tall, white-haired, immaculately-suited, black-gowned and unnervingly direct of gaze! He towered above me. On route to his office, he pointed out various School landmarks: Dining Hall, Staff Room, School Hall. The Entrance Hall had already taken my notice, in-between being somewhat intimidated by Mr. Pattinson's height. I had to crick my neck to look him in the eye...

I could see colour everywhere: carefully posted information, photographs, vases of flowers. Here was inspiration, care and friendliness.

"Mrs. Fox thank you so much". Mrs.Fox, introduced as the School Secretary served coffee and biscuits. I declined a biscuit. "Oh I would have thought you could have managed one," volunteered Mr. Pattinson. I wasn't sure whether he was sussing out my weight, or plugging Mrs. Fox's choice of biscuit.

'Hell, he's unnerving me!'

It was certainly a searching Interview, Ronnie, but I was so impressed with him and his lovely school. I would, however, hate to have been on the receiving end of his H.M.I.'s inspection!

There was much to absorb. The tradition of the School was its freshness, happiness, friendliness and pride. "That is the norm of Kelvin, Miss Uebel; we care for each other. We work hard and play hard, while remaining smart, courteous and enthusiastic. Children of all ages frequently under-achieve simply because no one expects much of them. We believe that what is necessary for growth, in its fullest sense, is that Teachers and Parents should have only the highest possible expectations of all Students. I should point out that I also expect the highest standards from my members of Staff. I believe that the only discipline worth having is self-discipline. You will not encounter a cane, detention or order marks here. You, as a Teacher, will have nothing to fall back on but your own charisma, energy and dedication. In my experience, when a Student is badly behaved in class, one usually finds that there is trouble at home, or, a Teacher's practice has not engaged the pupil. There is always a reason for modes of conduct."

'He sold it, didn't he, my darling!'

He did, Ronnie. On that morning, I put the seal on the following eight years of my Teaching life....

~

My last day at Northumberland Avenue School for Educationally-Subnormal Children was a sad one. I was leaving behind many people who had made such a difference to my life: so many people who had trusted me, so many who had created happiness, realisation and accomplishment.

I was left with a lasting and prophetic image as I made my way through the gates and out into the dusty, grey and sombre backstreet of Hull: a young boy was dragging a small cart which contained firewood. "Miss, do you want to buy some?" said he. As I carried four bundles across the road to where my Father's car was waiting, I felt the tears start and the strings pull.

"...no one expects much of them..." Bill Pattinson's words echoed through the still, foggy air. Such a gulf existed between a boy with a cart full of firewood and a boy born in sight of a window of chance and possibility.

'Perhaps, over the years, you took some wrong turnings, but you did not forget the boy with the cart and loyalty to his memory enabled you to realise an unswerving faithfulness that you did not know you possessed'.

Gran used to call it "a calling"...

'Interesting that you did not apply for either job. Opportunities arose...you clasped them...have you ever asked yourself why?'

KELVIN HALL SCHOOL

1964/1972

'They whom truth and wisdom lead, can
gather honey from a weed'

(William Cowper, 1731,
Nature and Countryside Poet)

I was invited to make several visits to Kelvin during the Autumn of 1963.

"Miss Uebel, you are to join my Staff here. I do hope you will be able to come along and soak up the atmosphere of my School. Before you arrive, it would be useful to gather as much information as possible. I know that Mr. Norris will be delighted to meet you."

'Bill was on your case, wasn't he?'

He was on everybody's case, Ronnie. His presence towered in more ways that one.

Stan Norris was responsible for Drama. He was an approachable, friendly guide; his help was worth its weight in gold. He introduced me to several members of Staff likely to cross my path by way of Play Production: those in charge of Art, Woodwork, Home Economics and English. Much later on, Jean Harrison, the Dance Teacher, let on that Stan had looked towards my visits with keen and animated expectation! "He scrubs up well before you arrive, Sue!"

'I know the feeling!'

In the course of these putting-wise meetings, I discovered that I would be expected to direct the Annual School Production every Spring Term.

'You were due to begin in a Spring Term!'

Yes, Ronnie, and I was already being asked for suggestions about choice of play!

'No!'

Don't worry, darling. I did my homework! Forewarned is for-armed! I had always loved 'Jane Eyre'. I dropped the idea in Bill's lap! He was quite stunned, I think, but didn't hesitate.

'A very wise move, love. Make the choices before he makes them for you!'

I chose to be ambitious, Ronnie. The play was a breakthrough. I knew its theme would appeal to both the Students and the English Department.

'Method in your madness!'

I had met Jim, the Head of Art. He would prove to be an important asset. The Set was also ambitious! Fortunately, he was intrigued…

'With you, or with the Production?'

Since you mention it, Ronnie, there did appear to be some interest in me. He advocated that we put forward ideas for the Thornfield Hall set over a drink!

'Such shenanigans usually rear their ugly heads somewhere along the line! Seriously though, it was good to get him on your side so early on in the planning…'

Jim was, undoubtedly, a colossal and prodigious support to my Kelvin career. It was early days in 1964, but once my passage was underway, a relationship between Jim and I developed. Over some years, it reached maturity, but not attainment.

'I reckon you'll mention it from time to time?'

Only from time to time, Ronnie.

~

'You have not spoken of life at Cerne Abbas while all this was going on…'

Sadly, as we neared Christmas of 1963, Grandpa died. He passed away peacefully, but it was the end of an era, a day of days. My Grandparents had meant so much to me…now they were gone.

Naturally, my Mother was distraught. Grandpa had been reminiscent of the final threads; she was an orphan. The loss of a Parent is manifold. We can no longer depend on unconditional love; the multifarious feelings and sacrifices that only a Mother or Father can afford. All at once, the difficulties that Grandpa had exemplified, seemed distant, irrelevant and secondary compared with the joy he had apportioned.

Nicky, I could hardly believe, was seventeen. For a year, he had been working for Delight Products, a Fancy-goods firm in which my Father had interest invested. Was this to promote some surety or guarantee for Nicky's future? I am unable to say. Nicky seemed to show promise, but not any surge of enthusiasm. Only time would tell…

'I suppose you were too busy keeping the plates spinning to attach much importance to it.'

My Mother was preoccupied. With hindsight….

'Mmn…hindsight…unhelpful and a bloody nuisance, in my opinion…'

I found her difficult. She had been introduced to Jim…

''ere we go again!'

She seemed to be agreeable, but before long I would be needled with doubt….I recall returning very late from an outing with Jim. "You've no business coming home at this time!" she announced.

'Were you twenty-four at the time, or five?!'

I was constantly dodging the bullets. All was rather mystifying and certainly unsettling. I tried to fathom it. Now, I'm inclined to think that my Mother had not bargained for the change which had come about. She, like me, had been hell-bent on my Theatrical career. Perhaps she was disappointed. She had, however, shown appreciation and pride in my Teaching success.

'I reckon it did not hold the same glory as a career in the public eye; after all, it would be difficult to live her life through you in the classroom!'

I was staying in the Parental home. Customarily, in the early Sixties, girls did not move out of it until Marriage. In my Mother's coterie, sharing flats or bed-sits with friends was frowned upon. As for couples living together before tying the knot – well, that would have been totally infra dig.

'You'd have been dancing with the Devil if the Sixties' Pill had been mentioned!'

Dear God Ronnie, even I didn't know anything about that!

So, while I was still living at home, I was obliged to observe my Mother's rules. I assured her that while I was under her roof, I would return at a fitting time and -

'Observe the sense of social propriety! Oh, I do I have a way with words!'

What's more, I was earning a good salary. I was in a position to alleviate and soothe my Mother's monetary worries. I had an opportunity to repay her generosity and care.

'One can't have it all ways, love'.

So, Ronnie, life on the home front had to progress in its own way. I was too preoccupied with Kelvin's multitude of complexity!

~

My first morning at Kelvin Hall School began with Morning Service. The usual terminology for such an event can be Assembly or Meeting.

Not so for Bill Pattinson. He wished the gathering to resemble Church Worship, complete with hymns, accompanied by the Head of Music. This was to be followed by an Address and Morning Notes from the Headmaster. It was impressive. The whole School congregated in the Hall where Mr. Venus, the hard-working and personable Caretaker, had arranged rows of chairs.

"Miss Uebel, do sit wherever you wish. The Students do not take up Form positions and all Year groups can mingle as they prefer. Staff very often sit in the body of the Hall and not formally on Platform or in a Group". This guidance was passed on to me by the Deputy Head Teacher, Miss Nora Harris.

I found the Service most enlightening. Here was consideration, respect, harmony and goodwill. School hierarchy, its ranking or pecking order, was not of prime importance.

'Was Bill on the platform?'

Oh yes, Ronnie. The hymn that first morning was 'Guide Me, O Thou Great Redeemer' and when we reached the line "feed me now and evermore", Bill obliged with the descant – "ever MORE!" It was indelibly printed on my memory for evermore. I always looked forward to that hymn being chosen for subsequent Services, if only for Bill's resounding, ringing, resonant rendering and the smothered giggles of all.

'He was quite something, Sue.'

His address was equally enthralling. He welcomed the new First Year Students, who were shivering with nervous tension; indeed, much as was I! "I hope you will enjoy your time here, working hard and looking towards success in the future. Always remember, everyone is good at something. I daresay that many of you will go on to be Doctors, Businessmen and Secretaries. I hope, however, that several of you will one day be able to lift the bonnet of my car and put right any problem it may have".

So, Ronnie, every child left the School Hall that morning with the promise of finding their place in the world.

'That's the kind of rallying call we all need...'

I was then introduced to Mr. Howard Adcock, Head of the English Department. In an inscrutable, baffling kind of way, he reminded me of Miss Sugden!

'Very little spit?'

Actually Ronnie, yes. How funny was that! Mr. Adcock was a Gentleman. He helped me to access my Timetable and Class locations. Most of my time would be taken with Drama, of course, but I also seemed to have a fairly extensive quota of English sessions. In those days, one took lessons in English Grammar as well as Literature! I was delighted to learn that Mr. Adcock favoured much time being given to Spoken English. I was home and dry, Ronnie!

One weekly class did unnerve me at first...

'In what way, darling?'

It was Liberal Studies with Sixth Form students! I was to meet these eighteen-year-olds for a whole hour!

'Dear God, how liberal were they?'

Bear in mind, Ronnie, that those boys (mostly huge boys, I hasten to add!) and girls were only six years younger than me!

I was terrified before my first lesson which had been prepared in meticulous fashion, needless to say. I was making my way along the corridor to find the staircase leading to the first floor classroom where the lesson was to take place. In a matter of minutes, I sensed I was being followed. Seemingly, some of my charges were close on my heels.

"Can I carry your books, Miss?" said one voice. As I turned to thank the thoughtful owner of it, another one added, "Can I carry you, Miss?"

'No! Oh Sue, how priceless!'

I turned. My helpful protégé was all of six feet tall!

'Well able to sling you over his shoulder!'

"Thank you, I think I can manage", was my prim reply, whereby we all fell about laughing. From then on, the Liberal Studies class got off to a fine start and our mirth could be heard echoing throughout the confines of the First Floor every Thursday afternoon at 2.00 p.m.

At 8.30 a.m. every morning the Staff Room buzzed with eager anticipation and preparedness. The Notice-Board displayed Notes from our Chief, Mr. Pattinson.

These Notes appeared at the beginning of each day and drew our attention to matters arising and those that…

'Had arisen?'

Indeed, Ronnie. These reminders were detailed, scrupulous and thorough.

'You missed them at your peril!'

Yes, Ronnie, I soon got the message, so to speak; I read and re-read!

These early morning turnouts of the Teaching throng provided Mr. Adcock with a time-slot to introduce other members of his English Department:

Jancis Loten and Lorna Pollard who were friendly, eager to be of assistance and most Professional. I so appreciated their willingness to be helpful.

'I reckon there was much to take on board…'

Tom Jones, John Ainsworth and Jean Harrison were in charge of Sport, Physical Education and Dance.

'Were they all very physical?'

They were, Ronnie. I found them rather intimidating. All three appeared to be absorbed in Departmental going-over as they prowled through the corridors clad in purposeful, strapping and robust gear targeted for the outdoors. Nevertheless, they were sociable. Jean, fresh from working in New Zealand, was a Geordie. Her manner was forthright, high-powered and eager. I liked and admired Jean.

As you know, I had already become acquainted with Jim of the Art Department and our 'Jane Eyre' meetings had gone well. These powwows had moved on apace; we were now well on the way to forming a fairly progressive relationship. I think it had been noted!

My days were full. I did have a few free periods whereby I could catch breath, but every moment was filled. Drama lessons took place in the School Hall. Each class numbered thirty plus boys and girls, from eleven to fifteen years. The Hall was large, parquet-floored and sun filled. Nearby, one could see the extension which housed the Woodwork and Metalwork Departments. The Hall Platform was adequate for Choir or Concert Performances, but I quaked at the prospect of setting Plays upon it. Once, engrossed in a Drama session, I noticed the Curtain tweak. It moved far enough for me to take in a very tall, bespectacled figure. The Gentleman was smiling and nodding. When the lesson closed, I wandered over to introduce myself. He shook my hand saying, "I'm Neville Taylor, my dear. I am a member of the Metalwork Department, but also most interested in Stage Lighting. Your wish is my command!"

The Improvisation lesson he had been secretly privy to, had ventured into a scene depicting domestic strife between Husband and Wife. "Puts me in mind of my Wife Myrtle and I. Do you want any advice?"

From then on, whenever I saw the knowing, smiling face between the Curtain folds, I knew that Neville had eavesdropped. He became a steadfast, true-blue pal; a virtuoso who was able to conjure schemes, stunts and ploys from a very temperamental Lighting rig.

'From whence do all your Guardian Angels appear?'

Several years later and many Plays later, I was devastated to learn that Neville had been killed in a car crash. The smiling face beyond the Curtain was no more....

Bill Pattinson began his School day with an 8.00 a.m. tour of the building. Long before Students and Staff appeared, he would be on foot inspecting corridor, lavatories and classrooms. He made a point of sharing greetings with Mr. Venus, the dependable, staunch Caretaker and Mrs. Harrison, the Kitchen/Cook Supervisor. As children began to arrive, he would know each and every one by name as he passed the time of day.

'Did that man ever find respite...? Lunchtime perhaps? No, you're shaking your head!'

He had lunch in the Dining Hall, sitting at tables with the children. It was an example that I'm sure he hoped the rest of us would follow.

"Sue," said he one day, "you learn more about a child while sharing lunch with him than you may ever do in the Classroom". Of course he was right.

'Did he have a beady eye on you, do you think?'

Oh yes, Ronnie. Oftentimes, I would be aware of a tall, white-haired Gentleman on the other side of the Hall's glass entrance door.

"Oh Miss Uebel, just popped along to see what happens in the Drama class."

'I get the impression that he was genuinely interested, not snooping. If he hadn't believed in you, he would never have allowed you into his School'.

I know you're right, Ronnie, but it was very unnerving. Also, he would suddenly appear at the back of an English Classroom! Then, strolling between the rows of desks he would find an empty seat and sit in it.

'Much to the abject horror or hopeless terror of the kid beside him!'

Well, suffice it to say, that there was an audible sigh of relief when, eventually, the Classroom door closed behind him.

The days were long. Lesson preparation, marking several sets of thirty English Composition books and planning the 'Jane Eyre' Production filled each waking hour. My lessons were exciting, thought-provoking and fun. The time was filled with laughter, teenage joshing and learning. We were all learning, all finding out and all progressing.

The setting for 'Jane Eyre' was complicated. Scenes moved from Jane's School to Thornfield Hall and on to St. John Rivers' house. Jim proposed to put the plans before the Woodwork/Metalwork Department. Thereby, a meeting was mooted with those in charge: a Mr. Bell and a Mr. Gooding.

'Do I detect a sharp intake of breath?'

Er, yes Ronnie. These two Gentlemen, from first moments, reminded me of a Variety Act. Both referred to each other formally...

'Oh Mr. Bell...Yes, Mr. Gooding....!'

Put that to music, Ronnie, and you've got it right. I was filled with apprehension. They seemed uncooperative. Jim placed the proposed Designs on the wooden bench. "Oh, that's not possible," announced Mr. Bell in military fashion. He was moustachioed, very upright of stature and daunting of bearing. Dear Mr. Bell, I did get to know him much better as the years went by and learned that his sergeant-major bark was far worse than his bite. "You see we have great difficulties here, for space" added Mr. Gooding, who seemed to be equally dismissive. I was on the point of despair.

Like his collaborator and work-mate, Mr. Gooding wore a buff-coloured coat by way of protective clothing.

'Bit like a form of heraldry, crest or coat of arms!'

Risible Ronnie! Yes, it was like a form of insignia. I never came upon either Mr. Gooding or Mr. Bell without such livery.

'Now who's being facetious?'

Over time, I learned that the most effective way of sounding them out, was to appeal in sympathetic fashion and empathise with the massive drawbacks they faced when constructing Stage sets.

'No breaking eggs with a big stick?'

True, Ronnie. In fact, I was devious.

'You...devious? I exclaim in utter disbelief!!'

I opened requests with "I don't suppose this could be possible? I quite understand if it cannot be done. It's a lot to ask."

'Did it work?'

Like a charm, Ronnie. There was, of course, much bluster, clearing of throats and "Out of the question! What do you think, Mr. Bell?" "Well, Mr. Gooding, we'll need to discuss this. It's not going to be easy".

So, that's how the Set for Jane Eyre came about. Indeed that's how the Sets for all Plays came about.

~

Jane Eyre was my first venture into Direction. I decided to handle the preparation of the play as I would for the Professional Theatre. Audition notices were posted in the School Entrance Hall. These caused a buzz; a hive of activity. Before, I had given a full explanation of my Schedule and its content to Mr. Pattinson. He was enthralled. Stan Norris, before leaving for pastures new, had been very helpful in putting me wise to Casting possibility. His prior experience with senior Students proved to be very useful. The leading Roles needed to be tackled with some skill and proficiency.

'You still relied on Audition performance?'

Oh yes, Ronnie. These were held after School. Feverish enthusiasm ruled. Many children attended for three-minute private slots and I ended up with an exceptionally talented and distinguished Cast.

Paul Henderson, a seventeen-year-old Sixth Former was to play Rochester and the lead, Jane, went to Valerie Wilson, a fifteen-year-old Fifth Former. I was stunned by the maturity of these young people. One of the most memorable Auditions came from twelve-year-old Frances Hewitt. She was quite remarkable; her vocal quality and precision of speech, extraordinary in one so young, was a matchless, peerless gift for Mrs. Fairfax, Thornfield's Housekeeper. In addition, the remainder of the Cast went down in the annals of Kelvin time as testament to a special group of young people.

Jim was, unmistakeably, a manifest asset to the launching of this first Production. He was a staunch, steadfast supporter, but also, possessed the facility and aptitude to engender unrivalled scenic results. 'Jane Eyre' was the first Play to be advertised by Front-of-House black and white Photography. Again, it was Jim and John Bebb of the Art Department who obliged with an authentic compendium of character camera wizardry.

'Was all this an added ingredient to the success of your relationship?'

I suppose it was, Ronnie. We worked so closely together. We were on common ground. I found Jim attractive. There was much to admire.

'Other than that, your lips are sealed?'

They are, Ronnie. Jim died some years ago. Thus, I do not wish to say more, except to say that he formed an intrinsic part of my life at that time. He was a fine man....

The Kelvin days were long. Rehearsals began at 4.30 p.m. and finished at 6.00 p.m. Fridays were late. Sometimes, we made our way through the School gates just before 7.00 p.m. It was not unusual for Mr. Pattinson to make an appearance...

'Just checking...?'

Just checking, Ronnie.

'Did he catch you with a Woodbine?'

Once Ronnie....he acknowledged the cigarette, looked searchingly, but never said a word. I did not take advantage. In those days, one was permitted to smoke only in the Staff Room. Other than that, my Woodbines did not see the light of day.

The First Night of Jane Eyre presented me with something of a trial. The Interval between Thornfield Hall and St. John Rivers' house was interminably long, largely because of the Set change.

'Oh Alice, I can guess what you're going to say...the Audience ended up with numb bums, waiting..'

Bill Pattinson, sitting on the front row with his wife, Freda, was very much aware of this novice Director's slip-up. When things eventually made a comeback and we reached the final Curtain – Neville Taylor, appearing within its folds once more and grinning from ear to ear in triumph – Mr. Pattinson was applauding with tumultuous appreciation.

'When did you get the summons?'

How did you guess, Ronnie. The following morning, Bill Pattinson nobbled me before class, saying, "Sue do you think you can get the Cast together this afternoon? I think we can work to tighten that gap".

'No, he didn't...you're not going to tell me that he buggered everything about?'

Yes, Ronnie, he did and because he did, I learned a very important lesson. Never again did I keep an Audience clicking its heels. I owe much to that very stressful afternoon. Not only did Mr. Pattinson save a very uncomfortable situation, he put great expectations on his Students. They came up trumps, remembered everything in detail that had been buggered about and steamed towards the second Performance as if to the manner born.

The next morning, Jean Harrison said "Sue, I don't know of anyone else who would have allowed Bill to interfere. It could have caused ructions! Those poor kids might have forgotten everything!" She was right.

The final Performance came to an end. My debut had been victorious.

~

That night had further significance. It was the night that Jim proposed. My uncertainty was supreme. For many reasons, that uncertainty was prolonged for a further five years; it put Jim's life in limbo. My behaviour was unfair. The relationship ended in 1969. The circumstances surrounding its conclusion, were deeply upsetting for Jim. He suffered, I am sure. I was unkind, unthinking and heartless. I did not regret my decision, but have gravely regretted the manner in which it came about and the desolation I caused.

Several years later, I was delighted to learn that Jim had married a former Kelvin Student. I hope that he found the happiness he so richly deserved.

'Souls need to grow....they grow when they are ready to grow'.

Towards the Summer months of 1965, I learned that my Parents were preparing to move once more; this time into rented accommodation. I had been aware of unrest on the domestic front: varying symptoms of discord, dissatisfaction, displeasure and ill will filtered through the walls of Cerne Abbas. Summing up the likely reason for such discontent, Jessica remarked: "Well I always felt that this was an unlucky house".

'Job's Comforter!'

I know such an attitude is not a positive one, Ronnie, but this development must have brought about considerable anxiety. My Mother, used to life in the leafy, kind environment of Anlaby, was no doubt, unnerved and filled with foreboding. It seems that my Father had made up his mind to retire. The promise of Supermarket shopping was on the horizon, small businesses such as his were feeling the pinch and Hull Council was snapping at his heels for compulsory purchase. As I understand it, he hung out as long as time would allow. Consequently, when it came to the crunch, Daddy received financial piecemeal when the Porter Street shop was sold. Things were on a downward spiral.

Charlie had worked hard over many, many hours for many years. Who could blame him?

'How old was he? Late Fifties? Retirement? Did he intend to retire completely?'

There was a yearning, a dream in the offing.

'If I may be so bold to offer a somewhat tart remark here...it's tricky to make earning-a-living dreams come true when in one's Fifties!'

My Father envisioned being Mine Host...in a Hotel... or Pub....

'Hell's teeth, he might as well have hankered after being an Actor! He'd be the Entertainer, always coming up with the goods; working unsociable hours!'

My Mother, far-seeing, sharp and discerning, would have agreed with you, Ronnie. She may have been dismayed, troubled and fretful in this whirlwind of change, but she faced the turmoil head-on and supported my Father.

'Had Charlie got any contacts, any inside information or plans of action?'

Difficult to know, Ronnie. I was not in on any immediate notions. To be honest, I was up to my eyes in Kelvin. I went with the flow.

'I reckon that applied to young Nicky'.

It seemed that Nicky would be encouraged to be part of the scheme. It could be a very promising opening for him. He did not seem to be straining at the bit to assume a position of consequence at the lack lustre Delight Products – any vim, zip, flame or motivation in that direction seemed to have been annihilated. So, for little Brother, there might have been a light at the end of the tunnel……

By the time the Spring months of 1965 dawned, Cerne Abbas was sold. Arrangements were put in place for furniture storage while my brave and long-suffering Mother set about packing.

'Poor darling…'

We were to move into Redlands Drive, Kirk Ella. The house was furnished and within easy reach of Willerby Square. The neighbourhood was pleasant and well appointed. This monumental change gave me an insight into how flexible my Mother could be. She set to with determination that was an incredible feat of resilience, pliancy and good nature. I have no doubt that she was deeply affected by the whole unsettling chain of events. She, like so many other women of her time, was dependent entirely on Marriage, the home and all being well, the adequate housekeeping allowance which was doled out on a weekly basis. This was agreeable if you were recompensed with generosity and even-temper. I suppose that my Mother squirreled away the odd quid or two for personal expenses. The whole practice depended on how resourceful she was. Hence, the dress-making Mrs. Sizer and "our 'ilary's" cast-offs.

'Was Charlie tight with money?'

There were persistent, unyielding arguments when bills dropped through the letterbox. I've hinted earlier that my Father gave way to irascible, tetchy attacks whenever outgoings materialised. Oddly, this occurred in the privacy of our own four walls. My Father was a showman. The outer world was treated to the bottomless pocket. Naturally, my Mother was aggravated. She was bitter. It must have been vexatious, to say the least, that the thriving business had collapsed and landed her in the mire. Especially, when she, quite justifiably perhaps, laid the blame at the door of my Father's retentive family who had squeezed their own sustenance and bread and butter out of it.

'Fuck!'

Precisely, Ronnie. Except that I didn't use those words then!

Added to that, my Aunts and their families were, by then, living off the fat of the land and nowhere to be seen when the rot set in.

'Double Fuck!'

Thank you, Ronnie.

'Bill Pattinson was right when he said that there is always a reason why people behave as they do'.

So, my darling, life was in a state of flux at that time. My animating force, however, was centred around Kelvin. The Redlands Drive house holds a touching memory. When I returned from School on that Moving Day, I saw a glow in the window. A fire was roaring up the chimney and a soft lamp was lit. Jessica, the home-maker, was at the ready.

'Bless...'

George White, History Department and Joan Liebrecht, Home Economics, happened to live...where?

'Redlands Drive?'

How did you know that, Ronnie.

'I'm a mind reader...! Especially when it comes to your whereabouts!'

Mr. White was a lovely man. He drove into Kelvin every day and offered, most generously, to be my chauffeur. When he was not around, Joan stood in for him. Joan Liebrecht was a round, jolly blonde lady who hailed from Tyneside. She always referred to her Husband as "my Michael"; so warm, affectionate and kind, as was Joan. She had taken the place of June Spence who had been so gracious when the Jane Eyre costumes had proved to be a mountain of extra responsibility. In those days, Drama teachers relied heavily on the capability and magnanimity of the Home Economics Department. Mr. White was a refined, courteous Gentleman.

'I bet he was not heard to voice profanities – I mean, like me!'

Who, Ronnie, could possibly be like you!

Mr. White was a fine teacher. He and his wife, Joy, hailed from the Isle of Wight. Much of their spare time was spent holidaying there and sailing was their main getaway.

If I was looking for respite after Jane Eyre, I soon came to know that another Drama Production was on the horizon. Younger Students were to take part in an end-of-Term Summer entertainment. This could be interspersed with Dance items so I was not wholly responsible for an entire evening.

'Something of a God's send!'

Well, it was time for a breathing space Ronnie. I chose extracts from 'Nicholas Nickleby', 'Great Expectations' or other Classics and adapted them for Performance. One huge success was the Poosticks excerpt from 'Winnie-the-Pooh'.

'Now I would have been an excellent choice for Eeyore!'

As it happens, Ronnie, I found my ideal in a twelve-year-old Pupil by the name of William Greenwood. Billy, as he came to be known, went on to become one of the finest young Actors of his time. He took part in many future Productions and his career spanned several years.

The Summer vacation of that year was taken up with deliberation and analysis for the main Production in the Spring Term of 1965.

'Darling, Teachers are supposed to have elongated weeks of leisure!'

I did manage to draw breath, but Kelvin was an enlightened, dynamic, accelerating house of learning. Kelvin became one's life. It was a life I did not object to. I relished it. I did not regard the hours of toil as a sacrifice. One was constantly making headway and moving on. Children were the beneficiaries.

I don't intend to go into elaborate detail about every Production. All were memorable for diverse reasons; each was chosen with a view to being distinctive, contrasting, enterprising and – perhaps – avant-garde.

'The Vigil' by Ladislas Fodor, my second choice, was a searching, thought-provoking piece. Biblical in content, the story follows the Courtroom Trial of the Gardener charged with the supposed body-snatching of Jesus Christ. Each character is called to give evidence.

'Must have been quite a Cast?'

There were huge opportunities for each Student.

'Did the subject matter prompt some discussion?'

It certainly did, Ronnie and by the time the curtain came down, the Audience was on the edge of its seat.

You know, Ronnie, as a Teacher, you never know how well you'll succeed. It's such a responsibility. A child's future could be held in one's hand.

'Go on, you're going to tell me...I know you've remembered such a child...'

I have – many of them. Frederick Hawksley was cast as Saul in 'The Vigil'. A handsome, dark-eyed young fifteen-year-old...

'Yes, don't stop there!'

Fred was talented. Quiet and reserved, he said little but, it seems, learned a lot.

'And....'

Unbeknown to me, when he left Kelvin, he embarked on Drama as a career. He had wished to be an Actor, but fate intervened. He became a Teacher and after several years in disparate British Schools, he found himself teaching at a School for Deaf Children, in – Newfoundland! He went on to be Professor of Drama at Memorial University there.

'How did you find out?'

Many, many years later, when our paths crossed via Kelvin's Alumni! By then, I was the old lady you now know!

'I know all right! Darling, what a wonderful gift...'

It was Ronnie. Fred had become totally absorbed with his school-day Drama lessons; in due course, he progressed to being a very notable authority on Drama in the Classroom. No doubt he influenced many fledgling Teachers. It prevails and perpetuates, Ronnie.

'What really happened in those lessons?'

The beginning of a lesson is vitally important. Your opening explanation needs to initiate a thrill, a rousing flurry of enthusiasm. One needs to alight on a subject which you hope each child can identify with...

'Such as...'

Family, domestic experiences, school experiences, the man in the street... followed by detailed class discussion to bring forth ideas. Then...one lets them loose...outline a situation, a climax ...divide them into groups and see where their imagination leads them.

'What about discipline...it must be bedlam...'

It's a very ordered row, Ronnie. It has to be while they prepare. Of course, it may be that some Children would prefer to sit out and watch. They may be inhibited, shy.

'What happened to them?'

I suggested that they do whatever they preferred to do. In my experience, they did sit out...at first...then, caught up in the momentum of their peers....

'They joined in?'

Exactly. They made their own choice. They were not being bullied and frightened into the unknown. Group performance follows. Each offering is evaluated by the class. Good, encouraging comments first!

'Then tactful criticism where it's helpful?'

To see thirty smiling, engaged children has its own reward, Ronnie. I loved every minute of it.

'I'd have carried you and your books, Miss!'

Spoken English classes followed a similar pattern but of course these took place in formal classrooms; that didn't hinder participation, discussion and warm animation. Volunteers abounded when it came to vocal involvement.

'Hey up, here comes another anecdote?'

A certain individual by the name of Paul Harrison was a particularly vocal young man. His version of the story goes as follows: apparently, I asked for someone to read a passage from the book we were studying at the time. I had requested someone with a loud voice (unusual for me – as a rule, I didn't differentiate between voices). Paul had raised his arm shouting "Miss! Miss!" It seems I lowered my eyes, looked across at Paul and said: "I asked for someone with a loud voice Mr. Harrison, not a big mouth. There is a difference!"

I wince on remembrance. Fortunately, Paul had a broad sense of humour. Laughter played an important part in my lessons. The Children worked hard. Fun, entertainment and merriment reigned. Countless precepts, morals and messages were absorbed through jocularity and jest.

Similarly, conduct, principles, ideals, ethics and a code of behaviour was subconsciously established; unbeknown to the children. We were a team.

Occasionally, there could be cause for concern. A class is a motley crew. There is always the possibility of an insubordinate member. I recall one, Christine Shufflebottom....

'No! You've got to be pulling my leg!'

That is absolutely true, Ronnie. This is a tale that will certainly appeal to you! Christine had problems. She had been at a previous school. It had not met with her special needs. She joined one of my Drama classes and for a while all progressed without incident. One morning, however, something must have rubbed the volatile Christine up the wrong way. She, erratically and without warning, rose from her seat, walked to the door, turned and announced to the open-mouthed class, "Ye can all fuck off, for all I care" and swept from the room. Uproar followed!

'To quote this erudite young lady, what the fuck did you do?'

I had to scarper post haste and in pursuit to the girls' lavatories where I had a pretty good idea Christine would be holed up. I was right. There she was – in some state of agitation. "Christine, I appreciate the fact that you wish to tell me and the class to fuck off, but it is very rude and I think you should apologise." There was a short, sharp and shocked intake of breath on my use of the F word, before Christine looked at me in utter disbelief, followed meekly back to the classroom, stood at the Teachers' desk and said:

"I'm sorry I said fuck off, but you got on my tits!"

'A girl after my own heart. There should be more plain speaking in this world...!'

Christine had problems at home. We can all identify with that.

'What had Bill said about reasons for everything?'

~

The Summer months of 1965 brought about more change. The weeks were interspersed with Pub viewings and domestic upheaval. The Redlands Drive sojourn came to an end and my Parents were hunting for alternative accommodation. We ended up in nearby Willerby where a rented house was available.

'All this must have done away with some cash...'

It was all very shaky and perturbing, Ronnie. My Father was unflagging in his determination to persevere. I guess my Mother, also indefatigably unyielding in her steady attempt to camouflage inertia and the doldrums, tagged along. I know the viewings were hardly encouraging and it became obvious that the envisaged idyllic, thatched Country Alehouse was a pipe-dream.

'Castle-in-the-Air? I reckon that one needs substantial financial backup. Did your Father wish to buy?'

Not an option, Ronnie. The search depended on Management or Tenancy.

'Where was your mindset when all this disruption was going on?'

I should not have been there. I was involved with Jim. I was involved with Kelvin and the acid test of meeting its prerequisites. I should have been unattached, unaligned and autonomous. Instead, I was a child-adult, afraid and desperate to please....afraid of...

'Jessica?'

Jim was not to her liking. My Mother was critical and quick to condemn. I knew it and although in agreement with some of her appraisals, I differed from her and recognised his praiseworthy characteristics, his attraction and unselfishness.

'Quite. Bugger that for a lark! You were in a relationship with him. She wasn't!'

The atmosphere of disapproval caused much misery. I was distracted, unhappy and constantly torn. Why did I put up with it? I could have left.

Jim's Parents lived in Dewsbury. I was invited to visit. They were homely, welcoming people and doted on their only Son. There was absolutely no reason why I should draw back. But – draw back I did. I cannot blame my Mother for my reticence. As time went by, I recognised the question marks, the flaws, the unsustainable, the signs for myself.

'Did you recognise the signs when you met me? Pointers to vulgarity, cursing and general unsuitability!'

Of course I did. But none of it mattered. I loved you and that was that.

'Sweetheart...'

When all seemed lost, a break, a chance came about. Townends, the Hull Wine Merchants, were advertising for a Pub Management post. This rescue, in the nick of time, was known as The Nag's Head, Routh, Near Beverley. Meaux Abbey, a Cistercian one, used to be close by.

'Rampant Monks all over the place. Typical!'

This news coincided with the beginning of the Autumn Term at Kelvin. Needless to say, I was far too preoccupied with preparatory work to really take much interest in this domiciliary flap of activity. I was so happy at Kelvin. Kelvin was my lifeline, my salvation. Jim was an integral part of that existence. It went a long way to explain the continuance of our bond. We were yoked together by common ground, common interest and by being cogs in that wheel. Kelvin was an affiliation, a fraternization with like people. We all functioned with a parallel impetus.

In the September of 1965, I became a Form Teacher for the first time!

'Did that mean Mistress in Charge?'

Not quite in the same context as you are imagining, Ronnie! Thirty eleven-year-old Boys and Girls made up 1U! We occupied a Classroom on the Ground Floor. Interestingly, I remember some of the little Boys in that class more vividly than the Girls. Perhaps because mischief abounded and antics were indelibly printed upon my memory. I have a constant reminder of those little Boys. Now, by my reckoning, they will be well into advancing years. Jim did pen n' ink drawings of their heads. These were arranged into a picture which hangs on the wall of my Hallway.

There, I can see Paul Smith, Graham Pepper, Colin Workman and Tony Menzies (complete with freckles!) They brighten my day! That was fifty-three years ago!

Christmas at Kelvin was memorable for so many reasons: Christmas parties, the Staff Christmas Panto – guess who was Snow White!

'Pestered, harried and molested by Male Staff; bottom-pinching Small People!'

Each Form collected items for Christmas Parcels. These were taken to nearby homes of the Elderly. Small groups visited each house, carefully supervised by long-suffering members of Staff!

'Bet that was an eye-opener....'

For the first time, Ronnie, I was exposed to the plight of less fortunate people. I had been so protected, cosseted and spoiled. I felt ashamed. Those needy folk were enchanted with the Children who made them laugh and chat. I learned a lesson that day, Ronnie. I saw how small, ostensibly insignificant gestures can bring about such gratitude, such hope.

It was humbling. It changed me...it changed my belief and my perception...much to my dear Father's horror, I never, ever, voted for the Conservative Party again!

~

Charlie was successful in his application for Management of The Nag's Head. Nicky was to deputise as Assistant Manager. Removals began. These were concurrent with groundwork for my Spring Term of 1966 and the onset of rehearsals for 'Pygmalion'. I had assembled a first-rate, masterly Cast. The leading lady, Eliza, was played by Janet Willis, a diminutive fire-cracker! I was fortunate to partner her with Michael Stanley, a handsome athletic Sixth Former: Professor Higgins.

'Did a lot of swooning go on?'

Most definitely, Ronnie. He was aided and egged on by Fred Hawksley as Pickering. They made a startlingly good-looking combination. My Eliza was more than able to deal with both, although only fifteen at the time. Rarely, one could detect her lack of sophistication, particularly in the Ball Scene, where her grubby, ink-stained fingers, from homework the night before, had been overlooked!

'Oh Bless! Did Bill put his oar in again?'

As with all Productions, Bill Pattinson, his wife Freda and various Guests were on the front row. Bill appeared for every Performance of four-night runs and applauded with enormous gusto. He sent written congratulations to me and never failed to show his colossal regard for every involved member of Staff. After First Nights, Bill would be in full flow at Morning Service, often speaking long enough to encroach on the first lesson. Not all Teachers were Drama aficionados and there was a hint of huffing and puffing. Nevertheless, nobody was left out. Each and every one was mentioned and awarded the appropriate recognition and acclaim. He certainly set many children free...'

'Guide us, Oh thou Great Redeemer!'

I never forgot his Teaching, Ronnie. Some say he was ahead of his time. Bill became my mentor and my guide. His ideals, his knowledge and probity became the bedrock of my Teaching career. His integrity, concepts and doctrines became my criterion and dictum. He was the Master.

~

The Nag's Head was a detached, red-brick building situated on the main road leading from Beverley, Yorkshire. Beyond, one could encounter several villages before reaching Bridlington or Hornsea on the East Coast. The Pub, standing on the roadside, spread over two storeys. The Ground Floor was comprised of a Small Dining Room and Cocktail Bar opening on to a Main Lounge at the rear which, in turn, looked out over Car Park, fields, and farm buildings. The Catering Kitchen –

'Oh God, who was going to do the Catering?'

I'll give you three guesses, Ronnie.

'Not that poor Jessica?'

The prospect of facing such a horror must have been quite dumbfounding, Ronnie. The cooking facilities hardly engendered waves of satisfaction, keenness or Cordon Bleu magnitude. To cap all, it was filthy.

'No industrial cleaners before you got cracking?'

That would have been crying for the moon, Ronnie. It was one thing to take on a Pub, but to be faced with the prospect of turning out twenty-plus steaks a night over two Sittings, was above and beyond the call of duty. Especially as my poor Mother was totally inexperienced. Even as a champion or ally, this was a comedown for her, a very sad fall from grace. My heart went out to her. The previous Landlord, a young man, had become noted for his Grills, so stepping into his shoes was no mean feat. Customers would draw comparisons and a reputation had to be nurtured and maintained.

I remember, with remarkable clarity, my Mother's horrified expression when I returned from Kelvin on that Removal day...

'How did you travel? Surely the upright, dependable George White drew a line at stepping into the breach on this occasion?'

I had no choice but to borrow Daddy's car. My transport story will come later!

'Hell, what am I in for?'

My Mother did not know which way to turn; to be honest, neither did I. My Father and Nicky were otherwise engaged with the doings of Bars and Beer. At least, a respite had come about in the shape of a Managerial Notice displayed on the Front Entrance:

'Go on...'UNDER NEW MANAGEMENT'!'

More importantly: 'THE DINING ROOM WILL BE CLOSED UNTIL....'

'All I can say is....'

Fuck! I read your mind, Ronnie. This was a farrago, a hotchpotch of disaster – a cataclysm, a catastrophe....

'I get the message...'

Brace yourself, Ronnie, I haven't got to the living quarters yet. These utilized the first floor. There was a large living-room and three bedrooms. Bare floor-boards stretched throughout. Along a corridor, an apology for lavatory and bathroom took up further space, with kitchen facilities large enough to make the odd cup of tea. Clearly, the previous occupant had camped out.

My exhausted Mother and I made valiant attempts to rustle up some appeal, some sense of resolve and initiative. We persisted with half-hearted conviction born of faith, expectancy and belief! When my Father appeared on the staircase and allowed his gaze to penetrate the far corners of this flop and ruination, even he breathed "Oh Jess...."

'You were landed then – there was no choice but to make the best of it...'

How right you are Ronnie. That's just what we did do and within a week or two the place was clean if nothing else and Jessica's steaks gathered a momentum of appreciation from all in the near vicinity.

'Oh petal, hope springs eternal!'

Routh was a small conglomeration of farms, tied farm houses, Clive Allen's garage and a Christadelphian Meeting House!

'What the hell was that doing there? Back of beyond!'

No idea, Ronnie. Just one more quirk of this unlikely neighbourhood.

Frank Goodlass's large farmhouse and outbuildings stood opposite to the Pub. Frank and his Brother were customers in the Old Bar, a minute Snug reserved for regulars. Both were colourful characters who rejoiced in their astonishing Yorkshire living language; dyed-in-the-wool natives, they regaled us with phrases and expressions which remained in one's consciousness for evermore: "chuntering" for grumbling, "cack-anded" for left-handed and "sat i't'chimley-nook" for sitting in the chimney-corner.

I'm too polite to mention the coarse, risqué and ribald ones.

'Oh go on....'

"E's pittled 'is britches" and "Let off" or "trump" – both should be self-explanatory. My Mother's education was broadened by the day! Jessica was always treated with the utmost respect and she became well-known for her ability to empty the Bar at closing-time quicker than anyone else – "Gentlemen, it's time to go home" was her genteel request.

Frank's Brother had very bad eye-sight. His spectacles were broad-rimmed with lenses resembling lemonade-bottle glass. Much to the amazement of all, he climbed......

'Pissed...'

... aboard his bicycle and careered in ungainly fashion down the middle of the road. His survival was miraculous. The Brothers' consumption doubled on Market Days.

'You were going to tell me about transport...'

Over the Redlands Drive and Willerby days, I had picked up my driving skills. Diamond John had been a first-rate Teacher and I remembered his schooling verbatim. All that remained, was to hone my Highway Code into some sort of accuracy and apply for a Test. I passed on the second attempt. My Father's car became a temporary go-between for the Kelvin commute, but I couldn't expect to rely on it indefinitely. 'Friendly'.....

'Who?'

'Friendly' was discovered on the forecourt of a garage near Beverley. He was hidden behind several other beaten-up vehicles.

'If you knew Susie....!!'

As my Brother Nick would explain, when I saw 'him' for the first time, it was love at first sight. Friendly was a 1960 Ford Popular, two-door and square in shape with a smart two-tone colour scheme of light and dark blue. Remarkably, he had leather upholstery in a matching light blue. He possessed chromium wing mirrors, bumpers and grill with the Ford oval badge in light blue on the bonnet.

'Petal, I must ask, why did you call that car 'Friendly'?'

The grill seemed to curl up at the edges with a headlight at either side. It gave the impression of a friendly face! He had very odd windscreen wipers, which worked on an engine-driven vacuum system; the faster you went, the slower they went and vice versa!

Friendly and I had an understanding, but coping with his moods and irritability was exasperating; galling to say the least. The Winter months at the Nag's Head could be frosty and cold, thus tempting the good nature of Friendly. Time and again he would refuse to start of a morning and Frank Goodlass's tractor would be called into service to tow me off. If this performance repeated itself at the other end of my day, the sound, upright Caretaker, Mr. Venus, would be at the ready to push!

'Approach at your own risk, presumably?'

Friendly did attract a bemused, baffled and flummoxed response among fellow motorists, I must admit. One Friendly episode still generates some embarrassment.

'Do I need to sit down for this?'

My Brother and I pulled into Clive Allen's garage on the way home, running over the bell wire which caused a strident ringing. Clive appeared and ambled over to the pumps. I explained that earlier I had lifted Friendly's bonnet in the hopes of finding out where the oil went...

'Dear God...!'

...and came upon 'FoMoCo'. I asked Clive if he would top it up as it must be getting low. "The what, luv?" he enquired, aghast. I pointed to the lettering. Clive then stuttered to my Brother, "You'll 'ave te tell 'er..." and seemed to be scuppered, incapacitated. "Sue, I think you are referring to Ford Motor Company", announced Nick.

'Darling, how were you supposed to know that!! Fancy expecting you to drive and know all that as well?!'

Are you being sarcastic, Ronnie? Believe me, Friendly was looked after like a Baby. He was always kept spotlessly clean and had travelling rug and...

'Make-up mirror?'

How did you guess. One rather terrifying thing happened on my way to School. Suddenly, clouds of acrid smoke began to bellow from under the bonnet. In panic, I pulled over and stopped. A very kind Gentleman came to my assistance and delved among Friendly's private parts, only to reveal the smouldering remains of a blanket I had spread, caringly, in order to protect the engine over the previous perishing, bleak and icy night...

'Oh dear....it gets more and more involved...I can't take any more....let's talk about something else!'

Jim was very supportive during all these trying events. At that time, he was living in a small ground floor flat near Holderness Road in Hull. His home did become something of a retreat from the hurly-burly and pandemonium of Pub life.

'He, like the others, Sue, seemed to be very long-suffering in the circumstances...'

Without a doubt, Ronnie, that is true. I'm sure, although he was fond of a drink, he was not hell-bent on becoming unduly involved with the process of Pub life. His interest was in me – not my family, nor The Nag's Head. Also, I was very tired at the end of my Kelvin days. I left home no later than 8.00 a.m. and sometimes, after Rehearsals, did not return until 7.00 p.m. Even then, I faced the marking of two or three sets of thirty-plus English Essays.

'Knackering....'

My Mother seemed to have little or no understanding of how exacting or time-consuming the work was. She was very caring in that I always came home to a nourishing meal, but other than that she could be dismissive, disinterested and indifferent. I remember arriving particularly late one evening after work and was met with "You should be down here!"

'Down where, for God's sake…?'

In the Bar, pulling pints. I could not oblige, I'm afraid. I did not have the energy to cope with that as well. What's more, I couldn't retire to the privacy of my own bedroom. Space was so minimal that I was obliged to share with my Mother! It really was intolerable – but – I stayed. I remained. Fear of the unknown and loyalty fought for supremacy.

'Those bloody pulling strings….!'

All came to a rather unpleasant head. I was about to leave to spend a couple of hours at Jim's home. I encountered my Mother in the kitchen where she was trapped between sinks, chip-fryers and the detritus of Catering. She entered into a tirade about Jim.

'Oh no, you didn't let her have it?'

Yes, I'm afraid I did, Ronnie. I accused her of finding fault with all previous suitors, bar Mr. Cayley, adding that presumably he had been on safe ground because he was married and therefore not in the running for a serious match. Now it was Jim's turn to come in for discredit. It was all awful. It was distressing. I had crossed the line. My Mother did not speak to me for several weeks.

'What about Nicky or your Father? Where did they figure in all this?'

They didn't figure at all, Ronnie. Neither seemed to care. They were absorbed in their own lives. Why would they be interested in Kelvin? Why would they understand or be interested in Drama? For them, the wheels were turning in a completely different direction.

'What about your Plays? Did either of them see your plays?'

No.

'Why not?'

I suppose they were running the Bars. I never really knew why. Pubs a absorbing. Pubs are greedy with one's time. Pubs take over. My Mother did manage to come along when the Dining Room was closed; no meals at the beginning of the week. To be fair, Jessica was an ardent Theatre disciple. She had been a dancer. She wanted to participate. One couldn't expect everyone to be earnest. Seeing the plays I had directed must have been as close as she could get to my being an Actress!

'Surely there must have been nights off?'

Of course. Nights for pursuing one's own interests. My Plays didn't warrant the effort. Nicky, almost twenty-one at the time, and my Father had other fish to fry.

Nicky found Pub life exhilarating, or so it seemed. The manual work, checking in barrels and organising cellar work, was arduous, but he was young and capable; more importantly, his link and harmony with Customers was appealing. He was good at his job. He had a natural connection with people. He was interested in them and their lives. Conversation came easily to Nicky. He had found his niche. Indeed, he, like me, was a product of our open, benevolent upbringing. We all liked people. Nick was outgoing, genial, hearty and jovial. He was blessed with a rich, sharp sense of humour. As Brother and Sister, in those days and despite the age difference, we were very much alike. Humour, drollery and the funny side of life, became a proven, clear and undeniable legacy bestowed by our Parents. Nick settled very comfortably into his new life. No doubt Jessica and Charlie were satisfied, possibly relieved, to know that here there could be a future, a vocation, for him. If they had had this in mind, the idea had promise of coming to fruition.

'At what juncture was the marital strife between Charlie and Jessica?'

There didn't seem to be much time for squabbling. To coin a well-worn phrase -

'They were rubbing along together?'

Perhaps they didn't have much choice. The erstwhile animosity and clashes were not quite so obvious. A peaceful existence oiled the wheels; equanimity made for composure all round. Providentially, my time was taken up with Kelvin. As a result, I saw little of the homestead and its intricacies. When I was around, the regular Customers were very friendly towards me. I liked them. There were some timeless, unforgettable favourites.

Geoff Whitfield, Brother of David, would call in for a pint on his way home to Leven, a neighbouring village. Outrageously handsome, fair-haired Geoff was a long-distance lorry driver. He worked for the Reader Company where his Father-in-Law was Director and Boss. Geoff heralded his appearance in full voice, which, incidentally, rivalled that of his Brother David. Geoff's "Cara Mia, mine...." echoed across the Car Park. He was noisy, fun and in possession of a scandalous sense of humour. Geoff was one of life's unique, special people. I have not forgotten him.

~

I could hardly believe that towards the Autumn of 1966, I was awaiting flashes of inspiration. What would be the Play choice for Spring 1967?

I enjoyed being a Form Teacher. It was a pleasure to be so closely involved with thirty individuals. Each day presented a fresh revelation together with an tinge of trepidation!

'What had the little buggers been up to this time?'

I fell for this one, Ronnie. Morning routine involved the Form Captain's collection of the Register from the Office. It was left on my desk ready for me to call the names. On the fateful morning in question, I opened the cover. The whole thing jumped in the air and lo and behold before me, lurking menacingly, was a bouncing, black spider!

'Hell!'

Well, all Hell broke loose. Of course I shrieked. By then, the whole class was utterly incapable, incommunicado! There was an initial lack of coherence from me coupled with disjointed, jumbled disorder. The noise must have brought all in the vicinity to a screeching halt! All at once, I realised how ridiculous the whole episode was and how hysterical my reaction must have appeared. I laughed, we all laughed – loud and long. Suddenly, a somewhat stricken face peered through the upper glass of the Classroom door – Mr.Adcock! "Is everything alright, Miss Uebel?" he stammered. Once reassured, he went on his way and I was left to steady my unruly Class. Needless to say, we were all late for the first lesson!

'How had they fixed that bloody spider?'

It was brilliantly clever, Ronnie. The spider was attached to a long rubber tube. There was a pump at the other end of it. When squeezed, the air inside moved the wretched Spider! Of course, it required a dextrous operator who needed to be positioned on the front row. Paul Smith had the aptitude and finesse for such a rascally feat of monkey business...

'There was one clue that you missed.....did Paul Smith usually occupy a front desk? In my experience, those with trouble in mind sat at the back!'

Ah, well Ronnie, we can all be wise after the event!

Bill's influence kept on coming! Especially when it came to writing my first set of Reports. Form Teachers were expected to compose a short paragraph about each child, after the individual input from Subject Teachers. Details could not revolve solely around Academic achievement. Thus, one needed to know each child very well indeed. Above all, every remark was to be one of encouragement. These Reports, for each and every child in the School, were read closely by the Headmaster; he then added his own final paragraph. Although time is a thief, every second of that important exercise was, for me, an abiding, infinite learning curve.

Form Councils were an integral part of Bill's democratic programme. Each week, Captains chaired class meetings. Minutes were carefully recorded and ultimately passed to the Headmaster for perusal. Bill took this discipline very seriously and was not slow to act on Pupil proposals or recommendation.

'Dare I go as far as to say that, in part, it was a subtle ruse to keep his eye on the ball?'

Undoubtedly Ronnie. For the same reason, he set an End-of-Term Essay for members of each Form.

'Go on....you're going to tell me that he read them all over the holidays!'

Ronnie, I have never met the like, before or since. As I look back, over the years, I am convinced that, for me, Kelvin and Bill Pattinson was life-shifting; a vital part of my decree of fate.

~

'The Crucible' by Arthur Miller was on the cards for Kelvin's 1967 Spring Term Production. I had, as usual, been fortunate enough to amass a stellar, commanding and energetic Cast, led by a clutch of powerful, gifted young performers. Robert Ramsden as John Proctor was to make his prodigious debut together with a very young Billy Greenwood, who managed to imbue the character of Giles Corey with grit and humanity. As ever, I was astounded at the Students' single-minded allegiance to the whole undertaking.

In the midst of this Academic, artistic experience I decided to have my hair cut!

'Eh?'

This monumental endeavour warrants some explanation...I had been to see 'The Sound of Music'...

'Yes, and....we're not back to Miss Gym and navy blue knickers are we?'

Certainly not, Ronnie, but Maria's rather fetching and drastically short hair cut gave me an idea...

'Yes, and....'

I found a very good Barber and requested he take the lot off! My hair, was, I hasten to add, very long....I mean, long enough for a French pleat. I was thrilled with the result and so was everyone else.

'Even Jessica, mistress of decorum, protocol and seemly appearance?'

She was delighted Ronnie – the style was de rigueur, refined yet...

'Way-out and unconventional?'

It was Ronnie. In the Sixties, my superbly-cut hair could be regarded as masculine, Spartan or spare. Mum was all for me being stylish, even flamboyant. To Mum, it all smacked of being the Performer, the Artiste and the unusual.

'Well, I won't argue with that – 'unusual' is only one of the terms I would use!'

The next thing I intended to work on was – my weight!

'What! You were hardly of gargantuan bulk!'

No Ronnie, but I had certainly put it on a bit. All was revealed in some very telling, explicit, unerring Christmas photographs. This mega, absorbing exercise, literally, came about just as my Parents were on the cusp of planning to move! 'The Nag's Head' had run its course and although providing a living of sorts, it was not in line for....

'Keeps...'

My Father got wind of a more upmarket establishment which was located in a village near Beverley. The Management of the Ferguson-Fawsitt Arms, in Walkington, was up for grabs. My Father applied and was victorious! There was to be an intermediary lapse of time before we could flit so, meantime, a small, detached bungalow in Leven was to be rented.

'Talk about being itinerant!'

Well, Ronnie, since you mention it, we might have been more comfortable in a gypsy caravan. The Nag's Head had left a lot to be desired when it came to Des. Res.

During the intervening, remaining time at the Pub, Brother Nicky was nearing the celebration of his 21st Birthday. My Father made some enquiries regarding Nick's hopes and desires.

'That could have been risky...'

Nick came up with a daft, glib and waggish proposal – "A Car" said he.

'Told you so....'

My Father came back with a further bid. "If you've got any savings, Nick, I'll match 'em and we'll see what we can do". The result was that Nick's princely sum of 50 quid was made up to a grand total of £100.

'Where the hell....?

This you won't believe, Ronnie. An advertisement appeared in the Beverley News for – a Bentley! It was a 1954 'R' Type saloon. To cut a long story short, it had been bequeathed to an elderly Gentleman for his Chauffeuring services. Since, the car, lovingly preserved and with only 86,000 miles on the clock, had been sitting in the garage waiting...

'For Nick presumably!'

The old Gentleman had not wished to make a profit. Now he could be sure that the car would be enjoyed and prized by a new, caring owner. So, Father and Son, in partnership, relished a rare, classic and definitive passage of motoring for several years to come.

~

The Leven bungalow was small but well appointed. We spent several months there, until our move to the Ferguson-Fawsitt Arms in 1968.

'How did your Mother survive this roundabout change of course?'

I think it was a welcome respite from the demanding call of the Catering kitchen. Leven village provided a local shop and Off Licence. This was a meeting-place, a detour and departure from the daily grind and chore. Here was a noticeable absconding from the difficult, taxing, and wearing responsibilities or obligations of 'The Nag's Head'. My Father pottered and took the window of opportunity to familiarise himself with the forthcoming expectations of his new assignment.

'Why did you mention the Off Licence?'

I thought you may be quick to pick up on that, Ronnie. Sooner or later, Mum was partaking of a sizeable amount of Sherry per evening and when available, I ended up with the mission to track it down. For Mum, this was becoming a habit.

'Did you feel the necessity to join in? And why Sherry for God's sake?'

Sherry was cheaper, I suppose. When one is knocking back a fair amount. I did find it difficult to refuse, Ronnie. I empathized with my Mother. I felt at one with her. I wasn't a teetotaller. I enjoyed the odd glass...

'Or four?!'

Well, that brings me to the subject of my diet. I was unflinching, even single-minded in my crusade to be sylph-like. Fortunately, this provided me with an excuse. I was able to justify refusal; booze was out, except for the occasional glass which put the seal on companionship.

'Clever little bugger!'

I was intent on following a very strict rations regime. In no time, I was losing a noticeable amount of weight. I knew it was working when Roy Butterfield, an outspoken member of School Staff, remarked: "Bloody 'ell, Sue, what's your secret? It's dropping off you!"

'If I may be so bold – first, your curls and now your curves!'

I remember feeling a bit under the weather, probably my blood sugar, which I knew nothing about at the time, was a little low....My Mother announced: "It's your own fault for starving yourself! I did tell you!"

'No doubt adding "have another Sherry, it'll do you good"!'

~

The Ferguson-Fawsitt Arms was an imposing building set in the centre of Walkington. The village had all the idiosyncrasies and hallmarks of stereotyped country living: pond, ducks, three Pubs, shop, Church Hall and Church.

Inhabitants were as varied as the residences in which they lived.

'There is a hint of disparagement in your voice...'

There was a definite distinction: kith and kin who had lived in Walkington all their lives and those who wished to set down roots within a self-styled country retreat. In time to come, this was summed up by the succinct comment of one of our Bar regulars – "Well, ye see, I'm a Countryman, not a Townie". Needless to say, we leaned towards the...

'Real McCoy?'

I knew you'd catch on, Ronnie.

The village was pretty, attractive and appealing. Cottage gardens spilled out over manicured grass verges and well-kept, rural lanes. After the encroaching traffic, dust and hay of Routh, we had found ourselves in a rustic, Arcadian paradise!

'And no danger of the ravaging Cistercian Monks of Meaux pillaging the stamping ground!'

I knew you would never forget those Monks, Ronnie! What I have been trying to explain is that we were catering for...

'Diversity! Now what was the Pub like? '

It was a mock-Tudor façade. The oldest part of the building was central and consisted of the original Bar; Snug close by. The staircase which led to the living accommodation, rose out of a Bar corner. A short corridor opened out on to the Cocktail Bar.

'Plummy, swish and sumptuous?'

Well it did seem to house or invite the top-drawer toffs and heavy hitters.

'That's something I might have said!'

The Cocktail Bar was a favourite. It had many of the original features including a red brick fireplace – Jessica's roaring fires come to mind. It groaned under the weight of brass, copper kettles and horse brasses. A large Conservatory had been built recently. Further along, this glass-roofed and windowed expanse served as extra seating and Cold Buffet facility. From here, three or four steps led to an expansive, capacious and commodious Lounge, complete with Bar. This new-fangled addition had the inspirational, original handle – The New Lounge! I was constantly reminded of a VIP Waiting area at an Airport. It was comfortable, but imperious, impersonal and detached. Although Coach Parties were discouraged, I did think it would have made an admirable rendezvous for them.

'Presumably, once more, you were living over the shop?'

Yes, Ronnie. Our chambers, rooms, or – barracks – whatever you care to call them, were definitely more conducive to off-duty relaxation than our previous berths. These consisted of large sitting-room overlooking the village street, a minute dining-room, an even more microscopic, Lilliputian kitchenette where my sorcerer Mother conjured up piquant Sunday lunches after closing time at 2.00 p.m.

'Ah…those were the days when you could call time…'

There was one large bedroom accessed by three perpendicular steps. All who traversed these came to grief in one way or another, largely because one forgot they were there. This room was big enough to take the twin beds, so, initially, this was a retreat for my Mother and me.

'Oh God, not again….'

There were two other smaller bedrooms for Father and Son. Eventually, an area to the rear of this upper floor, was converted into another space big enough for a divan and essential furnishings, so enabling the Family to somewhat unfurl. After a while, I did end up with a room to myself.

The sitting-room red-brick fireplace, similar to that of the cordial Cocktail Bar, was an ideal framework for my Mother's collection of brass and copper. Once our antique furniture was in place, the soft-green fitted carpets and chintz-covered sofas and armchairs complemented a fitting ambiance for this upcountry Hostelry. It was cosy, fire and lamp-lit. It was a tasteful home. Yet again, Jessica had worked her spell.

'She were a grand lass...'

I have never underestimated my Mother's cleverness, her sophistication and her refinement, style and grace. Her natural, innate insight was not lost on me, nor I believe, on anyone else. Mum could be difficult, controlling and ruthless at times, but I learned much from her. She aimed high, certainly for me; there's nothing wrong with that.

'True, even though, on occasion, her punches could be below the belt!'

The times I have been reminded of Philip Larkin's quote: "Your Parents fuck you up! They don't mean to, but they do"!

'What if I was to say that, in my opinion, they do mean to!'

The journey to Kelvin was much easier and Friendly coped admirably. School life was as busy as ever and I was toying with an ambitious idea for choice of Play.

"Now, Sue, what is it to be this year?" enquired Bill.

"Well," said I tentatively, "I may have a language problem, but not one in the usual sense".

"Try me," Bill went on.

'You've always tried me. Why do you dig these holes for yourself!'

I told Mr. Pattinson that I would love to direct 'Billy Liar'. I knew it had had tremendous success in the West End with our own Hull Actor, Tom Courtney, in the leading Role, so I had every reason to believe that Bill would want to jump on the bandwagon. The only obstacle would be the repetitive use of the word 'bloody'.

Bill, never caught wanting, agreed that the habitual volley of swearing from the character of Billy's Father, was indicative of a parlous lack of vocabulary; not gratuitous cursing used only for dramatic effect. He gave me his blessing!

'I bet you saw him hovering at Rehearsals a bit more often than usual!'

Well, Ronnie, since you mention it....!

'Did you find a good Billy?'

Two Sixth-Form Rugby players took the roles of Billy and his mate, Arthur Crabtree. David Boyes and Stephen Drewery created a memorable partnership of outrageous comedy and Northern realism. The ubiquitous Frances Hewitt, now a couple of years older, moved on from her unsurpassed Mrs. Fairfax to creating Billy's ailing Grandmother.

Neil Briggs was profoundly adept at turning the air blue and 'bloody' by the time the curtain fell, was ingrained, fixed and fundamental. One hardly noticed.

Bill's face was a study of pride. He had made allowances for something controversial. He had pushed the boundaries! Many complimentary letters arrived. Once again, my hard-working, faithful youngsters deserved the standing ovations they received.

One more string was added to my bow. Bill asked me to join his Pastoral Care Group of Teachers. The work was enriching, thought-provoking and progressive. To be placed in such a position of trust was an honour and a bonus.

'I think Bill held you in very high regard. Hadn't you sussed that out?'

No, Ronnie. Certainly not at the time. I remember a rather pointed question he posed one day. I was in his office where we were discussing background information about a boy in my Class. Bill was looking out of the window, watching Jim get into his Sports car. "Hasn't he asked you yet?" came the direct query. I suppose this intrusion could have been regarded by some as impertinent. Nonplussed, I had no idea what to say...

'Told you so! You always walked around with your eyes shut!'

Many, many years later, about twenty years in fact, I came to know what could lay behind that unguarded, searching remark. It was Bill's wife, Freda, who tendered a startling truth. Do you remember, Ronnie, when we were gathered at Bill's Funeral in Norfolk?

'I do. As we were leaving, Freda suddenly said "He loved you, Sue". Not only that, his Daughter agreed saying "If ever Mum had a rival, Sue, it was you!" What is more, it was said in full hearing of other Guests.'

That was an unforgettable moment. I had never thought of Mr. Pattinson in any other way except as my sage, my mentor. I had overlooked the man.

~

My Mother was settling into her new life. The Ferguson-Fawsitt Arms did not present the same snags and stumbling blocks as the Nag's Head. That had been a marathon run. Mum acquainted herself well with Staff: Cleaners, Bar helpers, Chefs and Waitresses. She was a thoughtful, generous Boss and certainly did not stand on ceremony. She encouraged teamwork, as did my Father; neither were pretentious or superior. In the main, none took advantage and the Pub ran like a well-oiled machine.

'Did you forget to mention the Restaurant earlier?'

Thank you, Ronnie. The Restaurant was imperative. At that time, Pubs were expanding: food was becoming a pressing, intrinsic component of the evening out. The

Ferguson-Fawsitt Dining Room was no exception. It was an impressive, sweeping, large-scale, oak-floored annexe built to the rear of the building, where it looked out on to an equally extensive Car-Park. The interior consisted of mock-Tudor pillars and beams. The jewel in its crown was a re-claimed oak fireplace; quite majestic, it extended from floor to ceiling and reigned supreme over innumerable groups of oak tables and chairs.

Ferguson Fawsitt Arms 'Grand Dining' 1969

'Known as 'covers' in the Catering trade...'

Trust you to know that, Ronnie.

'I was only trying to be informative!'

Once the tables were set with immaculate cutlery, glassware and flowers, the tone was set; the milieu intimate and inviting.

'I reckon that this was Jessica's domain?'

She adopted, with undoubted finesse, the poise and polish of Maitre d'Hotel and on busy nights added the title Major Domo to her curriculum vitae. Mrs. Sizer was called into action and produced nothing short of Designer kit. Mum looked lovely... elegance would belie her robust use of language as she whispered, "Makes a change from frying those bloody chips myself!" The Diners grew to know and like her. She remembered names and faces. She was an exceedingly popular asset. Having said that, Jessica and Charlie made a very effective double act. Despite the convoluted, complexity of their relationship and domestic life, they pulled out all the stops when it came to putting on the style.

'Not to forget that potent, seductive sense of humour...'

As an onlooker, most of the time, I realised what a crucial key that was to keeping one's powder dry.

My Mother was tactful and somewhat crafty in dealing with Staff. Not averse to playing one against the other, she moved her Chess pieces with a nimble, if somewhat crooked, aptitude.

'Oh do tell me about the Staff. It must have been a treasure trove for the fledgling Actor...'

Well, Ronnie, it was a big Staff and one needed all one's water on to keep tabs on each.

'Who worked in the Restaurant?'

A very haughty, magisterial lady by the name of Diana was on the Reception Desk. Everyone, much to Diana's exasperation and displeasure, referred to her as "D-eye-na!" Eventually, she gave up correcting them and gave in. Dina was a whiz with figures and could run circles around anyone trying to do or deceive her. She had her bills arranged in spruce, squeaky clean order and woe betide anyone who idly or inadvertently fingered them. She was the Keeper of the Gate and no one was allowed to be a fly in her ointment. Dina fascinated me; even more so when she closed a transaction. Her intransigent spearing of paid bills on a nail which protruded from its wooden block, was something to behold. The whole execution – execution being the operative word – was consummated with "Some of these Waitresses should be spoken to! Who taught them to write!".

The Grill was visible from the Dining Room enabling all cooking operations to be witnessed by customers. This was the engine room and space was at a premium.

Dennis, the Chef, was corpulent. There was much pushing and shoving to get him into place. Betty, a good-natured lady from the village, was his aide, abetter and putter out of plates. These skirmishes, a constant source of open-mouthed disbelief to the irascible Dina, made for entertainment which rivalled a second house at the Glasgow Empire. Betty was Dennis' support and an innocent collaborator. She was also the harbourer of village stories. The one I held most dear was the tale of the carpet with a hole in it: "Mrs. 'arris used to sit dog ovver it when Vicar were comin'"

'Don't stop there...'

Emily Robinson presided over the Old Bar. She officiated with the aid of a rude, rugged, prolific and fecund repertoire of malediction.

'In other words, her vernacular left a lot to be desired – wonderful!'

My Father was quite strait-laced and as I recall, never used bad language in my hearing or my Mother's. So Emily's colourful intercourse could stop him in his tracks. If I happened to be in the vicinity, Charlie would catch breath with "Hup" or something like that and hurry me in the opposite direction, whispering confidentially "Now come along, me lass...".

Emily had dynamic punch; other employees, or exacting Customers, crossed her at their peril. Cuss' and oaths were uttered with blank, expressionless ease. Emily's province was the Old Bar and I am convinced that Customers patronised the Ferguson Fawsitt on a regular basis just to witness this tour de force.

'What did she look like? I mean, did she cut a figure of undisputed sway?'

No Ronnie. Emily was diminutive. In fact, she had difficulty in reaching the pumps. She succeeded, after noticeable manhandling, but one expected her to remain, feet dangling, indefinitely. I would wait with bated breath for a barrel to go off. "Ahhhhhhgh! The bugger always goes off when I'm on me own!" In spite of small stature, Emily could defeat a resisting array of obstruction, hazard and handicap with remarkable strength; always accompanied with a fractious torrent of suspect patter.

Nick witnessed a remarkable and astonishing event. He had been called in at lunchtime to aid the imperious Emily. The Bar was busy and Emily was on form. A cultured couple made their way to be attended to. Nick served them with a Pint and a Gin n' Tonic. The Lady and Gentleman were polite and well-mannered. It seemed that they downed their drinks rather rapidly and returned for a top-up. They had the misfortune to encounter Emily, who barked: "Bloody 'ell, that's quick. 'ave ye dropped 'em?"!!

The well-spoken Gentleman, with a certain temerity, went on to ask Emily if she did sandwiches. Her reply was brief, that is, "Yes!" No more information, just affirmation. Nick intervened hastily and listed choice of food. The Gentleman, assuming that Emily had apt qualifications and would prepare his sandwiches, addressed her to give his order. Emily turned on her heel, walked to the rear of the Bar where a door opened on to the kitchen and shouted in her best cod-Posh accent, "Two fuckin' Beef samdwiches with Hoh-s-raadish Sewce"!

'How long did it take Nick to recover?'

Poor Nick, he was saddled with having to paper over the cracks on more than one occasion. Emily doubled as Cleaner, so she and Kath, a softly-spoken lady from Walkington, tackled the indisputable slog of scouring the Pub from top to bottom, aided occasionally by my Mother. I think Mum enjoyed the camaraderie, tittle-tattle and rich anecdotes. Needless to say, Emily was the oracular soothsayer; a raconteur and curator of village chronicles. So, Jessica, labouring with the eternal and incessant collection and laundering of tea towels, found diversion and merriment in the company of new-found friends.

Life at the Ferguson-Fawsitt Arms was absorbing and varied. I, too, became enamoured of its mood, flavour and spirit. I came to revel in its vivacity and scope; it was a mixed bag of interest.

'You joined in? Did it fill a gap in your life?'

Yes, Ronnie, it did. I began to see things I was missing. I didn't realise that I had missed them. Kelvin had taken over my life. Suddenly, I was presented with another dimension.

'Where did Jim fit in with all this?'

That was it, Ronnie. He didn't. I was aware of a hint of resentment. His perspective, socially, now seemed limited and noticeably at odds with mine. It was stressful. I was beginning to feel cut off and stuck.

Unexpectedly, I had more time at my disposal. Kelvin's Dance Department was now headed by a newcomer, Garry Harrison. She, a superbly proficient, clever Gymnast and Dance Specialist, was planning a major Dramatic Dance Evening to be presented at the onset of 1969. Garry became a close friend and work colleague. We shared a place within the Pastoral Care Group and became a devoted and zealous pair of advocates. Our ensuing friendship has lasted nearly fifty years.

So, at the onset of 1969, I was to be relieved, for the first time in five years, of planning the annual Production.

Life at The Fergie, as it came to be affectionately known, was a vital, engaging world of contrasts, people and situations.

'Akin to Theatre, my darling...it was seductive...and you were a Performer...'

Staff and Customers, in equal measure, brought about a cheering upsurge of escapism, distraction and recreation. I found myself joining in, being a part of this stimulating, witty and animated panorama. Laughter became a vital, component part in the mix. None more so than when Mr. Lee was on duty.

'Mr.Lee?'

A Chinese Chef who shared duties with Dennis. It so happened that Mr.Lee encountered Susan when she stood in for the masterly, exalted Dina! Now Mr. Lee took umbrage at Susan because she criticised his Staff Suppers. Susan, haughty and dismissive, did not care for Sausage and Chips. Mr. Lee took great satisfaction in approaching the Reception Desk and declaring, after the last Customers had left, "'loshish and clips, Slusan. You like?" Fred Bugger...

'Who?!'

Fred Bugger and his comrades were regular Friday night Customers. Fred, so nicknamed by all who knew him, used this maxim on a regular basis. Fred, Cliff and Jeff were a amiable trio and hugely popular with all Staff, largely because they were very generous and tipped in excess. Fred was an astute businessman. His tales about Miss Yapp, his Accountant, were legion. I found it hard to believe that she was really called Miss Yapp. Apparently, this was not a fabrication, but absolutely true.

'The mind boggles about the appearance of Miss Yapp!'

I think Ivy was perhaps my most favourite member of Staff. She was the irascible, peppery Emily Robinson's Sister-in-Law, but as different from her as chalk and cheese. I partnered Ivy on the Cold Buffet during School Holidays and when there was a Staff shortage. Ivy was patient, methodical and a slave to precision, especially when it came to her pristine dish-cloths. "I allus 'ave a good cloth, Sue. I soak 'em in Domestos. Some 'ave seen, used by those who shall be nameless, I wouldn't wash floor with!" Ivy was tireless, good-natured and had an infinite capacity for working all hours. On Christmas Eve, after labouring like a Trojan until Midnight, she would trudge home to her own Christmas cooking – cakes, Turkey, sprouts. There, she would be occupied until two or three in the morning. When I exclaimed, she would say, "Ye just keep goin', Sue, as long as ye don't look at clock"!

The significant Bar regulars, known to Emily and oftentimes greeted with "Aaagh! Look what the wind's blown in!" were humorous and exhilarating for different reasons. Sam, posh and a master of Queen's English, lolled on the counter, nearly always inebriated and referring to "His Lordship, Her Ladyship and the Honourable Sue". Charlie and Jessica accepted the Titles with wry, knowing amusement.

In those days, Broadgates Hospital occupied a site down the road from Walkington Village. This Sanitarium was home to many who were suffering from some form of mental illness. George was one such fellow.

'Go on, petal, don't stop there...you have a habit of doing that, just when I'm waiting for the next bit... presumably, he would do a runner but be safe to venture forth to the Fergie of an evening'.

He was, Ronnie. He certainly enjoyed a pint on several nights a week. Nick was very fond of him; in fact, acted as a caring, amused, minder.

George was slightly built and wore a vast, commodious, dark grey raincoat which almost reached the floor. It was impossible to determine what this voluminous creation obscured, for George never discarded it. He would take up his position before the substantial flames of a Jessica log fire, smoking his roll-ups. His cap remained in place, only being dislodged if an itching forehead precipitated a scratch. His sallow complexion almost blended in with his raincoat. His voice, high-pitched and shrill, seemed compatible with a perpetually affrighted expression. Without preamble, the voice would pronounce" 'ave got to make water!" Whereupon, George would make a rapid sprint to the Gents. There was a near miss one day.

"Summat's burnin'" hollered Emily. "Bloody 'ell, Nick, it's George!"

Lo and behold, George's raincoat, hanging dangerously near to the fireplace, had smouldered and eventually caught fire! Nick rescued him that night, before he went up in a shower of sparks. It was a tense moment. The sinister, grim and baleful smell of the simmering George took its time to be extinguished.

'It would have been an opportune time for George to make water!'

Bless George. Whenever the incident was mentioned again, he would smile covertly to himself as Nick treated him to another pint.

'Darling, what joyous memories....'

~

1969 brought about change in more ways than one. I learned via the grapevine that Hull Amateur Operatic Society was to present a production of 'My Fair Lady' at Hull's New Theatre in November.

'I used to belong to one of those in Hartlepool. It turned out to be a hotbed of sin and debauchery!'

I can imagine that you took to it like a duck to water, Ronnie! I toyed with the idea of making enquiries. I knew that Mrs. Higgins, a non-singing part, would be up for grabs...

'Darling, you'd be treading on the toes of all those middle-aged, big-bosomed warbling matriarchs who had their eye on the same thing!'

True Ronnie. I did, however, apply to Audition. I knew that I would have the time to Rehearse and was hankering after getting back into Performing. Of course I was new to the whole Operatic venture and when lined up in a corridor with the other applicants, I was studied and clocked by several – yes, Ronnie, they were conspicuously big-bosomed, chirruping and I might add – of a certain age – hopefuls.

The Auditions were held in the YMCA building, George Street, in Hull. On entering the Rehearsal venue, I found myself facing a barrage of Judges! I learned later that only two of these persons – the Musical Director and the visiting Artistic Director were Professionals! The remainder of the line-up were Officials, Chair-persons and -

'In short, the rest knew bugger-all about eligibility for parts!'

I think, behind the scenes, there was considerable dissatisfaction and unflattering comment when I was given the plum role of Mrs. Higgins.

'Well, to be fair, you were only in your Twenties and most of those old biddies could be pushing Sixty...no doubt waited all their lives for such a break! Then some unknown appears and whips it from under their nose!'

One comment, or rather summing up, came to my hearing much later. It was witty, self-deprecating and joyous. This older Lady announced, "Well, I knew I didn't stand a chance if they were looking for a beguiling appearance. My face always looks as though someone has stood on it to wind the clock up!"

'Delicious. Now...something comes to mind. How did Jim fall in with all these plans?'

Well, Ronnie, he fell in with them. He didn't have much choice, but nevertheless, he was not in tune and the wedge between us was beginning to widen. By the time the Show went on later in the year, the relationship with Jim had disintegrated. We parted. There were many instances of disaffection and the eventual split was very upsetting, but final. In all, the change in me was manifest. There was no going back. I was entirely to blame. I found myself experiencing continuous heartache, self-reproach and sorrow for Jim. I had taken up five years of his life.

'Did you regret your decision?'

No, Ronnie. This development, however, was complicated in that we were obliged to carry out our duties at Kelvin and there was, understandably, an atmosphere of discomfort.

'Must have been perturbation, to put it mildly, in the Staff Room...'

There was, Ronnie. Naturally, one sensed allegiance among friends. Understandably, loyalty became divided. We had been closely linked with Play Production. When the Play for 1970, 'The Taming of the Shrew', was being mooted, it was very noticeable that Jim was holding back. I needed to speak frankly when asking for his Artistic help and made it very clear that our differences should not affect the children. So, to alleviate awkwardness, Jim encouraged others in the Art Department to proffer assistance, when necessary, in an attempt to avoid uneasiness or misgiving. It was a miserable time, but Play progress was not halted and the Students benefited from ongoing skill and craftsmanship.

'No doubt it was a great relief when Jim formed a further relationship'.

As I said earlier, I was so happy for him. He deserved to find a partner who was much more suited to his expectations. It happened quickly.

In the many years that followed, I was alone. I did not, however, look back and grieve. My life was beginning to take a very different course.

The Hull Operatic experience led to many other opportunities. Mrs.Higgins was received with great approbation. Dear Bill came along with Freda, was unable to get good seats, but watched my whole performance from the back row of the Stalls – through opera glasses!

'I suspect that you had one very important ally in all this...Jessica.'

Yes, Ronnie, I did sense undisguised relief and approval of my actions. She did not make a meal of it for she was more than taken up with Mrs. Higgins! I suppose she could not mistake my absorption and obvious enjoyment and so, curbing the temptation to pass comment, she ceased to strive for a further coup.

On the strength of my appearance as Mrs. H., I received invitations from some very reputable Amateur Dramatic Societies in Hull: Hull Playgoers and the Garrett Players were recognised and held in high esteem. I had been noticed on the New Theatre Stage!

'Hmn flower...I always found you very noticeable!'

~

In February 1970, Kelvin Hall presented a rumbustious, uproarious production of 'The Taming of the Shrew' with a much more grown-up William (known as Billy) Greenwood as Petruchio. His Lady, Katherine, was played by the feisty Janet Willis, famous for her role as Eliza the

Cockney Flower-girl. To quote you Ronnie, it was a 'cast of thousands' made up of Townspeople, Peasants of varying size and demeanour, and Wedding Guests – not to speak of Dancers who were drilled by the diligent Garry Harrison.

Stephen Silvester (another burly Rugby player) took on Hortensio and became a very camp, flagrant Suitor for Bianca. In fact, Stephen almost ran away with the Show. Students packed the Entrance Hall where Front-of-House photographs were displayed; each and every one intent on finding out if Stephen "was really like that"!

'It's a knock-about Show...how on earth did you manage Petruchio's wooing of Katherine?'

Fortunately, Billy had grown into a portly, thick-set fellow. He was strong, agile and well able to hurl the tiny Janet around like a rag doll. I was careful to choreograph every move....

'I hope, with meticulous exactitude!'

Those are big words, Ronnie, but I do get your drift. The two of them always pushed me to the limit but safety was foremost. Janet was a shade bruised but never complained. Their belligerent, warring combat received well-deserved rounds of applause each night.

'Did you have time for anything else that year?'

It was busy, Ronnie. My life was rich, enhancing. Rewarding day-to-day Teaching and a Form Teacher's commitments were preoccupying. Not many days passed without incident and one was on-call from 8.00 a.m. until at least 5.00 p.m.

To cap all, my beloved Friendly breathed his last....

'Oh no....it must have been like parting from an old friend!'

Nothing could be done, Ronnie. He was incapacitated...

'It happens to the best of us, petal... how did you get in to School?'

I was thrown upon the good will of Daddy and a substitute car – not the Bentley, I hasten to add – until a saviour appeared on the horizon.

'Yes...and...'

There was a small, rather run-down Garage at the other end of Walkington's main street. Nick, browsing around, as was his wont where cars were involved, happened upon an aging Ford Zephyr Convertible.

'Oh no!'

Now, don't dismiss the idea, Ronnie. It was very beautiful and seemingly in "jolly good nick", according to Nick.

'Hmn, darling, I've heard that said so many times – people used to say that about me!'

The Garage proprietor assured us that this vehicle was absolutely roadworthy and for its age, quite a snip.

'They used to say that about me as well, long before I came to know the significance of the word snip!'

So, I had a test drive. All went like a dream and the deal was settled.

One thing I forgot to mention. The car was a dreamy shade of turquoise...

'I might have known!'

Now I did not, on this occasion, christen my vision of loveliness...

'No, but I bet when you pulled into the gates of Kelvin, the kids did!'

How did you know that, Ronnie? You're absolutely right. Apparently, it was known as "The Swimming Pool"! There was the odd occasion, reminiscent of the winsome Friendly, when this aquamarine extravaganza would not start. I was never short of a bevy of willing pupils at the ready to push me off.

That year, in whatever time was left over, I took part in several Shows. I was invited to play leading roles for the Garrett Players and made my debut with Olivia in 'Twelfth Night'. Edward Tilley, a remarkably able Amateur Actor, was Malvolio. Dear Teddie will be mentioned again much later. By then, he and his Wife, Joan, had become close friends whom I have revered and remembered ever since.

Ella in Ibsen's 'John Gabriel Borkman' and Mrs. Sullen in 'The Beaux Stratagem' followed. Yes, it was a busy, absorbing year. I made new friendships but there were no more relationships on the horizon.

'No chemistry, eh petal?'

No darling, no chemistry. Perhaps a few dalliances! But, Ronnie...I was restless. I was casting around, wondering where my life was going. Yes, I could remain at Kelvin, my familiar and lovely haven of work, for many years to come...I could play it safe...but

'Was something pushing again?'

Yes Ronnie, someone was. But who? I was soon to be pushed in a very unexpected direction. A puzzling direction...

'But, my darling, was it exciting?'

Well, Ronnie, it was certainly food for thought. I'll explain, for it was not the only thing which prompted deliberation and dialogue.

During the Autumn Term of 1970, I had launched my next Kelvin Production. It was to be 'The Diary of Anne Frank'.

'Wow! What an undertaking...'

I had long discussions with Jim Benson's second-in-command, John Townend. He was to design and oversee building of the very complex, intricate Set. I cast the Play and Rehearsals had begun. The skilled, masterly John intended, with the help of the trusty and upright Mr. Gooding and Mr. Bell....

Linda Palmer 'Diary of Anne Frank'

'Oh Mr. Gooding...oh Mr. Bell...!'

...who were primed and ready to spring into action, to construct, gradually, the Amsterdam Warehouse attic, its adjoining rooms and living-area. This was a really inspired, stimulating idea, for the Cast were then able, in Rehearsal, to develop specific, exact Performances as they became familiar with the limited and confined space. It worked. Not only was the School Stage transformed, but John also increased Acting areas by building extended platforms jutting out into the body of the Hall. Localised lighting defined the rooms when action moved from one area to another.

'Did you find Anne easily?'

Linda Palmer was heaven-sent, Ronnie. Small, dark-haired and blessed with a bell-like voice, she was superb. The resolute, steadfast Billy Greenwood was quite unforgettable as her loving Father, Mr. Frank. Both were favoured with a peerless, supreme supporting Cast which included Janet Clark as Mrs. Frank, Ruth Press as Margot and Alan Thorley as the finicky Dentist, Mr. Dussel.

'Was Bill there every night?'

You bet he was, Ronnie. He received countless letters of congratulations from his associates and contemporaries.

'Sue, this must have been your most difficult Play. It put emotional demands on boys and girls involved in a story and action out of their experience. I'd like to bet it brought tears to the eyes of many...I would have loved to have been there...'

I know you would Ronnie. Moments like those come only once in a lifetime.

Can you believe that in February 1971 I was taking the role of Mabel in Oscar Wilde's 'The Ideal Husband' amidst intensive 'Diary' rehearsals!

'Well, petal, you certainly were a glutton for punishment! Now what was happening on the home front?'

I think, during that time, the Ferguson Fawsitt Arms did not see much of me, except for holiday periods. All seemed to be coasting along on the crest of a wave. Of course, Jessica was also coasting along in the reflected glory of my many Theatrical ventures, so life was equable, even-tempered and unruffled!

'Why, aye flower. Wish life was forever thus...'

'The Diary of Anne Frank' ran until the middle of March. In May of 1971, I embarked on another ambitious exercise. For some time, I had had a yen to direct Charles Dyer's 'Staircase', a two-hander about the life of a couple of homosexual Hairdressers!

'Dear God, did you ever know where to draw the line!'

I broached my idea to two very straight, virile and strapping Actors whom I had met through the course of my adventures with the Garrett Players. David Ashdown,

Head of Science at Malet Lambert School in Hull and Frank Harris-Jones, Registrar at Hull University. Both jumped at the chance and the die was cast. The Play was presented in an intimate, miniature Theatre built and bequeathed to the Company by very generous members. Part of their own home had been made over to Stage and Auditorium. The piece attracted huge acclaim and all three of us were thrilled.

'And...something else happened, didn't it?'

Frank was aware of the fact that my life was on the brink of change and that I was unsettled. "Have you ever thought of University, Sue?" he asked. We were sharing copious glasses of wine at the time and I nearly choked! "You know," he continued, "Drama as an Academic study?"

'So, the die was cast in more ways than one?'

According to Frank, it seemed that Hull University was following in the footsteps of Bristol and Manchester Universities. All had created Drama Departments and resources for BA (Drama) Special Honours Degree Courses. The nucleus for Hull was centred in the Gulbenkian Centre, a new building at the heart of the University. "Could be just what you're looking for, Sue", continued Frank. "Have a go – apply – you've nothing to lose and perhaps everything to gain".

'Yes, and.....go on...I can't wait.. what happened?'

I spent hours mulling it over, Ronnie....

Most of August 1971 vacation was spent being involved with the machinations of the Ferguson-Fawsitt Arms. It was a quantum leap from my Professional life and in some ways became a form of refreshment; while helping to deal with its intrigue, contrivances and schemes, I was diverted from crucial, far-reaching and weighty decision-making. Life was frivolous and light-hearted. Others were in charge.

I worked hard. Ivy's Buffet was full-on and unstoppable. I met and greeted Restaurant diners while Mum had a few nights off and on a daily basis, cleaned the apartment and laid its coal fire.

'But…where were your thoughts kidda?'

All over the place, Ronnie. In moments of respite, on Summer evenings, I found myself leaning out of my bedroom window idly watching the world go by and wondering if my life was going the same way. Everyone I gazed upon seemed full of purpose, satisfaction and accomplishment. They were full of life. I suppose I was lonely.

'Now, come on…get it together Alice!'

I saw Frank from time to time. "Now, Sue, how far have you got with that application?" he would cross examine. I wasn't being let off the hook.

'Quite right, a man after my own heart…'

I took courage in both hands, told no one what I was doing and contacted the Hull University Drama Department Office. In due course, I received an Application Form which outlined, in minute detail, specification for qualifications and experience. It was daunting. I did not believe I stood a cat in hell's chance of being called for Interview. I reckoned that I could never be regarded as material for the world of Academia.

'Dear God…the prophet of doom…I sincerely hope someone gave you a kick up the bum!'

It may surprise you to know, Ronnie, that caution was thrown to the winds and the Application went off!

'I'd have been proud of you, pet…'

Well, having done the deed, I decided to get on with ideas to be set in motion for the next Kelvin Production. The Autumn Term was approaching and, as always, there was much preliminary work to be done.

'It was a Production line at that School! What was to be the next journey into the unknown or feat of strength and skill?'

Wait for it, Ronnie. I was well into the onslaught of the next Term and still toying with Play ideas, when a University summons dropped through the letterbox!

'Yes! Yes, go on...you always stop there....'

I was short listed and being called for Interview! This was to take place in the Gulbenkian Centre over the whole of one day in the New Year of 1972. I would be asked to take part in Workshops, Seminars and a one-to-one Interview. Also, in preparation, I was requested to prepare Shakespeare's 'Comedy of Errors'.

'Ugh...Shakespeare...I wouldn't swop places with you for that! I never liked Shakespeare...that's why I nearly always got cast as a Rude Mechanical or the Porter in 'Macbeth'.

Well, my darling, there's no one ruder than you! Of course, at first, I was thrown into complete disarray!

'Typical!'

What if I, in the wildest stretch of the imagination, was given a place! I would have to leave Kelvin. My life would be thrown upside down!

'Panic stations! Now, I'm sure you let common sense overrule all this and got down to the brass tacks of getting ready.'

I did, Ronnie. I decided on 'Charley's Aunt' by Brandon Thomas for the School play. In complete contrast to 'The Diary of Anne Frank', it would be a romp; a riotous and rollicking comedy which would go some way to providing my beloved Kelvin with a farewell gift of love and gratitude.

As always, I apprised Bill with my proposal. He was delighted. At the same time, I broached the prospect of my leaving Kelvin. If I was successful in my hopes for the

Kelvin Hall School
Miss Uebel and Paul Harrison 'Charley's Aunt'

University, Bill would need to advertise for my replacement. He needed adequate time.

'Must have been a shock!'

Yes, Ronnie. He was very shocked...but, as ever, he took my hand and wished me the greatest of good luck. He added, "Oh Sue, why aren't you at home, looking after an old man like me?"

'Sue, I expect that you were lost for words....I know I am...'

I had to get out of that Study very quickly, Ronnie. The tears were not far away. Here was a man who had taught me nearly all I knew about teaching young people. If I was successful, the wrench was going to be very great indeed.....Goodbye would be so final....

'Come on, petal...you're not there yet!'

I gave word to the Drama Department that I would be attending for Interview on the given day. After that, I had a play to Audition and Rehearse and also, to join the Chorus of 'Hello Dolly', the next production of Hull Amateur Operatic Society to be staged at the New Theatre, Hull.

'From the sublime to the ridiculous...'

Now then, Ronnie, I received some of my most valuable experience when taking part in the world of Amateur Dramatics. I owe them much....

'Sorry, pet, I did not intend to tread on anyone's toes... hmn...'

No, I know Ronnie. I suppose it did seem to be a wild, curious chain of events. Strangely enough, I did not look for the signposts in my life. They just happened to appear. It was up to me to choose which way I was to go.

'Was there much reaction on the home front? After all, this was promising to be a *hefty change for you'.*

I don't remember any noteworthy response. I guess there was pride.

'Perhaps that's why you can't remember'.

I have come to realise that others are pleased for your success and attempts to share it with them, but all in all, they are preoccupied with self and what self is doing. My Family had a busy life. There was much in which to immerse themselves; much to inhabit their thoughts and hopes. I was steering a different course and that was my objective, passion and responsibility, not theirs.

Work began on 'Charley's Aunt'. I assembled a supremely energetic, vigorous Cast. Also, it was exhilarating to behold many newcomers who had not acted before. Paul Harrison....

'Oh, of 'big mouth' fame?'

The very one, Ronnie. Paul took on the leading role of Lord Fancourt Babberley. Paul had no trouble in injecting his own take on the Character who appeared in drag – "I'm Donna Lucia D'Alvadorez from Brazil, where the nuts come from" – on several occasions; he was never at a loss for inventive whammy and bombard. Action did threaten to career out of control when I introduced a bicycle into these key scenes. We managed to obtain, on loan, something that strongly resembled a Penny Farthing machine. The stage business that ensued threatened to be a bridge too far. In the interests of safety, I had to design very accurate movement patterns in order to prevent the enthusiastic and reckless Paul taking out most of the Front Row!

'God, never work with children, animals and Paul Harrison!'

He was very ably supported by a versatile, upbeat and buoyant Cast. My nerves took something of a beating, however, for Paul was unpredictable.

Nevertheless, he turned in a superlative performance in March of the following year.

By the time the Christmas Holiday 1971 came around and 'Hello Dolly' was a thing of the past, I had accepted the part of Lady Teazle in the Playgoers production of 'School for Scandal' which would be presented in February of 1972.

'In other words, you used the Christmas weeks to learn words and study 'Comedy of Errors'. Your memory must have been in prime condition, that's all I can say!'

As I look back, Ronnie, I cannot believe that I actually did all this and in such a short space of time!

'I hate to remind you of this, my love, but you were very young!'

Thank you, Ronnie, just what I needed to hear!

While all this was going on, I received an Interview date from the University. I was to meet Donald Roy, Head of the Drama Department. This took place before the Main

Workshop Day. Mr. Roy was a long-haired, quietly-spoken and discerning Gentleman. He was casually dressed. I noticed expressive hands and carefully-manicured nails. His modulated voice was low; the diction precise. I sensed fastidiousness. His Office was ordered and exact. At the same time, surprisingly, he did not appear to be overly Theatrical. There was more of the Artist about him.

'Well, petal, isn't that the same thing?'

Well yes, Ronnie, of course it is, but he was totally different from what I had expected.

'Well, you were probably only used to Kelvin's male Staff – all with short back and sides! But, more importantly.... did he seem to be kind...did he seem interested in you?'

He did, Ronnie. He questioned me closely. He was most intrigued with my Kelvin work. He knew of my qualifications, so I was not quizzed about that. But, Ronnie, I was staggered when he went on to say that I was being considered for the Special Drama (Hons) BA Degree Course. It specialised in Drama only and was not a Joint Course teamed with a further subject. This was to be the Second Year intake and the Department had received over eight hundred Applicants. It intended to award eight places!!

'Dear God, did your heart sink, darling?'

Ronnie, I did not see how on earth I could be successful. Obviously, they were in a position to pick and choose.

'Now wait a minute, pet. How many of those people had eight years Teaching under their belt? Besides, you still had the Practical Day to come.....they were looking for a close-knit group of eight people. Not only Academia was at stake.'

I was invited to take part in the Drama Department's Workshop Day. This was to take place on a Saturday in mid-January 1972. It was going to be intensive.

Assembly time was 9.00 a.m. in the Foyer of the Gulbenkian Centre. The first Workshop was to follow. Breaks for Coffee, Lunch and Afternoon Tea were also on offer.

'You were undergoing social scrutiny as well...how sensible...no good choosing incompatible people'.

The Foyer was teeming when I arrived. Ronnie, I have never been so scared in my life. Everyone looked bold, brainy and bright.

'Oh give over...that's why you were there!'

A very pretty and welcoming young girl introduced herself as Adele, the Departmental Secretary.

'There's always someone at the ready to take your particulars down! Sorry, that's a very old joke....'

Adele was hurriedly ushering everyone into the Theatre beyond. It's difficult to say how many prospective Students were being steered therein, but it seemed to be swarming with eager, and......very young people....enough to put the wind up anyone as old as me at the ripe old age of thirty-two...

'Hmn...never heard of the value of a 'Mature' Student?'

The Gulbenkian Theatre was an affecting, outstandingly Dramatic space. Its black décor and tabs complemented an essentially efficient, workmanlike facility. It was designed for experiment, trial and error, research and development of its Students. This was new to me. I had been accustomed to traditional gilt embellishment, velvet seating, rich gold-fringed drapes and boxes. The Audience seating was retractable. On that day, it was in place, but...partially occupied by the whole Academic Staff of the Drama Department! In all, at least half a dozen congregated to observe.

'Presumably, all there to size you up and take notes!'

At that point, my mind went blank. I was frozen to the spot. Mr.Roy stepped forward and outlined the first task for Improvisation. Everyone shifted awkwardly. Fortunately, we were required to pair up with a Partner.

'Saved!'

All at once, a rather well-rounded figure appeared beside me. "'Well, pet, looks as if we're made for each other", twinkled my new friend.

'Oh Sue, what a saviour – a Geordie!'

Yes, Ronnie. Little did I know at the time that Jimmy Swan, as I came to know him, was to play a very definitive and ultimate part in my future. Jimmy, during the course of that memorable day, was an absolute joy. He was down-to-earth, very funny and extremely intelligent. Smart, intuitive, worldly-wise, warm-hearted and as camp as Chloe, he brought out whatever was the best in me.

From then on, my fear vanished. I performed. I relished the group discussions that made up much of the day and I knew then where I wanted to be.

'You will always recognise your Guardian Angels, my darling'.

One tense and trying moment or two came about, Ronnie.

'Yes, I'm waiting....'

Well, I had studied 'Comedy of Errors' very closely. I loved the play and imagined myself directing it. Jimmy and I took part in a Donald Roy Seminar. A small group was assembled. All at once, Donald referred to the elongated initial speech at the beginning of the piece, delivered by the Duke of Ephesus. "If you were directing, how would you handle this?" was the question posed to each Student. There did seem to be some very involved, Academically-sounding answers. When attention turned to me, I said "I'd cut part of it". A rather stunned silence ensued. What?

Cut Shakespeare! Jimmy saved the day by saying "Only an Actor could say that! I bet that's what we were all thinking!"

'Well, my darling, it would take more than that to gum up the works...'

As the Day came to a close, I was filled with buoyancy and optimism. What a dreadful disappointment it would be if.....

'Now come on, Alice...we don't live in hope and die in despair!'

Well, my darling, you know the outcome of course! I waited for several weeks before an envelope dropped on to the mat....I hardly dared to open it! Yes, there were the words: "We are delighted to offer you a place on the Special Hons Drama BA Course. Please notify us of your acceptance."

'Had I been there, we'd have painted the Town red.... my little Star!'

Oh Ronnie, if only.....

~

I knocked on Mr. Pattinson's door. He must have known, somehow....

"Well, Miss Uebel, I think Congratulations may be in order!"

The news broke. This was a gradual process, but Staff and Students alike were sad at the prospect of my leaving; all a little taken by surprise, but, at the same time, heartfelt and fervent in encouragement and support for this adventuresome life change.

As 'Charley's Aunt' drew towards its final curtain – mercifully without a Paul Harrison accident or incident – I began to take on the enormity of my decision...

'Come on, my darling, now's the time....'

Before I move on, my love, there are three things I have to tell you about. Three things that are lasting, enduring memories of my dear Kelvin.

In the course of my final week, I made my way home to the Fergie, parked 'The Swimming Pool' and made my way inside. All was very quiet. Yes, it was before opening time at 6.00 p.m....but, not a sound. It was all very strange...I climbed the staircase leading to our Apartment and opened the door...

Our Lounge was full of children! It was bursting at the seams with cheering, laughing children!

'Oh Sue...Sue...'

Mum came over and took my hands. "They've done it all, love. I've had children meeting here every week to arrange it. Can you believe, our Dining Room is full of food and booze! I don't know what Mr. Pattinson would say!"

That Party was one of the most memorable of my whole life. My own Form was responsible for everything and many more had joined in! Paul Harrison, of disorderly and disreputable fame, was, as I came to understand it, the main ring-leader and brains behind the whole endeavour!

'The power of love....'

Yes, Ronnie. That day brought much laughter and many tears...but, tears of joy....

'That rare, special day must have been stored in your memory box for always...a keepsake, a memento to be taken out and brought to mind again and again over the years that followed....'

The remembrance of Children never leaves you, Ronnie. For me, it was a bequest and a privilege to have been part of their lives....

Ronnie, do you remember me telling you about Kelvin's very detailed Report Booklets?

'I do, darling...'

Kelvin Hall School 1972
Susan & Bill Pattinson 'Leaving Day'

The Staff compiled comments in a Testimonial which was presented to me as a leaving gift! I couldn't resist letting you see it... the Report was entitled:

SUSAN ANN UEBEL: Classified information.
ADMISSION NO: 007

ART – Particularly good at painting faces
BIOLOGY – Fails to grasp her fundamentals
CAREERS – Drunkenly about the school
CHEMISTRY – More 'mystery' than 'Chem'
COMPUTER SCIENCE – Gets her wires knotted
DESIGN and TECHNOLOGY – Performs well under vices
ENGLISH LANGUAGE – Dificculty with speling
ENGLISH LITERATURE – Plays incessantly

FRENCH – A fluent command of the most unusual vocabulary
GENERAL STUDIES – Studies Generals very well
GEOGRAPHY – Presentable contours
GEOLOGY – Rocks well
GERMAN – Declines beautifully when asked to conjugate
HOME ECONOMICS – Burns water
HUMAN BIOLOGY – Disrupts lessons with dramatic outbursts
MATHEMATICS APPLIED AND…PURE? – Unbelievable
MUSIC – Can be relied upon to ring the bell – is always chiming in
PHYSICAL EDUCATION – Physically incapable but always willing
PRINCIPLES OF ACCOUNTS – No accounting for her principles
RELIGIOUS KNOWLEDGE – A most holy maiden
RUSSIAN – Always
SHORTHAND – Definitely
STATISTICS – Vital
PHYSICS – Has made a first rate contribution to the natural sciences
Conduct: Sober and upright
Deportment: Nerves in shreds
Speech: Luvly diction
Special interests and achievements: Cleaning out her drawers and collecting aged Cars and Gin Bottles.

'They must have been a wonderful group of colleagues, Sue. No wonder you were loathe to leave them…'

It was a pang and an ache, Ronnie.

Morning Service on my last Kelvin Hall day was a tearful affair for me. Bill gave a most moving goodbye Tribute. I think the ache was as great for him as it was for me. Of course, at the time, I did not realise how potent the emotion was, for I was too preoccupied with sadness to acknowledge it. Not until I saw the photographs of that final parting did I see how deep the connection went. I had travelled far since that distant day when I visited the School for the first time. A wealth of experience had been gathered along the way and many children had helped to mould me into a caring, steadfast and committed Teacher. This life, this engagement with young people had happened by accident...I had fallen into it...

'Mmn... accident? I wonder....you could so easily have walked the other way....but you didn't...why do we follow the map? I reckon that could be a question for Mother Cecilia...'

My leaving present was an unusual one. The whole school had made a contribution. As we both stood on the Hall stage, Mr. Pattinson took my hand and pressed a small, square box into it. Inside was a very beautiful ring. All had remembered my love for antique jewellery. The memories of my life at Kelvin were encompassed within that ring. It was a Talisman.

'Did you think you were leaving that world for good?'

As the Swimming Pool made its way through Kelvin's gates for the last time, Ronnie, I felt as if I was in space, a vacuum...a drifting place. My anchor was pulling gently away. For a time in my life, there was no looking back.... but...perhaps....one day, that destiny would beckon again....

~

The intervening holiday weeks spent at the Ferguson Fawsitt were busy. I was surrounded by noise, chatter, tasks and superficial thinking. I was filling in before the next unfolding and growth.

'I think I would have felt lonely.'

Yes, darling, I was lonely. I seemed to have thrown so much away....I had thrown it all away...deliberately. I so wished then that I had known you would be there...in the future...waiting...with your everlasting love....

'Lurking with intent, you mean! Now come on Alice..... don't stop there... you always do that!

GULBENKIAN THEATRE DRAMA DEPARTMENT – HULL UNIVERSITY

1972 – 1975

'Be not inhospitable to strangers, lest they be Angels in disguise'

(Inscription above George Whitman's English Language Bookshop, SHAKESPEARE & CO., in Paris.)

One member of our group of eight was not a stranger.

'The gay Jimmy Swan?'

Now how did you know that, Ronnie?

'I'm insightful and astute – that's how!'

I was such an ignoramus in those days, Ronnie. I was unaware and naïve about so many things; Homosexuality was an uncharted territory. Jimmy became my aide-de-camp in more ways than one.

'Camp, presumably, being the key word...'

It was comforting to discover that I was not such an old....

'Mature, my love....'

...biddy after all. Jimmy Swan was twenty-seven and Ian McAnulty perhaps twenty-five or six. Although thirty-two, I did not feel wholly out on an aged limb. The remainder of the group were, primarily, coming to the University straight from the Sixth Form. All were very different. All had manifold, multifarious experience to offer.

Timothy Reed was an eighteen year old six-footer who dressed with impeccable, expensive taste. Handsome, dark-haired and softly-spoken, Timothy was silent, even self-possessed and spoke when he had something to say. Thanks to Jimmy, he became Tim most of the time and Timmy when Jimmy was being come-hither and provocative! Tim would smile indulgently. He could afford to. His air, manner and presence appeared to be straight as a die.

Joan Hunter was eighteen and hailed from Lancaster. Joan had a two-year old daughter, Sandra. Sandra, as time went by, was gathered in to the bosom of the group and Child-minding was a forgone conclusion when Joan was occupied elsewhere. Sandra became a permanent fixture when future Rehearsals were in full swing.

Anthony Minghella, also eighteen and known forever by us as Tony, was very bright and very gifted. He sported an immense, grubby Afghan overcoat which reached the floor. It had certainly seen better days. Tony's curly, Italian hair reached his shoulders. Tony, I came to learn, was a kind, gentle and very sensitive man. I say 'man', despite his youth, for Tony was far-sighted, wise and remarkably knowledgeable about the ways of women.

'Are we talking about **the** *Anthony Minghella?'*

We are, Ronnie. Tony's Family home was on the Isle of Wight where his beloved Parents had an ice-cream business. Tony was devoted to his Family and whenever the whole entourage visited Yorkshire, he brought all, including Grandmother, to the Ferguson Fawsitt for dinner.

Ian McAnulty was a lithe, moustachioed fellow...

'Was it the Che Guevara variety of the time?'

It was certainly rather droopy and his fingers were forever adjusting its position. Mac, as he came to be affectionately known, was quietly spoken and thoughtful. He mooched. He didn't walk, he mooched....I remember his smile so vividly; paroxysms of laughter followed it, invariably instigated by the scandalous Jimmy. Mac was a competent Musician and regular on excursions to the Jazz hotspots of Hull.

Jon, pronounced Yon, Gunnarsson hailed from Reykjavic, Iceland. Tall, blonde, good-looking and of princely carriage and conduct, Jon was frequently thrown into disarray by the incorrigible Jimmy who was heard to mutter in hushed tones, "Erken, sherken, flerken, derken" in send-up and take-off of Jon's broken English.

'The poor lad. Didn't anyone rise to his rescue?'

Laughter rose to his rescue, Ronnie. This teasing was usually followed up by Jimmy chiding us all with "She just doesn't understand the language!!"

Jon, totally perplexed, came to recognise this ribbing as a compliment! 'She' could be applied to most Male individuals, Staff and Students alike.

Jimmy had a repository for the most apt prefixes. Tony, however, did not always take kindly to being referred to as Mary Minghella or worse, "When are you going back to sell the ' isa creama"!

'Wicked!'

The use of 'she' began to rub off on me. I remember applying it to a sound, stout but fulsome and effete member of the male chorus in the Operatic Society's rendering of the 'Student Prince'.

'Dear God....!'

Er, yes Ronnie. That met with a stunned but, I have to say, very appreciative audience.

'You were being edified, nurtured and elevated to the world of gay expressionism!'

Absolutely Ronnie. It was all such fun; so diverse, so engaging. I lapped it up and thirsted for more.

The remaining Students to make up the eight-strong group were Peter Bainbridge and Jenny. I can only refer to this pretty, endearing and winsome young lady as 'Jenny' for beyond first meeting, she was snatched from us. Her Mother became gravely ill with Cancer and Jenny was called away.

Peter was a Northumbrian. Peter was dark-haired, amiable, handsome and.... Oh, that accent...!

'I keep telling you...all Geordies are of unique calibre! They have the stamp of greatness upon them...'

You're speaking personally, of course.

So, Ronnie, we became an Ensemble of seven. Us girls – Joan and I – were outnumbered by the Male fraternity. Nevertheless, in all, we became a clan, a circle of intense fellowship, trust and affection for each other. Hugs, kisses abounded as we formed our individual, exclusive and immovable stronghold. We developed our own kinship, language, potential and power. We became the idiosyncratic Second Year Specials.

'What about the First Year Specials? Did you have much contact?'

All I can say, Ronnie, is that they seemed rather aloof and awesomely able. Bob Carlton terrified me. He was very large and imposing with piercing gaze. I always looked the other way when he appeared around a corner. Many, many years later, I was to discover that Bob became a humorous, skilled Theatre Director. He cast me in a York Theatre Royal Production of 'The Ghost Train'. I had misjudged him. He had noticed me. He had valued me. He was a star. It was with great sadness that I learned of his death such a long time after, when age had caught up with us all.

'In contrast, Jimmy must have been an absolute enigma!'

That is only one of the descriptions I could apply to Jimmy. He was a one-off! Clad in fashionable but exaggerated flares of the time, he sported elevated, Cuban-heeled boots and a liberal dollop of Strawberry Aftershave. That Strawberry aroma hung around the Gulbenkian for several days after James had passed through. He wore his hair shoulder-length and was prone to tossing his head seductively when the time was ripe for unfurling this coiffure in wanton abandon. His moon-faced grin perfected a very dear image. I loved Jimmy. We became very, very close.

'Glorious!'

The Group embarked upon a programme of practical and theoretical skills. We explored Classical, Contemporary, Renaissance and European Drama where we delved into specialist areas of Production, divergent Periods of Drama and Historic cultures.

The Kabuki Theatre of Japan was particularly interesting, largely because Jimmy evolved a devastatingly funny representation of the Kabuki style. Kabuki was geared to bizarre, exotic, alien and somewhat exaggerated movement and expression. There was weird, chilling vocal accompaniment which consisted of freakish sounds and a grotesque guttural clearing of the throat resulting in an alarming screech. Jimmy mastered this to perfection and his rendering of "ooooooo – eee – ooooo – eee!!" rose to an alarming crescendo. His hands moved in unseemly fashion and as he cupped round face between fingers, he brought the whole Performance to a close with 'Eh, Betty, "Viddy, viddy, vadar"! in broad Geordie dialect. Jimmy was also fond, in his own inimitable style, of using a dash of Old Polari where appropriate! Our Lecturer, the illustrious Thespian grandee Harry Thompson, joined us in unrestrained mirth, which must have stopped short the Gulb Foyer and all in its vicinity.

'Jimmy was a jewel, Sue...'

The days were full. Lectures were absorbing, tense, crammed and overflowing with Academic detail.

'I'd like to bet your Shorthand and Typing came in very handy? But...so different from Mr. Cayley's "Sue, letters!"'

Oh Ronnie, so different. But you're right. I was able to get on top of the many notes I needed. It stood me in very good stead when it came to essay writing. Since I mention it, that did become something of an issue for me. I recall that I hadn't written an essay for nigh on ten years! My Grades were not very good to say the least....

'Darling...'

It worried me even more when John Harris, a scholastic, gentle giant of a Lecturer, who specialised in Restoration Drama, reminded me that as one advances in years, one's brain cells either drop off, or cease to operate efficiently!

'Well petal, genius is irksome to the less gifted!'

Viv Bridson's Movement and Improvisation sessions provided a hiatus and lull from all this brainstorming. Physical knocking about and cavorting in tights and leotard, as we mistakenly thought, was an excuse for slacking off.

'Camperama, eh? Chilling out and hanging loose...as they say in France! At least you didn't have to parade in navy blue knickers!'

Shall I say, Ronnie, that we were in for a rude awakening. Viv, or "La Vivienne", as Jimmy alluded to her, was a task master.

'Hell's teeth, not a reincarnation of Miss Gym?'

Viv's classes were held in the Gulbenkian Theatre. Our initial sortie to this venue was alarming to say the least. Horrified, we were confronted with Ballet Bars!

Jimmy's opening elucidation was Bette Davis' quote from 'All About Eve' –

"Fasten your seat belts, pets – it's going to be a bumpy crossing!" Jimmy was given to the wisdom of Bette Davis on a number of occasions and gave a very eerie approximation of her vocal technique. In fact, Jimmy's knowledge of 40's Cinema masterpieces almost rivalled mine.

La Belle Vivienne was a petite Lady. Dark, short curly hair framed elfin features. She smiled frequently; often, I think, in triumph as we strove, without favourable outcome, to lift leaden legs, feet and hands in balletic poise, finesse and dare I say it – elegance. It was easy to feel inordinately clumsy in Viv's presence for she was athletic and....

'Bendy?'

Very Ronnie. Very bendy indeed. We were not bendy. Not bendy, at all.

In fact not at all....

I should add that we Specials were all shapes and sizes. Fortunately, the Men, in the main, were well endowed in the physical department. Mac mooched, Tony was of sinewy, wiry build, Jon was an Icelandic God while Peter played Rugby, which spoke for itself. Jimmy...well...roly-poly might suffice.

I was overcome with gratitude when darling Jimmy encountered Joan and me outside the Ladies Lav which doubled as changing-room and announced, "Sue, darling, you look absolutely lovely in your leotard". Poor Joan, who was battling with a debilitating dose of 'flu' at the time, was just saved from running, hell for leather and in misery, back to the comfort and confines of the Lavatory.

Fortunately, Jimmy was our saving grace for, as hinted at earlier, he was not blessed with the physique of an Adonis himself, so made amends by greeting Joan with "Behold Araminta, the fruit of my loins!" whereby all knife-edge strain was appeased. Nevertheless, it may have been opportune to post a Class notice stating 'Abandon all hope all ye who enter here'!

Never mind, we struggled with knee bends, hip bends and anything else that would bend. Jimmy referred to it all as "tappy-lapping" or "sashaying his bits"!

Whenever Viv appeared to be utterly despondent, Jimmy would enthuse with "Take heart, Vivienne, the bairns are doing their best!"

'How did you all take to the exposure of Improvisation?'

Not terribly well at first, Ronnie. Tony was a great help. He was an innate musical genius – a natural. This was the early days of his intuitive feeling and sixth sense. I was almost taken aback, unsettled or unnerved by his brooding intelligence. Tony was quiet, thoughtful and instinctive. He and I had an unspoken understanding.

'Each recognising the other's inborn predisposition'.

The difference in age was of no consequence. This time, I was not the Teacher. I followed.

The Group did progress. Cohesion developed. Viv coaxed the driving force within and after a shaky start (which produced a mind-blowing feat of Academic Improvisational proficiency entitled 'Wanda the Wood Nymph'!) we came through victorious. She must have known where we were going and oiled the wheels; facilitated our strength, staying power and stamina.

'I think she knew what she had in the palm of her hand'.

I didn't realise that until much later, Ronnie.

There was much to engage us during that first Term. We embarked upon a course entitled 'The Hollywood Musical', so Jimmy and I were in our element! Both of us had backgrounds of detailed appreciation. We remembered the Saturday morning Cinema and the everlasting fascination of Gene Kelly, Fred Astaire, Debbie Reynolds and Ginger Rogers. Perhaps we were enthralled even further with the magic of Busby Berkley and the beginnings of The Follies.

It was a feast of remembrance, constantly punctuated with Jimmy's vocal portrayal of Bette Davis "Nothing can hurt us now. What we have can't be destroyed. That's our Victory...our Victory over the Dark!"

'From guess what? 'Dark Victory'!'

Brace yourself, Ronnie. Here's another from 'Now Voyager' – "Jerry, don't let's ask for the moon. We have the stars!"

I'll leave you to imagine Jimmy's fluttering eyelashes and pouting lips while delivering these gems! Imprinted on my memory forever....

We also coped with John Bernasconi's History of Art Course while all this was going on – poor Betty Bernasconi, he was fighting a losing battle – we were nearly dropping off with exhaustion. In spite of a draining fatigue, we won through to enjoy his Lectures enormously. This cornucopia of visual cognizance was imprinted upon our consciousness in preparation for whatever was to follow.

My allegiance to the Hull Operatic Society did not diminish. Much of my social life at that time, when there was space or span for it, centred around friendships made within the round of Rehearsals for 'The Student Prince', due to play at Hull's New Theatre in November 1972. I was invited to play the Grand Duchess, which was a Part small enough for me to balance the commitment alongside the more fiercely concentrated demands of the Gulbenkian. News of this caused much hilarity at the University; nonetheless, a Fan Club built and many turned up on the First Night, led by the gregarious James Swan.

I came to know Ian Butler who acted as the Society's Musical Director. Ian, Head of Music at Malet Lambert School in Hull was not only a master Professional and Maestro – he was arch and devilishly funny.

'I seem to remember you mentioning him as something of a dish!'

He certainly was, Ronnie. Tall, athletic, dark-haired and – er – 'hot' I suppose one would say now, he had a cutting, sardonic repartee and badinage. Ian was at his blasting best when faced with the exasperating, vexing lack of zeal or purpose from the Main Chorus. Most of his wit went over heads; Ian was a Theatrical and as seen by the ordinary man as an eccentric beyond the bounds of average or pedestrian experience. His accurate and often withering comments were wasted on all except me! So, we became very close friends....incidentally, Ian's close confidante was Malet Lambert's Curate – a John Hall. Amiable, studiously quiet, affable, attractive, bespectacled John who went on many years later to be Dean of Westminter.

'Name dropper!'

Another Pal, Alex Simpson, was Amateur Actor and camperama extraordinaire! Alex stayed by my side on many future adventures...

'Camp follower?'

Thank you, Ronnie....yes, most definitely...but a loving Buddy and giving companion. He has remained so through length and breadth. Ian Butler's death many years later was a devastating shock and great sadness for me. Ian was fifty. So much laughter and love dissolved with Ian's passing.

Guess what, Ronnie...towards the end of that first Autumn Term, Donald Roy launched his proposal for a production of Moliere's 'La Malade Imaginaire'. This new translation of Don's was to be entitled 'Sick in the Head' and presented in the Gulbenkian Theatre in March 1973.

'Yes...go on...you said 'Guess what?'... well, what?'

Jimmy was invited to play Argan, the Invalid and I was asked to play Toinette, his Maid – both leading parts! The play, an illustration of Moliere's style designed for Court performances, was a mixture of Comedy, Farce, Satire and Burlesque; not forgetting integration of Theatre and Ballet convention.

'Sue, what a great start!'

It was a steep Academic learning curve for me, Ronnie. This exploration of a new mode and style of Theatre was utterly compelling. The whole presentation was lit, as in French Theatre of the period, by candlelight!

That was somewhat nerve-wracking, for a lot of flickering and spluttering of wax went on. Jimmy's moon-face gleamed in ghostly, spooky aura and needless to say, added to his hilarious and brilliantly sustained performance. We worked together well and when Toinette was disguised as Argan's Doctor, thus becoming an "itinerant Physician", I hit on giving him a wee Scottish accent reminiscent of Andrew Cruikshank's Dr. Findlay!

'Thank God it wasn't Andy Stewart or...Moira Anderson perhaps?!'

Try to imagine Jimmy's feedback – it was all I could do to carry on; Jimmy's relentless ingenuity knew no restraint. I was skewered!

Of course the Specials were not the only Students engaged in Drama. Many studied on a Joint Course teamed with a further subject, so the Department had a wealth of talent to draw upon when Casts were large.

We were acquainted with many who became great friends. All this took place after the Christmas vacation.

'Ah, I wondered when you were going to return to life at the Fergie...'

I was completely knackered after that First Term, Ronnie. I had roughly three weeks to draw breath. There was, however, little opportunity for that. I had much homework for the University: Toinette's vast amount of lines and a couple of tricky essays. Fortunately, I did possess a typewriter, so some of the slog was taken out of the copying up. Most of my College work was done in the very early morning, that is, round about 6.30 a.m. when the alarm went off. I was not a night owl and could not concentrate beyond 10.00 p.m., so, I functioned best as a lark…

I worked on Ivy's Buffet during the day. Christmas was busy, but I still oversaw my customary Christmas missions or obligations: buying everyone else's presents, bar Nicky's, who just about managed those himself; decorating our flat's Christmas tree; wrapping most of the family's gifts, including those for two Aunties who, traditionally, spent the Day with us; making the car journey into Hull to collect the Aunties; washing up the Dinner detritus single-handedly in order to relieve my Mother, who, in inexplicable fashion, days before, had insisted on scouring out every cupboard in sight. I remarked, "Look Mum, what's the point? They're not going to inspect the cupboards." "Oh well," she replied, "they've always been so particular. They might think it's mucky". I realised that there was no answer to that. Finally, my concluding task on Christmas Day, at 10.00 p.m., as the revelry drew to a close, would be to chauffeur Auntie Annie and Auntie Elsie to their respective homes.

'No help?'

Everyone else was working in the Pub and Restaurant. You know, Ronnie, real work. Teachers and University Students are only playing at it!

'Now then....don't be waspish!...now how was Jessica doing?'

Jessica covered a lot of ground, one way or another and appeared resplendent every evening to greet her Guests. This was a marked contrast to the front she donned pre-Aunties' arrival.

'You're not going to say sackcloth and ashes?'

No make-up or hairdo, but apron and impression that it wasn't going to be easy, but she would struggle through any inconvenience. The overall image was hitched to harassed air and aspect.

'You've got to take your hat off to that Jessica!'

She worked extremely hard, Ronnie. Also, in view of her soldiering through past feuds and family rifts, I think that Mum did rise to the occasion with more that a fair share of generosity, particularly in her protective defence of Auntie Elsie, who, in the past, had also come off worst when it came to the petty injustice of her kinsfolk.

'I found out, via the grapevine, that years ago, Jessica cared for your Auntie at Lowfield Road, unaided, solo and without help, during Elsie's post operative, convalescing weeks. Don't you remember when poor Elsie had everything taken away and a gas stove put in!'

Trust you, Ronnie, to come up a realistic, rude and rugged explanation! But yes, I do remember. I was only very small at the time.

I believe that life at the Fergie, although busy, became a refuge for my Mother. The gossip and intrigue spurred on and filled the waking hours and took her a long way towards some form of relaxation. It was Theatre! Her nightly soirees in the Dining Room, on occasion with trusted customers and friends – over one or four gin 'n tonics – charged her batteries. Come to think of it, they charged mine also. I hasten to add, however, that when booze is on tap, it can become a habit. Perhaps I was on the brink….

'If I remember correctly, circumstances intervened before that could happen…'

True, Ronnie. That was some time later….

The most entertaining pastime or diversion was watching Dina in action.

'Oh yes, I love Dina….'

There was a very convenient corner of the Dining Room where one could park without attracting too much attention. It was a fortuitous vantage point as far as Dina's antics were concerned. Her moods varied. Glasses perched on the end of her nose, Dina could feign vibes of superiority, an assumption that she was too remote, too stylish and classy to be behind the desk at all. Far too la-di-da to deal with the hoi-polloi. I think she branded a large percentage of the human race as rabble; or the masses. Some evenings she would overdo the gush and smother one with garrulous, chatty and loquacious prattling. Customers would hasten to the door at breakneck speed. If she was the wrong side out, however, it resulted in a no holds barred attack. The Waitresses came off worst. Her classic riposte to an innocent enquiry: "Well, what do you expect me to do about it? If there isn't a table, there isn't a table...I'm not a magician"! or "What's this...on this bill...how am I supposed to be a mind-reader?" Fortunately, when Mum appeared on the scene, equilibrium was restored and all one could hear would be "Oh, times have changed...! I can remember the day when they wouldn't have got away with it!" Unfortunately, this cast something of an aspersion on Mum's management. A besprinkling of criticism perhaps?

'I'm sure Jessica was a big girl. She could take it...'

Oh true, Ronnie. For me, it all made for a luscious indulgence of the ridiculous.

You ask how Mum was doing. I think she was fairly content. Certainly more comfortable and settled. Also, don't forget she was at the centre of a life that was stimulating and also, at the hub of her Daughter's progress. Backstage action during 'The Student Prince' fed her Theatrical yearnings. She was a part of all doings there. She had acquaintances from years ago; people who could reignite experiences and longings.

'Added to that, there was no inamorato of yours diverting her thoughts...'

I don't think that would have mattered if the lover had been to her liking.

Any wooing gallant needed to fit my Mother's...

'Bill?'

Surely Ronnie...not just mine. That Suitor needed to be someone who could be steered...manoeuvred...someone who would fit in with the plan. I can see it much more clearly now.

'Nothing wrong with thinking that...it didn't stop you loving her.'

No, never, Ronnie. I didn't think of these searching psychological explanations then. I just pandered. It was easier. I was approved of and that made for peace of mind. I was doing what was expected of me and according to my Mother, no unsuitable interloper was getting in the way. I knew peace. But... my thoughts....they were my own... and .... one travels far....

~

Harry Thompson's Jacobean and Elizabethan Lectures opened the Spring Term of 1973. Harry was an inspiring, animated man who imbued us with motivation and creativity. He sparked and galvanized us into thought and action. Harry painted verbal pictures. One was tempted to relinquish the pencil and listen, enthralled. Incessant note-taking became an unnecessary chore. Harry's vibrant, dynamic descriptions of the Elizabethan house and life within it, remained sharply etched on my memory. I recalled those graphic Harry images in evocative, life-like detail nearly three years later, when I faced my Final Examinations. His words came back to me as if I had heard them only the day before.

Rehearsals for 'Sick in the Head' ran in tandem with thought-provoking Academia. Life was busy...

'I was wondering how you got in an out to the University – was 'The Swimming Pool' still in service!'

Alas, no, Ronnie. I had an alarming escapade en route to nearby Beverley. The brakes failed. I narrowly missed a very decorative front garden and came to a shuddering halt on the pavement.

' "I'm not afraid of dying. I just don't want to be there when it happens..."

Spike Milligan took the words out of my mouth!'

That was that, Ronnie. Daddy stepped into the breach and loaned me a Cortina saloon which he had purchased a few months before. It was a Godsend. I know he was so relieved that I had walked away from disaster unscathed.

This car of Daddy's was also very useful if I needed to help Joan manage little Sandra's needs. Joan was very courageous in her determination to keep her Daughter by her side. She had no intention of farming her out to Parents based in Lancaster, however willing they appeared to be. Joan was eighteen. I was thirty-two and marvelled at her stoicism. I dare not contemplate how I would have survived. She did not complain, nor did she explain. I learned little about Sandra's Father. I did not ask. He was not around, ever. It didn't seem to matter....

'What about child care?'

Most of us took it in turns. I remember that Tony had distinguished, de luxe qualifications in the area of Baby-sitting; he seemed more than capable when it came to high-powered conversations with a two-year-old.

'Bless... don't forget the importance of Italian life. It would mean everything to Tony – I bet he looked after his Brothers and Sisters. Don't you remember, I did that in Hartlepool...it's something you do....'

Yes, darling, I do remember...

Eventually, Joan was able to find Family-orientated living accommodation, where the Lady of the house was only too pleased to watch over Sandra when Joan was at the University. Whenever Joan seemed fraught and frazzled, I brought her over to the Fergie for one of Dennis' wholesome suppers! When Rehearsals were in the offing, we worked it out between us…somehow….

'It was an exercise in flexibility!'

The Group had two excursions to Elizabethan houses with a view to embellishing and fleshing out our Lecture notes. These trips were to Hardwick Hall and Haddon Hall in Derbyshire.

I don't think Harry had envisaged carting a coach load of Specials, plus the incorrigible Jimmy, on a voyage of discovery and hassle to Stately Homes. His expression frequently betrayed the look of hopeless, dismal submission! Like someone who had undergone aversion therapy!

'Poor bugger….!'

The bus was driven by David Edwards who was the Gulbenkian Lighting Box Chieftain. There were intermittent 'lavvy' stops and constant searching for Jimmy's bits, which seemed to find themselves in inaccessible corners of the seating – most important being his hairbrush!

Haddon Hall was particularly atmospheric. Bathed in the warm afternoon sunshine, the wooden interiors "glowed in firelight", as Harry recalled the use of tapestry and wall hangings; how they covered all, enabling the rooms within to be cocooned, remote and hidden from the outside world. Once more, the word portraiture conveyed all. It was mesmeric.

The subject matter of these excursions was Academic but the behaviour of those taking part was anything but. It resembled a rowdy, unruly and disorderly coach-party bound for Bridlington-by-the-Sea. I think much to Harry's delight, these peerless inroads and incursions to Drama Student life was the nonpareil!

'Did you stop for fish n' chips?'

Ronnie, of course we did! Most of all, we were together. Those times were unequalled. I think it took Jon a long time to recover.

'Ah well, she didn't understand the language!'

I didn't notice that that made any difference to his obvious savour and zest for the whole day out. Jimmy's final observation "Here's to Reykjavic and all who sail in her"! brought closure to two very noteworthy, celebrated and unusual days of mayhem and ....

'Commotion?....'

'Sick in the Head' came and went in March of that Term. Jimmy and I, judging by some very complimentary Reviews, had made our mark. James, very ungraciously, concluded that Mum had written mine! Needless to say, my Mother was slave to Jimmy's spell....

Little did we know that La Belle Vivienne had a further ploy, a tactic up her sleeve. She was about to divulge detail of a bold, intrepid and ambitious assignment!

'Go on....go on...you always stop there....!'

After Easter 1973, Viv outlined her proposal for the next Second Year Specials' Practical exercise, or....Trial-By-Production! We were in the middle of studying Open-Air Elizabethan Acting traditions in 16th Century London. The aim of Viv's notion or conception was to re-create as accurately as possible those elements of production as performed in an Elizabethan Courtyard.

'Oh yes...and...?'

Well, Ronnie, we had concentrated on the Social, Moral and Political values which governed the actions of characters in such Plays. Ladies, by tradition, were excluded from Elizabethan Acting companies. So....

'Had Jimmy got his frock ready?'

Ronnie, you're telepathic. Viv proffered the idea that the Play extract she had chosen would be cast, not to suit the Players – us- but to stretch their creative imagination and inventiveness.

'No ladies playing ladies, in other words. Go on then.... what was it?'

'Twelfth Night'.

'I'll have one guess at casting Toby Belch! You!'

You are a soothsayer. I hasten to add that padding would be imperative! Mac was to play the dreamy Orsino...

'With his Che Guevara?'

He was allowed to keep it! Pete Bainbridge was Feste – fiendishly magnetic and impertinent; Jon, a gangling Icelandic Andrew Aguecheek; poor Joan, Malvolio; Tony, somewhat shorn of Italian mane, Viola. Olivia, the six-foot Tim who possessed hands like shovels and last but by no means least, to crown all, Jimmy Swan, Maria the Maidservant!

'Dear God....I can't wait....tell me about it...!'

Various other parts were played by Joint Drama Students. Don Reed, a great Geordie pal of Jimmy's and referred to constantly as Dolly Reed, made a very good job of Antonio.

A smart, conspicuous and astute Joe Richards took on Sebastian. Little did we know at that time that Joe would transfer and become yet another Second Year Special. Many of the Joints became great friends and made repeated visits to the Gulb. On this occasion, many, who were skilled Musicians, accompanied our extravaganza on Harpsicord, 'Cello, Flute, Percussion and Guitar.

'Where on earth did Viv envisage all this taking place?'

Our extract was destined for the Courtyard of St.William's College, York, on 6th June 1973.

The Rehearsals were, in the main, a hilarious mixture of inspired characterisation, howlers, errors and blunders. My Toby did create something of a stir. I was able to drop my voice....

'Not your pantaloons, I'll wager....'

...to a lower register and resorted, rather frequently, to a 'Ha Ha, Ho, Ho' brand of jocularity in the vain hope of personifying Sir Toby's bluster. That, and my obvious padding, doublet and hose (which kept wrinkling), brought about a gleeful Review, post Perf. "Susan Uebel's Sir Toby, so reminiscent of an out-of-work Father Christmas"!

'Cruel bugger!'

That, Ronnie, alas, came about several weeks later. Our preparation was intense and La Belle Vivienne did not let anyone off the hook. She devised an alarming swordfight between Viola, alias Tony, and moi – Sir Toby. This confrontation became rather volatile on occasion: erratic, mecurial and....

'In a few words: unsteady, up and down and altogether unstable!'

Thank you Ronnie. I couldn't have put it better myself. I was quite determined to pursue each turn of Choreography with impetus, verve and gusto. Little Sir Toby became noticeably more blustery, tempestuous and light of foot.

'Ah...now what is it that goeth before a fall?'

You may well ask, Ronnie. A fall it was!

'Which part of your anatomy came in for it?'

My right knee. I was...er...lunging at Tony, or rather Viola, sword in hand – and...slipped. I felt an excruciating pain and sank to the floor. In an instant, I was surrounded by very concerned mates and a mortified Vivienne. The shock was momentary and I scrambled to my feet far more rapidly than I should have done. Little Sandra, who had been perched on a Theatre seat beside Viv, burst into tears.

'I do hope it was Viv and not the resolute Jimmy who administered First Aid.'

Oh darling James did his best, wailing yet again "Oh, Betty! What I would give to have a man about the house!" This time his summing up was very accurate. Jon chipped in with some very illustrious Icelandic curses, I seem to remember.

'Were you carted off to A & E?'

Not on this occasion, Ronnie.

Hell's teeth, that sounds ominous!'

I was able to drive the car and once safely sheltered in the harbour of Fergie's Cocktail Bar, our very agreeable GP, Dr. Platt...

'Are you sure you got that title correct?'

...was summoned. My very swollen knee was exposed, examined, prodded and poked. "It's the Cartilage, Sue. I think you've torn it. I'm going to refer you for Physio" announced Dr.P. "The exercises will either strengthen the muscles and you'll be OK, or, the cartilage will pop out and it will mean an operation."

'Dear God, and William's Courtyard all thrown into shambles, jumble and disunity!'

That's putting it mildly, Ronnie. We were, by then, nearing the conclusion of our Rehearsals. Jimmy had really pushed the boat out and shaved his chest in preparation for his cleavage-bearing Maria gown. My knee problem could never be allowed to sabotage his self-sacrifice and drag!

'Only Bette Davis could pull you through – "That's our victory! Our victory over the Dark!!"

You took the words right out of Jimmy's mouth, Ronnie!

So, bound we were for St. William's Courtyard. Indeed, I was certainly bound, bound up with what seemed to be yards of crepe bandage! Dr. Platt had been right. My knee had stood up to some pretty vigorous Physio and for the time being, I was mobile.

Most of Hull Operatic Society was due to join the Audience. Anticipation was rife. Gradually, seats were filled, some with unsuspecting American tourists.

'Had audience participation been taken into consideration?!'

By that time, Ronnie, all probable misfortune had been thrown to the winds. The Courtyard was quite beautiful and the early Evening sun was dipping down to bathe the golden stone of College façade in a glimmering bloom. The building's frontage was our backcloth. At various intervals one could see the latticework of the windows.

We had one Dress/Technical Rehearsal which took place during the afternoon of 6th June. We dressed and prepared in a couple of anterooms situated at the rear of the College. A rash La Belle Vivienne had let it slip, in Jimmy's hearing, that the mesh/grille windows were operable and opened out towards the Court.

The Rehearsal came to a juddering halt, mid the Toby/Aguecheek meeting, when the lattice was flung open and who should appear framed within fretwork but Jimmy, a.k.a. Maria – thrusting his shaven, pulsating booosom forth in womanly invitation and pursing lips the while… all Professionalism was lost, never to be regained.

'I have an amendment here – never act with children, animals, Paul Harrison and Jimmy Swan!'

In point of fact, Ronnie, James could nearly always be relied upon to save the day.

Harry Thompson had generously provided a sizeable hoard of Pick 'n Mix sweeties backstage. Jimmy, me, Tim and Jon were on stage awaiting the entrance of Tony, other wise known as Viola. Much to our horror, Tony was off! He didn't appear. Jimmy filled in with a barrage of improvised rubbish – "Hie thee hence – see where he cometh – if he cometh! Whereth can he be? I will hie thee hence and see where he hath went"! So, with a flourish of skirt, Jimmy disappeared. We were abandoned!

Apparently, Mary Minghella was smoking a fag in the Dressing-Room and sucking one of Harry's boiled sweets! Like Dolly Reed, in his resume of the incident, I recall hearing "Gerron that fuckin' stage, before a strangle yer!" Jimmy proved to be a man of few words when disaster struck!

Hull University 1973
The Second Year Specials

Sir Toby, Maria and Sir Andrew

Sir Toby, Jimmy as Maria and Yon as Sir Andrew

Susie as Sir Toby Tony Minghella Viola

The Performance was a hit, a winner and a victory! The Audience rocked, we rocked and my knee rocked – or, rather, was knocked – painfully – resulting in my needing to be carried, literally, around the Stage for the whole of the Second Half, by the lusty Feste. He was the only one strong enough to bear all of my 8.0 stones. After the Curtain Call, I was harried forth into York A & E for knee resuscitation. Fortunately, the Cartilage remained intact, which is more than one could say for poor La Belle Vivienne, who looked as if she was on the verge of a nervous indisposition.

'Sue, we are the stuff that dreams are made of – this was all pure, wondrous comradeship and love of our Art'.

I think that Viv's prophetic programme note was inspiration of a genius:

"We hope to please and entertain you – and, as Shakespeare would say:

'...piece out our imperfections with your thoughts...'!!"

My ailing knee was not the only casualty of this gamble and crusade.

'Yes...what?'

I failed my History of Art examination.

'Oh, darling...viddy, viddy, vadar!'

Once all the excitement had died down, I was in considerable pain. Revision was put on the back burner and the Art Exam came to grief. Fortunately, I was able to join forces with poor Jon, who also missed out.

'Ah well, poor bugger, she didn't understand the language!'

The day of the Exam was gloomy for I had no choice but to make my way across the vast University Gymnasium, on crutches!

'Very Bette Davis, my love'.

The Supervisor, accompanying my limping labours towards the allotted desk, announced in jocular fashion "I 'ope you've left that parrot outside!"

'There's always a comedian.....'

~

The three Summer months that followed were filled with enforced inactivity, a life of crutches and sticks. There was, however, much time for reflection and catching up. I missed the Specials.....

'Was a bit of loneliness creeping in?'

I suppose so, Ronnie. The Ferguson Fawsitt was lively and I was lucky to have companionship and support while nursing something of a disability.

'Makes you think, pet. Think that this was only a temporary setback for you...'

Never fear, my love, I took that on board and didn't allow any interval for languishing! Besides, that History of

Art needed attention and the Academic ties were binding in the form of essays and reading. Our Studies were moving towards Restoration Drama of 1700. I was in harness to say the least…

The bond with Hull Operatic Society chums remained strong. Ian Butler and I became close friends and there were many gatherings where we yielded to corresponding, risqué sense of humour and like-minded speculations or conjecture. Ian was easy and great fun…

'What was his next Show?'

Since you mention it, Ronnie, it was to be 'The Desert Song'!

'I'm old enough to remember John Hanson, you know – oh, and all those bloody Riffs!'

Like the fool that I am, I weakened and gave in to Mum's persuasion yet again!

'You Auditioned for that dirty little Slave-girl, Azuri, who lived in a cave!'

Ronnie, I did! I Auditioned on my crutches! Completely ignoring the fact that Azuri was a dancing Slave-girl!

'And…I suppose you got it! Toby Belch, then this!'

Well, it all seemed a long way off… November…I was not looking ahead! I had long phone calls with Jimmy and Joan and so kept my Academic feet firmly on the ground. All of us were off doing this and that to earn holiday money, so, in spite of having time to let, we were not in a void. We did not become disengaged.

'How was Nicky getting on? Did he seem to be engaged?'

Nick seemed happy. No doubt there were Dad-clashes; not a bowl of cherries working in such close Parental proximity, but he had security and a certain freedom to do what he wanted to do. He didn't seem short of companions and Girlfriends. He was twenty-five and no longer the little Boy who needed Nuna!

'You were distant...looking towards another skyline...'

Yes, Ronnie, but old habits die hard...

Jessica found my connection with home very comforting, I have no doubt. There were complementary interests and opinions....

'And....Gin!'

A wicked comment, Ronnie, but an accurate one! It became an accessory to companionship. It soothed, of an evening, to retire with the odd glass, or three, to the part privacy and seclusion of the Restaurant Corner. I gave in to complacency, refreshment and the beer and skittles of life!

'Hmn....'

It became my other life, a handing over; surrender, if you like. Oh yes, it all fitted in very well. I fitted in. There was no argument, no crossed swords...just peaceful compliance. No one seemed to think it odd. Odd that a thirty-two year old was sitting there alone, with her Mother, in the Corner, still at home.

'Nobody puts Susie in the corner, my love...!'

I felt exposed and conspicuous. Why? It was no one else's business and to the onlooker I must have appeared content. Did the word 'unusual' ever spring to mind?

'Bystanders are usually too swept away with their own affairs, pet...the perceptive few, however, are curious.... many do see controlling forces....and are intrigued...'

One could have moved away; found digs and moved out – but – there would have been an inquisition; ill feeling and disappointment. The sentiment was remindful of the regular formula for Christmas homecomings. My Mother allowed no license for being elsewhere. My duty lay at home, as it had always been. How often I heard her phrase "Now all my chicks in the nest". One day, that nest would fall apart...

My thoughts were elsewhere....perhaps to my future home, a husband and children, perhaps to St. William's Courtyard where the apron strings ceased to tweak! I travelled far in hope and dreams....Gin complemented my dreaming...

I did not heed warning and curb the further offer of "have another one".

'None of us did. The danger of that sort of dependence was something we all chose to ignore! Yes, you were still at home, but you were reaching up and out, my pet. Nothing in your life was standing still...if only you could have seen that then....'

Jimmy's influence at that time was of supreme importance to me. Yes, Jimmy was an exuberant personality; Jimmy was different, worldly, but Jimmy was generous, open – very often damning – but, sensitive and wise.

I learned that, before University, he had been Administrator and Actor for the Bruvvers Theatre Company in the North East – Newcastle, I believe. There he was known as an inspirational leader who believed in the Educational potential of Drama. That led Jimmy to work in Community Theatre. We had much in common. I came to know that Jimmy had considerable intellect which rode in tandem with his unconventional style. There was much to love and admire.

'I think you came to understand Homosexuality on a much deeper level because of your affinity with Jimmy.'

Undoubtedly Ronnie. I suppose when one knows that there is no sexual conjecture, one is able to prize and value the whole person; to love them entirely for who they are. A deep and affectionate friendship endures. So many are hung up on the sexual component in relationships and what is normal. Normal? Perhaps Homosexuality exists in all of us, to a lesser and larger degree. So many reach for what is accepted as the norm and cruelly ridicule and persecute those who do not accede. I wonder, if those who are so vociferous, when in the seclusion of their innermost thoughts, harbour frightened feelings that they, too, might be different! The Sexual Act, how or with whom it is performed, has always seemed to be the singular, sinister element.

Fortunately, time has moved on and the Sexual climate has moved with it. Now, to cite an instance, one doesn't need to exchange the view that sex between 'normal' couples must be connected to love. It is widely accepted, according to commonplace conduct, newspaper article, film and television programmes, that Sex can be executed quite easily without it.

'Some still find that thorny to accept, petal...'

Nevertheless, when one is lucky enough to have both....

'Sex is a bonus!'

Well Ronnie, we came to know that all too well! Love, however, is where it falls....our liaison was not without complexity. Acceptance for us was a long time coming!

I have encountered numerous and varied Homosexuals as the years have rolled by and so many have become a stay in my life; constant, abiding and firm friends. I owe dearest Jimmy a great debt of gratitude. He opened my eyes to such variety, scope, a multiplicity of principles and codes.

Jimmy, my lovely Jimmy, died at the age of 62. After his University years, it did not surprise me to learn that he went on to become a Lecturer at the Tyneside Metropolitan College where he made a selfless commitment to getting the best out of his Students. He became their Mentor: personally, Academically and intellectually.

It is with great joy that I have remembered Jimmy. He enlightened and made me aware. Most of all, he gave me courage and a lasting belief in myself....

'He was your "Angel in Disguise"...'

~

That Summer of 1973 consolidated much in my life. It was time...

'To move on, pet?'

Ever heard of Claude Debussy's Opera 'Pelleas et Melisande', Ronnie?

'Er...yes...should I be waiting with bated breath?'

The Autumn Term moved us into another Viv Bridson exercise in Practical Theatre with regard to the span of Theatre History we were to cover. A Play from the repertoire of a little known French late 19th Century Dramatist, Maurice Maeterlinck, was chosen. Written in 1896 it was immensely popular with the Pre-Raphaelites and 19th Century Romantics.

'So 'Pelleas and Melisande' was born....'

There was a collective groan when this flight of fancy was first mooted.

'Poor Vivienne...why..?'

It transpired that the Play defied conventional Staging...

'Oh you mean realistic stuff; scene to scene, situation to situation...'

Exactly Ronnie. So, we set on evolving a Piece, through Improvisation, which became our response to Mood, Colour and Movement within each scene. It became a symbolist Poem, a sleepy processional of light and shadow. No single member of the Cast would leave the Stage during Performance. Everyone and everything, we concluded, became an adjunct to the principal action taking place on stage.

'Of course you're talking about pure Ensemble playing...'

That's not all, Ronnie. La Belle Vivienne added another element into the mix: for the exercise to fulfil its aims, we were to involve ourselves in every facet of the Production. The Costumes, Set, Lighting Design, Stage Construction, Décor and Presentation were to be created by us!

'Now then....a minor consideration...we come to the Music...would Debussy turn in his grave?'

Guess what, Ronnie?

'Oh not again....what?'

Tony composed an original Score! And....he played the whole thing himself!

Dear Viv, she gave the impression that we were on our own, but, there she was, our Belle Vivienne, Directing, unobtrusively and from afar!

'One of Jimmy's phrases come to mind...."Bless that bairn!" Oh, you forgot to mention...who played who?'

That was a Team effort, Ronnie. I was fully expecting to be cast as Genevieve, an aging Parent, but, much to wonder, shock and marvel, the whole Company bestowed Melisande upon me! All in spite of me pleading that I was...

'Such an old bugger...!'

Quite, Ronnie.

'I hope that, by this time, Melisande did not have to resort to crutches!'

Thankfully Ronnie, no. I was discharged from Physio by then, with strict instructions to lay off sword-fighting for the time being...Pelleas was allotted to Jon. Jimmy gave his accustomed blessing with "Well, she's the Moonchild of my loin, God Bless her!"

I don't think Jon was as confident in his ability to pull off being anybody's Moonchild! The poor love was prone to the odd wobble.

Tim proved to be a legendary Lighting magician. His Plot for the Play was a glorious combination of golden shafts of light, shadows and pools of luminous iridescence. The dark contours of the Stage became a brooding accompaniment for the loveliness and symmetry of Tim's creation.

Mac assisted Viv and Jimmy devoted in-depth energy to a new Script translation. Joan, in the main, gave succour to me when Rehearsals had thrown up a sudden or untimely spanner in the works!

'Who took on the Costumes?'

The Gulb was fortunate to have the sturdy, able-bodied Ruth Stuckey as Grand Dame of the Department's Wardrobe. Jimmy hobnobbed frequently with Ruth and could be found within her lair "shushing his bits" or, "feely-faxing his Bopling-Box!" God knows what that was, but very evocative of Radio's 'Round the Horne' and Julian and Sandy. Dolly Reid was known to keep them company. Poor Ruth! Two was above and beyond the call of duty.

Many Joint Students were involved in Backstage help, so our Group of seven swelled to encompass Technical Assistants, Sound, Electrics and Front-of-House.

Earlier in the Term, we had been disappointed to learn that dear Pete Bainbridge had decided that the world of Theatre was not for him.

'Well, it's a special place and it doesn't suit everyone...'

Joe Richards joined us and became a great asset to the workings of our Specials troupe.

'That can't have been a walk-over – you were all very attached...'

Well Ronnie, Joe was soon referred to as "Josephine" by you-know-who. He took it on the chin. From then on, immediate acceptance held sway. Besides, Joe had a great intellect. He was an unusual man; a Mature Student, he was watchful, composed and athletic. He was a boon.

Tony originated a haunting, evocative, poignant and unforgettable Score for 'Pelleas & Melisande'. It enabled the Story to be told in melodramatic, wistful, fragmentary episodes; filled with harmonic unity, atmosphere and the spirit of Maeterlinck. Our Play, over that Term, became a visual and aural delight. The Scene Stations and Tableau Vivant dissolved into a series of fluid movements which allowed the Group to achieve an unbroken coherence of mood. It was Symbolist Drama at its best.

'Well, my darling, Melisande must have been sublime...'

She was indeed, Ronnie. Tony entrusted me with the Opening Music. I was to sing, alone on Stage. The Piece was geared entirely to my vocal register and written just for me. As the Musical Rehearsals progressed, Tony and I became very close. I think that working intimacy, filled with trust and mutual understanding, produced a very significant, captivating Theatrical relationship.

'And what about all that hair – apparently Melisande was enveloped by it!'

Ruth gathered yard upon yard of diaphanous material to form a circular, voluminous drape. As the lights came up on the opening of the Play, I was shown, standing in the centre of these folds – my 'hair'. As the strains of the Melisande melody came to a close, each Character in the group held the fabric aloft, allowing it to scintillate and cascade in fiery flash...

We laboured long and hard that Term. Of course the Play imbibed most of our attention, but Lectures and the day-to-day workings of our Departmental life were kept up to speed. Nevertheless, Opening Night drew near in January of 1974.

'How did Lady Wishfort figure in all this?'

Susie as Melisande in 'Pelleas & Melisande'

Ah, well Ronnie. That was another story. John Harris was hell-bent on directing 'The Way of the World' in March, only a couple of months after Melisande! I was invited to take on Lady Wishfort!

'You little bugger – what a glutton for punishment!'

But, Ronnie…

'She stammered….!'

I couldn't turn that down, could I?

'Am I also right in remembering that you took on that grubby little slave girl, Azuri, in November?'

Ronnie, I did! And apart from being covered in bruises as I was manhandled out of my Cave, I really revelled in it…and…the Specials came to cheer me on!

'Oh….Susie….'

Christmas of 1973 came and went in a flurry of activity. I oversaw and held sway over the usual ritual and established practice…

'Aunties, Tree and Presents….?'

Thank you Ronnie. I hesitate to appear glib or gloomy. As always, the Festive Season at the Ferguson-Fawsitt was happy. I would pause for thought before the word glorious comes to mind, but… it was full of glad tidings. I worked in one Department or another during my vacation, but baulked at the prospect of Bar work, not because I considered myself to be bungling or gauche, but rather that the contemplation of making the Till balance as evenings drew to a close, was too much, too far. I quailed at the thought of appearing dozy and incompetent.

'Oh, Mrs. Arithmetic…you fucked things up good and proper!'

I was also attempting to get on top of Melisande's lines. I was nearly there for the Term's Rehearsals, in juxtaposition with constant Musical preparation, was work in progress and I surprised myself at how much I had already soaked up.

'Lines and moves go together; one prompts the other... oh, she knows, ye know!'

Now it's my turn to say 'Bless'!

'Thank you darling...now what about that Family of yours? All going according to plan?'

It cruised along without incident, I think. Much depended on routine and repetition. I suppose Customers and Staff acted as a catalyst. Therefore, at that time, the climate, for me, remained square, dispassionate and placid.

'That must have come as something of a relief?'

There was no cause for me to complain, Ronnie. I didn't. I was fortunate. I basked; reclined upon a foundation of support. While that was in place, I could allow my day-to-day thoughts, my Academic premise and the groundwork of committing to memory the words of both Melisande and Lady Wishfort to take precedence. My mind was uncluttered and anxiety over the welfare of my Family, one or the other, took a backseat...

'For once!'

When the hurly-burly of Hotel life was in full swing, I didn't notice any meaningful communion between my Parents. They tolerated each other and were practised at putting on a good face of it, when others were around. As always, there was a marked pretence, an act, if you like; a dishonesty. Then...after... silence betwixt...it was very, very sad.

So many years later, I am reminded of a reunion with Joan, long after she had emigrated to Australia with the no-longer-little Sandra. Joan visited family in Lancaster and got in touch. In the course of our reveries, Joan said "I always thought you seemed lonely, Sue".

'Intuitive...'

Joan did not know how unerring that viewpoint was, Ronnie. I was lonely.

My life was filled with incident, people and the promise of success. I seemed to be waiting....

'Of course you were, petal...you were waiting for me!'

That's not as daft as it sounds, Ronnie.

~

Melisande was a triumph beyond compare. The play was acclaimed by Students and Academics alike as a smash hit, a jubilation. There were, however, a few gremlins and glitches.

'Go on...I love hearing about those...!'

Poor Jon did have trouble with the language! Not entirely his fault. Many of the exchanges between Pelleas and Melisande turned out to be romantically trite and insipid. Jon did seem to be unfairly burdened with lines that Charles Boyer would have blushed to speak!

'Who the fuck can remember Charles Boyer?'

That poor Jon had a line finishing with the words "... the truth, Melisande, the truth". In spite of Jimmy's diligent coaching, Jon could not master the "th", so "de trut" was repeated ad infinitum, much to Jimmy's aggravation. After all, he was in charge of the translation!

'Poor bugger – that was one thing that was lost in translation!'

Half way through the run, Joan caught the mother n' father of all colds!

'Poor love, she seems to have a constant allergic reaction to the Drama!'

Ronnie, it was an incessant stream of water! At one juncture, the whole group, bar Jon, who was busy with a soliloquy somewhere stage right, was gathered together within the shadows; Timmy's lighting catching the guttering of make-believe candles. All at once, as we were closely huddled, Joan's rosy-red nose began to drip – copiously! It became profuse and plentiful until the floor beneath began to form into a noticeable puddle. In order to stem the snot, Joan began to make some disgusting, catarrhal-type sniffs and swallows, whereupon the rest of us went. We ended up in a tottering, quivering and convulsed gaggle. I could not behold the face of James! It was excruciating. Meantime, Jon tussled manfully on with "de trut", until the lights dimmed us, the rest of the group, into the shadow where we could lapse with a modicum of decorum and character incentive... which seemed to have slipped, disturbingly, in the midst of Joan's drain bursting...

'All you needed was a cloud of dry ice wafting around and you'd have been home and dry!'

All that aside, Ronnie, the spectacle in general was marvellously effective.

The decision to stage the Play in a series of fluid movements with all Actors on stage, worked remarkably well. It exploited us as an unbroken, faithful Ensemble of powerful Players. I will never forget it.

~

'You were half way through your Course...'

I know, Ronnie. My essay Grades had much improved, so I was holding my own on the Academic front. Constancy and perseverance went hand-in-hand with laughter, revelry and rave-ups.

'Not such a thing as raves in those days, pet...'

I keep forgetting how old I am, Ronnie!

'I don't!'

Chivalry was always your strong point, my darling. One thing for sure, we did not seem to draw breath. The days were full. John Harris was raring to go on 'Way of the World' and I was in awe of him.

'I'm not surprised. He was the one who suggested that your brain cells die off after the age of thirty!'

The Rehearsals were exacting; John's notes and approach, detailed and intellectual. Thank goodness, Jimmy was around, playing a leading Part and sashaying his bits. This time, he was a male Character, Mirabell, so there was no likelihood of a bare-booosomed teeter and swing.

The play, 'Way of the World', was Congreve's last Comedy and first performed in 1700. Again, Tim Reed was to be congratulated on his Design and re-creation of Setting and Conventions, with which Restoration Actors would have been familiar. In fact, it transpired that little furniture was used and the Actors remained on foot most of the time. There was a great use of Tableau and stylised patterns of movement. Timmy devised 'boxes' on either side of the stage. Moving shutters 'revealed' the characters, singly or in groups.

'Were you thus revealed in all your glory as Lady Wishfort – and, er, did she 'wish for it'!'

She did the way I played her, Ronnie! Lady Wishfort was an absolute spree, a prize, a jackpot. One remarkable line lives with me forever and I might add, would be entirely applicable now that I'm an old lady!'

'Go on… reveal all!'

Lady W. is found en tableau, with her Maid, mirror in hand. "Oh, I look like an old peeled wall!"

'Before the advent of Elizabeth Arden!'

The Play went ahead in March of that year. Melisande was barely out of the way, but I went on to master some of the most difficult dialogue I have ever encountered. It proved Congreve's genius as an observer and caricaturist of the foibles (in fact L.W's Maid was called Foible!) and fripperies of London's high society during the Restoration.

Susan as Lady Wishfort in 'Way of the World'

'I say, darling, all that Theory that Marjorie drilled you with all those years ago, must have become manna from heaven...'

It was the basis of all my Technique, Ronnie. From an early age, I had been Classically trained. Marjorie's vision had been propitious.

'Was Jessica there?'

Oh yes, Ronnie. Jessica was always there. She was very proud, I'm sure. I think she was enthralled with the University, the Gulb and all that it promised. She was greeted with affection by Students and Tutors alike. It formed a very different feature in her life. In return, whenever the Department chose the Ferguson Fawsitt as its venue for Staff Dinners, Jessica was on the front line to welcome and receive.

'Did she come alone to Plays?'

Yes, she did. It was her forte, her metier. Not everyone shares, or wishes to share such an 'idee fixe'...

'Eh?'

A preoccupation...

'You could have said that in the first place...stop showing off! So this interest was not Charlie or Nicky's cup of tea?'

They were very busy and needed to be on Fergie duty. I understood, Ronnie.

My Mother's immersion with my life in Theatre, engineered in part by herself, certainly formed a bond. It is easy to see, now, that my Father remained on the periphery. I empathized entirely with my Mother at that time; her needs and preferences became of prime, dominant importance. My Father, over the years, had been shut out. In no small way, my Mother had brain-washed. So, she took precedence. It was wrong. I was to think long and hard, in the years to come, when my Father's death brought about change of thought; a melancholy soul-searching. When I was weary of recrimination.

'Now then...don't get lachrymose...'

Now who's using big words!

'Well, sorry for yourself or weepy...that's what I meant!'

I didn't have time Ronnie. We were on the crest of a wave and getting ready for the next Production. This time it was to be another Satire, 'During the Interval' by Richard Cooper and set between the Wars; it concentrated on a super-idealism which appealed to the upper classes.

'Oh God....'

The characters, or caricatures, resembled Prime Ministers and notable personalities of the day. I was to play Lady Nuthatch who closely resembled Mrs. Simpson and portrayed as being on the brink of an affair with Chetwynd Minto, son and heir to Fortescue Minto, Lord Crossbill; hereby played by Anthony Minghella.

Susan & Tony Minghella in 'During the Interval'

'I can't keep up with the versatility!'

It was a bit of a romp, Ronnie. This was supposed to be part of the Summer vacation course and a lead up to the Theatre of Brecht in our Third Year.

The Costume Department found a wonderful vintage dress for me – black and purple crepe. I coveted that dress for evermore.

'Didn't they let you keep it?'

Alas, no. I have a feeling it was a treasured piece and irreplaceable.

'Bit like you, sweetheart…'

Thank you Ronnie.

We worked in the Gulb Theatre for several weeks during that holiday and as no one was in the building, we gave vent to gales of laughter, raucous behaviour and take-aways. The consequent aroma must have been quite nauseous. Late one afternoon and much to our horror, we noticed Don Roy framed in the entrance. It had been a tiresome day and we were ready for unwinding….! Also, Sandra could not be left at the Nursery during vacations, so, whoever was not on Stage, kept her amused. Chaos reigned. Don did not utter, but looked on in profound astonishment and beat a hasty retreat. "Bollocks! It was Herself!" remarked Jimmy.

No reprimand, however. I think Don realised that all had been in the interests of artistic furtherance. He did not interfere. After all, a large percentage of those Students involved were supposed to be Mature ones! Grown up!

'I reckon that, by then, he had come to be acquainted with your original or unwonted method of working! You always came up with the goods…'

~

Little holiday time was left after 'During the Interval'. We had pulled the Show out of the bag, as I suppose poor Don knew we would. The Play did much to launch us into the stringent and inflexible demands of our Final Year. We were to concentrate in depth on Bertolt Brecht's contribution to German Theatre.

This year we encountered a Lecturer we had not worked with before.

Tony Meech was a gentle, very humorous man who wore incredibly tight-fitting jeans!

'What a way to remember an Academic Man of Letters!'

Poor Tony, soon to be known as Mary Meech by the ubiquitous Jimmy, became a firm friend. I think he really understood the Second Year Specials!

'That must have been an achievement in itself!'

We faced a difficult year. Academia really took charge. By then, I had developed an efficient and productive method of study. Much time was spent at the crack of dawn – learning, re-learning, revising, recording, making notes, essays and constant assimilation of fact. Into this farrago, this medley, Mary Meech dropped Brecht's second play: 'Drums in the Night'. It was to be part of the Group's Third Year assessment; adapted and Rehearsed by the increasingly adroit and ingenious Tony Minghella.

All were involved. As ever, we were lucky to have back-up from the Joints. This time, a hugely able Musician, Gary Yershon came on the scene.

'Didn't he, many years later, go on to do great things?'

He did Ronnie. Gary, like Tony, was a lovely man.

Much to everyone's amusement and to my chagrin, I was cast as Augusta.

'Why were you mortified?'

She happened to be a bloody prostitute and at the mercy of the sexy Joe Richards!'

'Inspired Casting!'

The Production photographs proved just how much I had caught the flavour of the moment!

'Would the word 'tart' be appropriate?'

I was a Brechtian tart! All in the name of Work in Progress and scholarly calling!

'What did Jessica think to that?'

To her, it didn't matter – because I was an Actress. Actresses have to do those things in Plays....not in real life! My Mother could be extremely broad-minded when she wanted to be.

Thereby, in December 1974, at the onset of our last Gulbenkian year, Tony Minghella's Brechtian enterprise played to packed houses. Tony Meech watched over the project with the help of yet another newcomer to our band of Lecturers – a Bob Cheesemond, who sported an even-tighter pair of jeans!

'These must have drawn comment from James Swan?'

Jimmy was never known to let such allurement go by and christened him Roberta Cheesemond!

~

Michael Walton, a senior Lecturer in the Drama Department, presided over much of that Brechtian period of our study. He was learned, erudite; meticulous in approach and manner. A stern expression could give way to radiant smiles. In that moment, his face was transformed. Slowly, I overcame a lurking reticence whenever our paths crossed.

'Why?'

I kept thinking of my cells dropping off!

'Hell's teeth!'

One day, my neurosis went up a notch when he asked me to remain behind after a Lecture!

'Oh no! Order marks a go-go!'

I found myself rooted to the spot as Mike (I always felt I should address him as 'Mr.Walton') outlined his purpose...

'I trust it was honourable?'

He explained that he had always wished to mount...

'I knew it!'

give over, Ronnie...he had wished to mount a Production of Durrenmatt's 'The Visit' but had been unable to do so because there had never been a Student in the Department old enough to take the leading part!

'Was he in the habit of giving back-handed compliments? Well...I know what's coming!'

There and then, I was invited to play Clare Zachanassian, a woman of advancing years, in a new adaptation by Tony Meech. I did not know the Play, needless to say! It was a magnificent story, a tale of revenge taken to extremes and so unusual it almost defies logic. The scene is set in a nondescript Central European town in the grip of economic depression. When a native of the Town, a very rich old lady (Me!).....

'Type cast, except for being rich!'

...revisits the place of her birth, the townsfolk set out to extract money from her. She promises a vast sum on condition that they kill the man who seduced her many years earlier and left her with a child.

'The cad! Yes, and...you always stop when it's exciting...'

They refuse to sink to such an inhuman act, but gradually and almost imperceptibly, the whole Town gives way to the lure of wealth...

'Filthy lucre!'

...and carries out the Lady's gruesome conditions. Of course, Brecht's macabre theme, on a deeper level, points to the kind of conflict between moral and material values which beset society.

'Sue, what a part!'

Well, you can imagine, Ronnie, I was flabbergasted.

'Overwhelmed and overcome....!'

The Cast was enormous...

'Darling, all those Townspeople....poor little buggers....!'

'The Visit' was to open at the Gulb on 3rd March and run for a week. Thank God I would have the Christmas Vac to break the back of the lines. Needless to say, there were a lot of them!

'I have every faith in your memory – it's like Methuselah's!'

Timmy was, as had come to be expected, crowned with the title of 'Lighting Design and Design Supervision'. Jimmy took on Publicity with great aplomb, although he was mid-Rehearsal for his own Student-led Production of 'The Maids' by Jean Genet. 'The Visit' was a mammoth undertaking and again backed by a multitude of Joint Drama Students. After, many became lasting friends.

'When did you start, darling?'

Mike went into Rehearsal towards the end of that Autumn Term 1974. He made the Gulbenkian Stage as large as the building would allow. He dispensed with wings and backcloths to form an Acting area in the middle of the Theatre and an expansive darkened border, the perimeter, where costumes, the fearless and heroic Ruth Stuckey needle and thread in hand, props and Off-Stage Actors were clearly visible.

'Authentic Brechtian practice and protocol...now, how easy was that to work?'

Off-Stage boundaries were 'frozen' when the Acting area was lit and Scenes were taking place. They took life between clips and segments.

Claire Zachanassian was a complicated, bizarre woman. Not only was she timeworn and decrepit, she was crippled and infirm...

'Poor old bugger... how flattering of Mr. Walton to cast you!'

I'll dismiss that comment with the contempt it deserves. In the solitude of my Ferguson Fawsitt boudoir, I contemplated how the bloody hell I was going to convey all this! I take my place in a breed of Actresses who find a particular trait or quirk applicable and build the rest of the persona upon that.

'Yes, Dora Bryan used her Character's shoes...'

I searched for Claire's voice.

'Dicey, for your own voice is light...I hesitate to say girlish! One must give credence where it's due!'

Richard Williams & Susan as Clare Zachanassian 'The Visit'

You're right though, Ronnie. On instinct, I knew I needed to lower it a few octaves...so, I grappled for ages, knowing that this was the key, the peg on which I needed to hang everything else. Soon, I resembled a woman who was in the habit of smoking sixty fags a day and imitating Paul Robson singing 'Ole Man River'!

'Incidentally, were you still smoking?'

I was, Ronnie...the amount fluctuated, depending on how much stress I was enduring at the time! I had graduated, however, from Woodbines to Benson & Hedges tipped!

When I first experimented and put Claire's voice to the test in Rehearsal, there was an eerie silence before Mike said "Well, where did that come from?" Interestingly, a sentiment also expressed by Tony Minghella as he watched this metamorphosis from the Audience on the First Night. In Performance, Claire's method of transport was by sedan chair!

'Surely no poor darlings Auditioned for lifting!'

Perhaps a bit of press-ganging went on there! Two worthy Joints stepped into the breach; servants to Claire and named Roby and Toby.

'Sounds like a pair of Chihuahuas!'

Not every Artiste gets the opportunity to make a first entrance hoisted aloft by two burly henchmen; veiled, in full bridal dress and looking like a Brechtian Miss Havisham!

'Bless that bairn!'

I was totally engrossed, rapt in the invention; the concept of Claire. She monopolized my Christmas vacation and dominated the opening weeks of the Spring Term 1975.

Again, we played to overflowing houses and the vibrant response we received inundated the Gulb. Mike Walton was overjoyed....

'Do you think you came up to his expectations? After all, you were a very old Mature Student – he'd been waiting for you for years!'

I received a card from Mike on the closing night. It read: 'You were beautiful, Klari.....'

'My darling, that's all you needed to know....'

~

Three more months! That was all that remained of my Specials Course! Where had the time gone! The weeks that followed the triumphant 'Visit' were spent being deeply engrossed in...

'What do I do next?'

Quite, Ronnie. This proud, victorious catalogue of events had brought me to yet another crossroads. This incredible collaboration, focussed on encounter, trial and tests, had provided the transition between Teaching and dipping one's toe into another world; the Theatrical world where uncertainty, financial irregularity and fate, chance or the haphazard, ruled supreme. It was a gamble.

'I suspect you had made up your mind!'

The Academic work was all encompassing in the weeks that followed. I had re-taken History of Art and much to Betty Bernasconi's delight, Jon and I vindicated ourselves. We passed muster – and the exam!

The Course demanded one more practical Assessment. Each Special was to Direct a play by Harold Pinter!

'Not a walk in the Park, my darling…'

I did freak at first, Ronnie, but took myself off to the Library pretty quick…. and…came upon a little-known One Act Piece called 'Landscape'. I had a shrewd guess that it would be an unusual and compelling choice. Set in a farm-house kitchen, two Characters talk of their Marriage; they sit in isolated pools of late-evening sunlight on either side of the Stage. Their conversation is scattered, disconnected. The poetic prose of the dialogue complements a momentous depth of feeling. On first reading, I was hooked on the Play's lyrical possibilities.

During 'The Visit' Rehearsals, I came to know a couple of Welsh Joint Students: Wyndham Perkins and Pippa Thomas. Both had been involved in several Gulb shows. Wyndam reminded me of a very young Richard Harris, complete with beard!

'Oh Sue…two Welsh voices…wonderful…'

Ronnie, those voices were out of this world. I could hear the cadence in my head; the lilt and pulse of the language. They were delighted when I asked them take on the Pinter play. As with everything I have directed, I could visualise the finished composition; the sound, colour, mental picture and the image.

Wyndam and Pippa were profoundly moving. Accomplished Actors, they endowed the delicate, dreamy and searching play with unforgettable intuition and beauty.

'The language of the Welsh is a poetic illusion in itself… seductive, hypnotic…'

Wyndam and Pippa made a magnetic pair. Both had charisma and drawing power; an entrancing, alluring presence.

'How did you stage it?'

I used Pinter's placing of two pools of light and within each, created symbolic kitchen ambience; brass and copper kettles, two rocking chairs, knitting for Pippa and a pipe for Wyndam. Tim Reed came up with firelight warmth which bathed the characters in homeliness and contentment. Only the dialogue disclosed and laid bare the light and shade of a Marriage.

'You were thrilled with it, weren't you?'

I am reminded of that play, Ronnie, whenever I open a carved wooden trinket box which Wyndam and Pippa gave to me when the play closed. It represents friendship, sensitivity and the Theatrical bravura of two very young people.

'One does not forget....'

~

Practical Assessments were now finished. All that remained were the Final Written Examinations.

The Specials did not see much of each other over the coming days. They were incarcerated, holed up and shackled to notes, play texts, essays and innumerable cups of coffee. All had different methods of study. Jimmy could work until the early hours. My day started at 5.30 a.m. when all was still and the air was fresh. I devised a regular, systematic and structured pattern of study. There was an element of risk involved. I hoped and prayed that I was on the right track.

'How petal?'

I speculated, took a chance on certain areas of study coming up and planned how I would answer. By the time

I'd finished, I knew them backwards. After that, it would be...

'Fingers crossed?'

On the rare occasions when we got together, there was much chat about Grades. We were all hopeful, but in the main I knew I would be thrilled, satisfied and astounded just to pass!

'Darling, what was it like? Go on...don't stop there!'

Ronnie, you'll hardly believe this, but I made it! I was awarded a B.A. Special (Hons.) Drama 2.1 Degree!!

'Darling....I expect that, for once, you were speechless!'

All the Specials passed. Jimmy also got a 2.1 and of course the brilliant Tony came away with a First, as did Josephine!

'So, was that it – after three wonderful years, did you all go your separate ways?'

Well, almost Ronnie. Before that painful parting, however, Tony Minghella tendered a Swansong for contemplation. It was to be something that was quite out of the ordinary; for me, so bold and brazen that I never thought I could be part of it.

'I'm on the edge of my seat!'

Tony's farewell Piece was to be entitled 'Hull University Department of Drama Green Room Club Production of 'Mobius the Stripper'!!' The Musical Play was based on a short story of the same name by Gabriel Josipovici. The story was part of a collection which won the Somerset Maughan Award for 1975. Set in a seedy Soho Strip Club, the tale centres around the lives of both male and female Strip Artists. Having secured kind permission from Mr. Josipovici, Tony had written Dialogue and Music for the Dramatisation.

The Production was scheduled to go ahead in the middle of June 1975 and staged at the Gulbenkian before

Susan as Beaujolais Rose in 'Mobius the Stripper'

moving to the Humberside Theatre, Spring Street, Hull for a further week.

'I would love to have been a fly on the wall when you broached this to Jessica!!'

She never batted an eyelid, Ronnie! This was Theatre!! All part of what a girl does – for Theatre!

'You are evil – I love it!'

Tony cast me in what proved to be one of the most renowned Theatrical Performances of my career. Tony's awareness, his innate recognition of whatever ability I possessed, was a consummate endowment. Consequently, his fashioning, his moulding of my Beaujolais Rose was phenomenal.

'Sue, what was she like?'

Needless to say, Rose was getting on; a most definite has-been. Her story was a sad, reflective resume of a rough, abused existence. Tony's plaintive, soulful Score was the accompanying embodiment of Rose's life and background. Her final, haunting Song beginning "Beaujolais Rose, I take of my clothes...." brought rapturous applause at each staging.

'Who played Mobius?'

Why Jimmy of course. He was absolutely superb; poignant, tragic, heartbreaking.

Some Joint Students took part and the Technical/ Musical Crew had their work cut out mastering this very detailed, ambitious presentation. Once more, Gary Yershon led a striking team.

'How did you manage the steamy, raunchy environment?'

Very easily Ronnie! Once we got the hang of upfront, open and unreserved expression, we sensed an epoch making release of doing something so sensual and erotic! Guess where we Rehearsed?

'Not, I hope, in some seedy Hull joint?'

Brace yourself, Ronnie! The University's Catholic Chaplaincy!

'You Specials had no shame!'

Tony needed us to prepare for taking off our clothes – down to underwear I hasten to add – in a private venue. This hallowed place was the only one on offer that Saturday afternoon. It's a wonder that we were not investigated, for noise reached manifold decibels. Jimmy was largely responsible for this racket and ballyhoo: "Eh, Betty, me Mam never thought a girl like me would stoop to this! I'm not shushing my bare bits till the First Night!"

In point of fact, none of us shushed our bare bits on the Night. The girls, Beaujolais Rose, Juicy Lucy and

The Duchess sported bra, pants, suspenders and black stockings....

'Hell's teeth...that was more erotic and lascivious that being starkers!'

We began one of the songs clad in Kimonos and brandishing fans! My outfit was really hideous. Ruth Stuckey had gone to town, literally, and found an emerald green frilled blouse, skin-tight black slit skirt, a fun-fur collared coat, platform shoes and a moth-eaten brown wig. Oh Ronnie, it was all such wonderful fun! Wonderful, shocking fun!

Opening Night at the Gulbenkian Theatre was packed out. Audiences soared.

We took the Show on to the Humberside Theatre, where again we played to houses bursting at the seams. This Musical Play attracted waves of attention and queues formed outside and down the street. Extra Performances had to be arranged! Jimmy said, wickedly, that he had observed several prurient-looking, lewd men in raincoats!

'I hope they employed heavies to see you home!'

Oh Ronnie, what an absolutely dazzling, divine way to bring one's University career to a close! 'Mobius' had been a succès de scandale!

~

So, my darling Ronnie, that was it. Once more, I was in limbo, a strange rudderless place....The Second Year Specials were dispersed, disbanded. It was over. I was lonely....incredibly lonely. Work, three years of very hard, animated, inspiriting work, had been a substitute for so many things. My life was unbalanced, one dimensional....

'How so, flower?'

No real plan was in place. I had marked time. No partner, no lover sustained me. I was alone. Work had been the surrogate, the replacement...I could have drifted...but I did not...all that remained was a driving force...

'Now come on...I know you...I have no doubt that you sashayed your bits pretty quick!'

I did, Ronnie. One more event tied me to Hull University. The Graduation Ceremony was to be held in the Hull City Hall on Saturday, 12 July 1975.

My whole Family attended. It was a proud day. It seemed to be a very significant, crucial day for Charlie. I was close to my Daddy that day...

~

The day after Graduation, I wrote several letters to Regional Repertory Companies, applying for an Audition. The decision had been made....there was no looking back....

'Well pet, God Speed! You were off!'

I was scared, Ronnie. I had no idea what to expect. I had no experience other than that acquired in my beloved Gulbenkian Theatre. I was armed only with potential, proficiency, courage and the steadfast belief that others had in me...

'You would be helped....'

The Specials may have been displaced and divided, but threads of phone conversation kept us together. Joan married Jim Lambert, the Gulb's Lighting Technician, Jimmy took on Front-of-House Management at Oxford Playhouse and Tony remained in the Drama Department as Lecturer no less....

Timmy went on to do wondrous things in Lighting Design, Josephine took on a post at Dartford College and Mac married fellow Joint Drama Student, Sheila. Jon was somewhat uncommunicative and we didn't hear from him for some time. We did discover, much later, that he had, presumably, recovered from his perplexing trial-by-

Jimmy and moved on to accomplish feats of Dramatic excellence back in Iceland! No doubt he now understood the language!

'Not that he would need it in Reykjavic!'

I played the waiting game. As usual, I filled in with work at the Ferguson Fawsitt. I was diverted.

'How had your Mother reacted? I reckon there was much support in favour of your decision to move on?'

Unanimous Ronnie. The fruits of one's labour, I suppose. She was full of encouraging comment: "Oh you'll be all right...you'll be fine once you've settled in".

In point of fact, my Mother had absolutely no idea whether or not I would be all right! She had no conception of what the world of Theatre was like. She was not the one who was jumping in at the deep end! I was thirty-five years old, green and afraid.

'Age don't banish fear, petal...but...one thing was for sure, someone somewhere had your back....'

I received two phone calls. The first from the Belgrade Theatre, Coventry and the second from The Library Theatre, Manchester. Both were offering Auditions.

I was asked to appear before the Artistic Director of the Belgrade, armed with a Shakespearian Piece and an extract from a Modern Play. To cap all, I would be requested to sing! The Audition was to be held in Soho!!

Manchester issued the same invitation but in a much more convenient venue! That was to be before David Scase, Artistic Director based at the Library Theatre in the Central Library building.

'What did I tell you? Someone had you by the hand....'

At that crucial turning point in my life, I had no idea that, in the not too distant future, three of my beloved friends – Jimmy, Mac and Tony – would die at a very early age. Sometimes, it is fortunate that the future is shrouded in mystery....

'Has it occurred to you, my darling, that, in the years to come, it may have been they who had you by the hand?'

THE THEATRE

1975 – 1979 The First Years

'I love Acting. It's so much more real than life'

(Oscar Wilde)

I had had some Production photographs taken after Guildhall. I squandered all my hard-earned holiday job money on the panache of a Professional Theatrical photographer, John Vickers of London. Those finished, superior pictures which expressed so gracefully my characteristic features, became a trademark; a stamp of individuality and potential.

'In those days, Photographs went a long way towards being called for Audition..'

I'm sure I owe John Vickers commission! The Belgrade Theatre and Manchester's Library Theatre both received those Photographs.

Soon, I was aboard the train for King's Cross and Soho!

'I hope you weren't wearing anything too revealing!'

Well, Ronnie, Beaujolais Rose was part of my Audition Repertoire that day but I did not wear Ruth Stuckey's carefully-chosen Costume!

'Now, what extracts had you chosen?'

I decided to do the Duologue between Titania and Bottom, playing both parts, then something short from Noel Coward.

Audition Photos

'Tell me what you wore..'

I wore a full-length and lustrously-patterned Indian dress complete with beads and shush...

'Ethnic...very fashionable then...'

I was shaking with nerves, Ronnie, as I made my way along the narrow, bustling backstreet of Soho. This was an utterly alien, seemingly hostile environment and I thought longingly of my Interview with Bill, long ago; so sheltered, protected and sequestered. What the hell was I doing here, in the heart of Soho, about to sing Beaujolais Rose's Stripper song for my supper!

'The Lord knew what he was doing....'

I hoped so, Ronnie. The Audition room was approached by a winding staircase and seemed to be above a Bookie's. It was small. Three men rose to their feet as I approached. They introduced themselves as: Artistic Director – Ed Thomason, Assistant Director – Jon Tarlton, and Peter Skellern – Singer/Composer.

'Peter Skellern – didn't he come up with that Chart-topper 'You're a Lady..'

The very same Ronnie.

They seemed very pleasant and invited me to start with the Shakespeare.

I did and you could have heard a pin drop. I carried on with the Coward and you could have heard a pin drop. It was all a bit silent and I experienced a certain sense of foreboding....

'Go on...go on...'

Peter Skellern asked if I required any accompaniment for my Musical choice. It was then that I noticed a Chap peering from behind a piano in the corner. His eyes opened a little wider when I said "No, I can sing on my own, thank you".

So, I did. By then, the afternoon sun was streaking across the floor. It threw shadows and pockets of darkness here and there. Looking back, I suspect I couldn't have chosen a more timely or befitting frame for Beaujolais Rose. As I finished the closing notes, there was an even longer silence, broken by Peter Skellern, who said: "Who composed that beautiful song?"

'"Anthony Minghella" – she said with pride!'

Dear Tony. What flair, what genius....how lucky I was to have known Tony.

'Some things are meant to be at certain times in our life. That was one of them...'

It was time to leave. Ed Thomason announced: "Susan, please will you let us know at once if you receive an offer from another Company".

'Ah, they were with you, petal. That's a classic request if they're thinking seriously about taking you on'.

It was a relieved, but excited, journey home. I knew Mum would be waiting, breathlessly, for news and I looked forward to the comfort of sitting in The Corner once more, armed with a Gin n' Tonic and safe, while watching Dina crack the whip! What a tumultuous life it had become....

'Now, go on...tell me all about Manchester!'

It was a simple train trip across the Pennines to Piccadilly Station. The Library Theatre building was situated in the City Centre and was of rotunda shape, complete with dome.

'I'm rotunda shape...but – not complete with dome!'

Thank you Ronnie. It was quite a trek and I made my way through some very striking shopping arcades, certainly surpassing and a cut above those in poor old Hull. In the days before the Humber Bridge came into being, hardly anyone visited Hull unless they had a definite purpose in mind. One omnipotent Actress was heard to exclaim: "Oh

God, I always feel as if I'm going to fall over the edge if I go there!"

'Silly cow!'

The Library Theatre was situated in the Basement of the building and was semicircular in shape. The seating rose in tiers from the Stage area, also half of a circle with backdrop and wings.

David Scase and his Associate Director, Howard Lloyd-Lewis, were there to greet me. David reminded me of the Actor James Robertson Justice. He was bearded, thickset, smiling, jolly and thoroughly nice. Howard L.L. was also bearded; his being a luxuriant, black full-set. David was of stocky build while Howard towered above me. When he laughed, frequently, the sound was reminiscent of a fairytale giant.

'How did they compare with the Belgrade Directors?'

No comparison really, Ronnie. Here were two sound, hardy, jocular and lusty fellows who possessed very roisterous laughter and a pragmatic, down-to-earth sense of humour. The Belgrade men were remote, cool and a shade haughty.

'Had you got the feeling they were not Theatre men?'

Well, in contrast, I identified at once with David and Howard. They were hearty and warm. I was instantly at home and relaxed with them.

'Not intellectuals who sat behind the desk?'

Nail on the head, as usual Ronnie!

I was much more at ease this time and the Pieces went well. Again, there was a noticeable silence when I'd finished. "Where did that wonderful song come from?" enquired David.

'I hope you sent messages to Tony afterwards!'

Of course Ronnie. Again, I was asked to inform the Library at once if I received an offer from another Company!

'Darling, it looked as though you were going to be placed in the rare position of being able to choose!'

I didn't take it in at the time Ronnie. I suppose I was punch drunk and certainly thrown by the whole experience; it was curiouser and curiouser.

'Don't forget, petal, you had rocketed yourself into a completely untried way of life. There was bound to be psychological reaction....I'm such a wise old bugger – I surprise myself. Now, go on...I bet you ended up getting offers from them both!'

I did, Ronnie. I did. The only difference was that the Belgrade offered Play-as-Cast only, whereas the Library wanted me to Assistant Stage Manage as well as Play-as-Cast. Added to that, there was a salary difference.

'Ah Ha! Well, pet, that is always important...go on, how much?'

There was a fiver in it. Belgrade came up with £35 a week and Manchester £30.

'Now, it occurs to me, being such a wise old bugger, were you settling for extra cash as opposed to the possibility of emotional comfort, fun and ordinariness, which the likes of David Scase could put before you?'

It's easy to be wise after the event, Ronnie. All will be revealed! I had to chalk the following events up to experience.

'Oh eck!'

The Belgrade Theatre of Coventry did have an added draw. It was in possession of Theatre Flats. These were set aside for Actors, Lighting Technicians, Stage Management and Set Designers.

'Were you keen to live alone?'

Stop jumping the gun Ronnie...being alone had not really taken on the importance it should have done.

'I would have thought it would have been top of your list! Homesickness and all that....'

All I can say is that at the time it seemed to be so convenient.

'Oh yes, go on.....'

I accepted the Belgrade.

'Hmn...'

David Scase, I think, was disappointed. When he phoned with his proposal, he went on to say, "Well, Susan, please let me know immediately when you are free, or, when your present Contract comes to a close".

'Bloody 'ell, Sue...I hope you wrote that in your Diary!'

~

The Belgrade season began in September 1975. I was awarded a Theatre flat and asked to report for Rehearsal at the end of August. Of course the news of such an achievement was thrilling. There was excitement on all levels. Mum was delighted, Jimmy was delighted, as were all my Pals at the University and Ferguson Fawsitt....

'You were delighted, weren't you darling?'

Oh yes, Ronnie, of course I was....

'I know Susie so well....there's a but coming...'

Ronnie, darling Ronnie, I was frightened to death.

It was at this junction that Alex Simpson and his loveable partner Kevin intervened with plans for action. In no circumstances were they willing to allow me to make the Coventry switch alone. They would offer unconditional assistance to up sticks!

'Now, I'm trying to keep up....was this the Alex a la 'Student Prince'?

The very same, Ronnie. Of course I had known Alex, a dear friend, for some time. He was the ultimate in optimism. No clouds messed up Alex's horizon.

'Needless to say, he was just what the Doctor ordered..'

Kevin was an even greater boost to my rather doleful mood. Kevin giggled most of the time.....he giggled when

I was reticent and withdrawn...he giggled when Alex dropped the cases and he giggled when it rained! Kevin had a chirpy, ebullient attitude to life. His voice was light, gentle, even girlie, but his six-pack physique made a nonsense of any apparent weakness. Kevin was a very good-looking young man, much younger than Alex who, in turn, didn't giggle quite so much. When he did, however, all in proximity knew about it.

'Why?'

Alex had a high-pitched cackle; no other word for it. That cackle could make itself heard in a full-house Matinee at Hull's New; a Theatre that could seat a couple of thousand! One became accustomed to astonished, flabbergasted stares. All this made for an eventful evening out! I loved them both...

'Sounds like that love was reciprocated a thousand fold...'

I'm sure it was Ronnie. There are some people to whom you can trust yourself, no matter what. Alex and Kevin will always be remembered as the archetypal Guardian Angels.

I did not receive any further communication from the Belgrade Theatre; no Cast List, no Call Sheet and more importantly, no indication of how I was to be cast.

'Lackadaisical, lazy buggers...'

Mum decided that she would help to mastermind the whole junta.

'I'd like to bet that Alex and Kevin managed her very well!'

To the manner born, Ronnie.

So, one sunny Summer day in August I was bound for the unknown. Meantime, Daddy had disappeared into Beverley that same lunchtime, just before my departure. When he returned, he pressed a small box into my hand. Inside, glistened a very beautiful amber-stoned ring which he had chosen himself.

"Good Luck, love," Daddy whispered. I thought my heart would break. I loved him very much. It is only now, when I am old and it is too late, that I wish he could hear me say "I love you too".

'Oh Susie, he hears you.....'

~

The Autumn Season at the Belgrade was to open with Shakespeare's 'The Merchant of Venice'.

'And that was as much information as you received?'

Yes, Ronnie.

It was a long journey to Coventry. Most of the time, silence pervaded.

The Boys did their best to instil some nonsensical chin-wags and tete-a-tetes but I found it difficult to respond with any familiar, witty banter. All was strange; repartee was laboured and contrived. I felt as if I was on a cliff edge...just waiting to jump. I longed to hear that familiar voice saying: "Eh Betty, pet, we miss you!"

The car was loaded to the gills with my belongings: clothes, kitchen utensils, books, make-up and a bottle of Gin. Mum made a point of packing that! All could be solved with a few slurps of the hard stuff!

'Bless....I daresay she was as bewildered and bereft as you, petal'.

I'm sure that was true, Ronnie. Mum was never known to hide her feelings. Every trip from home, or the nest....

'Now then....'

...would be punctuated with the sight of a tear-stained face at the window.

So, it was always an effort to bounce with rapt anticipation.

The Belgrade was situated in the heart of Coventry and approached from the main High Street. At that point,

I did not take in much of the City tenor or complexion. We arrived late afternoon. The Flat in question was on the first floor of the Theatre complex and above a row of shops overlooking the street. Several Apartments were accessed by a narrow flight of dark, concrete steps at the rear of the Theatre building, which opened out on to a railed pathway serving each residence. I had been advised that keys could be collected from whoever was to be my next door neighbour. He turned out to be Terry Parsons, the Designer.

'So that was it? You stepped over the threshold of what was to be your home for some time....I won't ask you how you felt...I know!'

The Flat was really quite well proportioned and consisted of a kitchen near the front door opening on to bedroom, bathroom and sitting-room.

'As Theatre digs go, darling....five star!

I think we were all impressed, Ronnie. Mum, nevertheless, delivered one of her timeless, classic deductions and said: "Oh well, it's not what you're used to!"

'And that was the proverbial that!'

Couldn't have put it better myself, Ronnie. Never mind, all hands were put to the wheel. Before long, my goods and chattels were in place and it was time to part. I was trembling inside, Kevin started to giggle and Alex said, "Oh well, sweetheart....time to..."

'Gather your bits?'

Quite, Ronnie. I took one look at this new home and proclaimed, "I'm coming back with you!" Mum looked startled, Alex said "But....how will you get back in time for Rehearsal tomorrow?" and Kevin giggled.

"On the train," said I. "I'll do it..."

'Dear God, Alice...'

So, I travelled all the way home to my beloved Yorkshire for one more night! My Father, Nick and all at the Fergie, could not believe their eyes!

'Were there hugs all round?'

You bet, Ronnie. I downed a few Gins, slept fairly well and boarded the Coventry-bound train at the crack of dawn the following morning. In many ways, this unexpected detour and circuitous route to my destination, was beneficial for I found my way, unaided, to the Theatre, let myself into the Flat, got my bearings and reported for duty.

The Theatre was buzzing with people. A very friendly young man came along, introduced himself as Will Thompson and added that he had come looking for me the previous evening, thinking I would be his Flat neighbour! I was too embarrassed to confess that I had hot-footed it home and felt too lonely to be on my own!

'He might have jumped to the conclusion that you were a shade odd!'

That's what I was afraid of, Ronnie. He'd have been right!

'Now, how old were you Susanne Ubble?'

Advancing years do not solve the problem of loneliness. It hits us in the most unexpected ways, so do not mock!'

'I was lonely if you weren't there. Now come on.... what happened next?'

The obliging Will took me on a journey of exploration. I found out where the Backstage areas were, Rehearsal Room, Calls Notice Board and Greenroom. He was so helpful.

'So you found your Calls?'

There was a Cast List for 'Merchant' and my name was on it, but no Character!

'No!'

There was a Readover scheduled for that afternoon. The Cast List was impressive. I was in the company, it seemed, of some notable Theatrical personages!

'Hmn, I've 'eard it all before!'

Linda Thorson of 'Avengers' fame was to play Portia; Geraldine James (then an unknown ingenue) Jessica; Ian Talbot from Regents Park Open-Air Theatre, Gratiano and William Gaunt from TV's 'The Champions', Antonio.

'And....Susanne Ubble, the most notorious of all... now come on, no more name dropping....incidentally, Ian Talbot was a great mate of mine, but long before I met you...'

I attended for the Readover. No one said a word. Ed Thomason kept a low profile...

'What I said...from behind the desk?'

How did you guess, Ronnie. When reading was finished, I thought I'd better find out what was what. I found Ed and asked him if I was in the right place! With that, he seemed to get a grip and went into some very vague explanation.

'Nothing surprises me about these people...'

"Oh, er, something you did in your Audition gave us an idea. When you played both Titania and Bottom, we thought it would be most interesting to introduce a Jester for Portia. A sort of Hermaphrodite figure..."

'Oh Eck!'

"We have decided to begin the play with a Musical Introduction to all the main Characters. This will be sung by the Jester and this same Jester will appear in all the Belmont scenes as Portia's servant. Consequently, all the Casket scenes will be set to music and sung."

'Were you about to say, what the blazes has this got to do with me!'

I was too inhibited to put it quite like that Ronnie, but yes...I found it all rather alarming.

'I think I can guess at his bolt from the blue!'

"We would like you to play the Jester, Sue. George Fenton will be writing the Music and as soon as the Score is in place, we'll call you!"

'What were you supposed to do in the meantime? Ha! Bloody Directors! There again, in all fairness, darling, had it occurred to you that they were paying a a compliment? To base something so significant on an Audition performance, was a risk. They must have had great faith in you.'

No Ronnie, that didn't cross my mind. All I was concerned about was being able to pull it off! I think the rest of the Company were totally disbelieving and not a little scornful....

' I reckon that they did away with the idea. One hears of Shakespeare being buggered about, but surely, in their snotty opinion, this was beyond the pale...eh?'

So, for the first week of Rehearsals I was cast adrift. George Fenton did not appear with my Music; I was redundant for the time being. I was not called.

One would imagine that Theatre Flats could be a hive of harmony, congeniality and togetherness; a fraternity of like-mindedness and amity.

'I think you're going to say you were lonely...I could have foreseen that..

In retrospect, which as you know is always a bloody nuisance, I think you may have been much happier in good old Theatre Digs, where some jolly Landlady would have mothered you.'

Hindsight, Ronnie, is a wonderful thing...but yes, I think you were absolutely right. The Flat, although comfortable, was the loneliest four walls I have ever known. Actors occupied other flats, but no one seemed to offer any companionship; no one congregated. Alone, I spent hour after hour exploring the streets of Coventry.

'I guess the rest of the Company were called for Rehearsal?'

True Ronnie and added to that, many lived in London which was within commuting distance. A short train trip took them home.

Coventry appeared to be a rather soulless place. The City had suffered terribly during the War and I wondered if it had ever picked up. The famous Cathedral was impressive, but, having peered into every corner of it on my solitary visits, I would not bother if I never saw it again. Shopping Malls were prosaic, banal and commonplace. Poor Coventry, it was trying hard, but without much success I fear.

I came to the conclusion that hiring a Television would be a good idea.

I made the necessary enquiries only to discover that the Belgrade building was not furnished with appropriate aerials. So that was another blind alley.

'Now then, don't give in.....what helped you through pet?'

Phoning home, most of the time, I'm ashamed to say. I think that even if I'd been working all hours God sends, I would still have called home. I came to realise how emotionally dependent I was on hearing my Mother's voice. That link was my salvation at the time, but it troubled me to know that I was well and truly needy and over-reliant. It was not healthy or benign.

'One or two things had somewhat backfired on Jessica, hadn't they? Do you think she ever recognised her culpability?'

I'm sure that my restless unhappiness unsettled Mum, but, strangely, while I gathered strength and championship from her, I could function in this foreign, contrary land; in return, she was sustained. To all onlookers, I have no doubt that I appeared to be certain, secure and self-assured.

'The Swan gliding by, feet paddling frantically below...'

It occurs to me now, when I have time to think on such quandaries, that power wielded by Parents is intractable. They hold a warrant to dominate. How easy it is for them to withhold favours if one steps out of line. The Child looks for emotional approbation and praise. There is a deep and lasting need embedded in the search for approval, goodwill and espousal. My Mother was a past master at exerting power, but its hold was subtle, almost Machiavellian.

'Did it ever cease to be?'

Oh yes Ronnie. Just before I met you. I was helped to sever those strings, but I don't think my Mother ever recovered or wholly forgave me or my aide.

'How then did you find the courage and wherewithal to do the things you did?'

Knowing that my Mother was my sponsor, I could forge ahead with guts that came from an obscure place beyond my ken. That is how I faced melancholy and heartache. I was following the permitted mandate. Jessica acknowledged my achievements with pride. They enriched her own lonely and unfulfilled being. Mum's chosen resume or synopsis of her life was summed up in the exposition: "I'm so sad...." She often remarked on how many others had noticed this sadness, so evident in photographs and pictures.

'True. Don't you remember I had picked it up on her Wedding photos?'

Sadly, I could do nothing about that. I drew a curtain over it. But...it was sad, terribly sad...

'So, when were you eventually called for Rehearsal?'

About the second week in, Ronnie. I'd managed short intervals at home, so felt fortified for whatever may come to pass. Weekends in Coventry were particularly bleak and even though getting away from it all involved Saturday to get there and Sunday to get back, the few short hours of respite were worth the aggravation of travel.

I was closely teamed with Linda Thorson at Rehearsal. She was an interesting woman who sported much varied and costly kit . Here, I came upon green nail varnish for the first time! Linda's hands were expressive. She was in the habit of flinging them about at any given time, so one couldn't help but notice those phantom, eerie extremities. Linda was bold. Her stare was bold. She was tall, angular; it wasn't until the First Night of 'Merchant' that I saw her in slightly different light for she was transformed by a baby blonde, bobbed wig! She regarded me with some incredulity and not a little wariness or scepticism.

'Perhaps your Jester put the shits up her!'

Linda travelled from London daily and to this apprehensive Yorkshire Lass, she represented browbeating pressure; each day we were treated to contrasting, very lavish, extravagant ensembles, typical of a Bond Street fashion-plate of the mid-Seventies.

'Did you think she was going to launch, Kung Fu, over Ed Thomason's desk and attack you Avengers style?'

She had the boots for it!

My Music still hadn't materialised, nor had George Fenton. One morning, I was fed up with this and decided to invent my own tunes, a la Belle Vivienne's Improvisation sessions. Everyone fell silent....

'Oh to be a fly on the wall!'

When the Scene came to a close, the phlegmatic, stolid Ed actually rose from his chair and said to me "I say, I'm so glad that the Music has arrived. I think it's going to be great!"

'Actually, Mr. Thomason, said you, I have just made up the whole lot. That is my Music, not bloody George Fenton's!!'

Well Ronnie, I did say something to that effect. There was a bewildered and embarrassed silence whereupon a tea break was called for!

'Got the bugger!'

Never mind, my love, I had overcome my nerves and gave them a dose of improvised inspiration! Linda never looked at me in quite the same way again and at the next Rehearsal whispered, "I say Sue, I love the clothes you wear!" I couldn't wait to phone Jimmy, just for the satisfaction of hearing him say: "Bona, Sweetheart Sue, that's given Edwina Thomason something to stuff in her Rehearsal Plot!"

'I bet that wasn't the only thing Jimmy told the impassive Ed to stuff!'

Amazing what wins through in the end, Ronnie. Always the unexpected.

~

Running in tandem with these events were forthcoming plans for a family Wedding.

'Things must have been moving on a pace since last I heard about the homestead'.

For some time, Nick had been seeing a young lady called Angela.

'We used to call it 'courting' in my day!'

Nick and his Lady seemed very happy and I was happy for him. So preoccupied was I with Coventry, my Mother and a very worrying Heart condition for my Father, which had presented itself in recent months, that I had put any thoughts for such an occasion on the back burner.

'Did Jessica meddle in Nick's affairs?'

I wasn't in direct contact, so am unable to offer any clue on that one, Ronnie. It did, however, transpire that a strategy had been put in place.

'In other words, petal, interference!'

By this time, my Parents were definitely within reach of taking things a little easier. So, it had been suggested that

Nick move steadily towards running the Ferguson Fawsitt, thus stepping gradually into my Father's shoes, while Angela would give my Mother's rank and status a go.

'You've got to be joking!'

Now Ronnie, don't be waspish! That's an accusation you are inclined to level at me!

So, a September Wedding date was clinched. As it happened, I was still in Rehearsal for 'Merchant' and able to be around for the Celebration. It became a very rapid Weekend dash, but I was present...

'Certainly not correct, that's for certain!'

The Wedding Reception was held at the Fergie and it was a light-hearted, merry and auspicious day. I liked Angela and could see no reason why she would not make my little Brother very happy.

'Nuna raised no objections?'

No, darling, Nuna did not...

My Mother, dressed as usual with cultivated and select taste, made...shall I say – the best of it. Times were changing...how was she going to react?

'At a guess, I would say with repressed disapproval... I've come to know that Jessica very well indeed!'

The story goes...via report from Nick...that on return from a Honeymoon lasting approximately a couple of days, he made his way to the family Flat, only to encounter my Mother at the top of the stairs brandishing a kitchen knife and ready for whoever she thought may be a burglar!

'I always said your Mother should have been cast as Lady Macbeth!'

Poor Nick, imagine his distress. My Mother was implicit. She was suggesting fear, neurosis and unease at being left alone to watch over my ailing Father in a sizeable building which could be prone, indeed predisposed, to intruders.

'Poor Nick, poor bugger...how do you get round that one and try to enjoy the bliss of early married life at the same time?'

With enormous difficulty Ronnie. I sympathised with both. Nick was going to be as torn as I had been in the past; torn between allegiance to an exacting Mother and rightful devotion or duty to his new Wife.

I commiserated with my Mother for she had never lived alone. For the whole of her life she had shared a home with either her Parents or a Husband and Family. Naturally, she was frightened...

'Ah, interesting, pet. So why did she not empathize with you when alone, homesick and fretful? Strange how our chickens can come home to roost...'

Perhaps she didn't want me to be like her, Ronnie. Perhaps she thought that too much compassion would wean me away from the Theatre-Land she so avowed. Shall I tell you of the outcome?

'I think I know!'

Nick and Angela had, initially, taken a Caravan within easy reach of Walkington and the Ferguson Fawsitt. It was cramped but served as a miniature first home.

'Then there was the episode of knife plying...'

Which hastened a change in the life of Nick and Angela. They jettisoned the Caravan and moved into the Family Flat at the Ferguson Fawsitt.

'Doomed!'

My Mother's tactics were not quite so successful with Nick. Nevertheless, such manoeuvres made their mark and over the years, my Brother knew repeated bouts of regret, remorse and contrition as a result of not fulfilling Jessica's jurisdiction. Several years before, I recall her telling, artful judgement: "You can't shame Nicky".

'Presumably she had already tried that one...but why, for God's sake?'

Just a form of control and influence. At that time, I know I, too, carried guilt. It hovered and lingered over me like the black dog. My Mother could twist, exploit and steer. I came to realise that such Parental pull, that force, even spell if you like, can exist beyond the grave. It may be interesting to mention that, in the future, when both Nick and I needed to seek treatment for threatened nervous breakdowns, we presented with identical symptoms.

I estimate that Nick's marriage lasted a couple of years. It's impossible for me to go into detail, for I was not there, but later, at the time of his Divorce, I found myself writing numerous letters to Nick's Solicitor in the hope of exonerating him from any blame; all part of my ingrained, innate protection of Nick and my Mother. The part I played was not a fair one; both Nick and Angela suffered. It was a miserable time. I came to bitterly rue and deplore any influence I may have exerted, in a matter which had nothing to do with me.

'Does it hurt to go back, pet?'

Yes, Ronnie, it does. One tries to make sense of the past; to find reasons. I can only hope that, over the years, my Mother acted as she did for what she thought would be best for both of us. I will never know....

~

I returned to my Jester.

George Fenton appeared in about the third week. He was young and very appreciative. The Score was clever, but complicated. Fortunately, I was pitch perfect and found no difficulty in singing unaccompanied. Oh, but where were you Tony?

'I know, darling, it's difficult getting to know another's methods...'

Most important, I liked George. We got on. Which was more than I can say about my connection with Linda.

'Now what?'

She was not generous in the Casket scenes and seemed to think that I was not 'giving' enough to her Performance. On one occasion, she took me on one side and was quite objectionable.

'Oh yeh....go on...'

One thing I have never erred upon is selfishness in Performance.

'La Belle Vivienne would not have put up with that... ever!'

Thank you Ronnie. I crept away to the Flat and burst into tears. I had tried my best with that bloody Jester and now enough was enough. As it happened, Miranda Forbes (Nerissa), who realised I had been attacked followed me and insisted that I explain to Ed Thomason what had transpired.

'Sensible advice, petal. It could have affected the Scenes. He needed to be told...'

His was a very kindly and somewhat unexpected reaction. He seemed to be on my wavelength and said "Oh I'm surprised to learn that you are so upset, Sue."

'Perhaps you had given the impression that you were a tough cookie?'

No advice was given. There was, however, a very interesting development. The following day, Linda called in sick with a throat infection!

'Justice! It reaps its own reward!'

That's exactly the same reaction I received from the rest of the Company. The word had got around that I was being bullied and I sensed an element of protection!

The proof of this came about in a most endearing way. My Birthday was imminent. Someone had got wind of this and on the Day, I received a very thoughtful, caring gift from the Company. It was David Niven's Autobiography

'Bring on the Empty Horses', which was a bestseller of the time. Each member of the Cast had signed the flyleaf. The messages were affectionate and fond.

'Others are not daft, you know Sue. They can read between the lines...'

My Birthday that year was memorable. Presents and cards arrived from the whole Family. Mum sent a very beautiful gold necklace – through the Post! – with the message "Thinking of you all the time..." She had sought the craft of a Beverley jeweller who had advised that "fashionable people are wearing these fine gold bands morning, noon and night"!

'You were realizing her hopes. Perhaps she wanted to compensate?'

This time, very proud and loving cards came from Daddy and Nick. It was the second time for me to shed tears. I missed them all very much on that day.

'Now come on Alice, onwards and upwards...the First Night must be getting nearer...'

Linda reappeared. Now, knowing that I had the support of the Company, I gave that bloody Jester all I had got! She piped down and fussed over her blonde wig!

I was called for a Costume fitting. Ronnie, the design was breathtaking. I was open-mouthed. A cat-suit shaped the base of the rig-out. The piece de resistance was the circular overskirt. This was embellished with brilliant stones and beads. One can only imagine the effect when under the lights!

'Dear God, did the Designer have it in for Linda as well!'

Well, Ronnie, through no fault of mine, it was upstage ammo! The final touch was to be a white Clown's face. My very short hair complemented as the inherent key to the Character. The Jester was complete. A surprise was in store...

'Yes, yes, go on…'

Mum was coming over for the First Night! One of the Waitresses, Audrey, was eager to see the Show and volunteered to drive my Mother and a couple of friends over!

'That was some journey, darling…'

I threw myself into a frenzy of activity and raided shops for preparations. It would be a flying visit for them, but I tried my best to come up with some appetising sandwiches and cakes.

'God, Sue, while dealing with jitters and jinx!'

Well, it was worth it Ronnie. The Show went brilliantly well and we had a glorious Opening.

'That reminds me of a very old Theatrical gag associated with First Night cards: "May you have a warm hand on your Opening"!'

True Ronnie, that one is very old! After, I had to say Goodbye to Mum, who was tearful but very proud, before the capable, vivacious Audrey loaded her little combo into the car in preparation for the long overnight crusade to Yorkshire.

The Show and its unusual representation was very well received. Commendation and acclaim came my way. I had been on edge. After all, who anticipated that a trilling Jester would open the play? Even School matinees behaved themselves; only once were we aware of a suppressed giggle or two.

'How about Linda?'

Peace on all fronts, Ronnie. Besides, she was too busy seducing Lorenzo to pay much attention to me! She had mellowed!

~

'How long was your Contract to last, darling?'

Until December 1975, Ronnie. Several new Actors joined the Company. One or two to take part in a Peter Skellern Musical. Jacqueline Tong, famous for her role as the 'Upstairs, Downstairs' Daisy for Television, made her presence felt and I enjoyed meeting her. My next appearance was to be in 'Skidaddle', a daytime Children's Show. I was pleased to see Jacqui's name on the Cast List. By this time, I was getting used to my new life. I say getting used, but I wrestled with the thought that I may never get used to it. Loneliness still pervaded and I found myself resorting to the Gin bottle. It was a useful device. It induced sleep. The nights were long. 'Skidaddle' consumed the daylight hours, but I spent some desolate evening dusks gazing down into the uninviting, unattractive Coventry street.

'Now come on Alice, why didn't you invite a few of the others over? You know, they may have been feeling low too...'

As a matter of fact, Ronnie, that's just what I did do. I was delighted that everyone seemed to jump at the chance, including John Tarlton, the Associate Director. I laid on a few sandwiches and bottles of wine; the evening went with a swing!

Sundays could be problematic. The whole day stretched before one. Often, the Flats could be almost deserted when a large percentage of the Company decamped to their London homes. Lo and behold, I was rescued by my old friends, Joan and Teddie Tilley, who had been such loyal supporters on Hull's Amateur Dramatic scene. They had retired to Kenilworth in the heart of Warwickshire. Their generous invitations to Sunday Lunch were an oasis of peace in my often troubled world. I would take the train and then walk through tree-lined streets as the smell of countless Sunday lunches would waft under my nose.

'It wasn't called 'leafy Warwickshire' for nothing...'

Joan and Teddie were notable Thespians and had lost no time in becoming members of the tiny one-hundred-and-sixty seat Priory Theatre, the home of the Priory Company. I was given a guided tour and on the odd free evening from the Belgrade, Teddie would ensconce me in the Auditorium while a Rehearsal was in progress. I remember having a painful attack of homesickness; a longing for God's own Hull Garrett Players and the Playgoers, where Teddie, bless him, said I had cut a dash.

'You had a job with those tears...'

I did Ronnie. I buried my nose in a tissue and complained of a cold! After, Joan and Teddie returned me to the Theatre; Joan worried about my traversing the gloomy steps which led to the Flat; dear, kindly Joan. Actually, I worried about traversing the bloody steps!

'Poor little bugger...never mind, you lived to tell this tale!'

Joan and Teddie died many years ago, but I remember so clearly Teddie's unforgettable Malvolio, his vigorous, earnest chuckle and his "Queen's English" as he called it! His speech was impeccable.

'I was always recognised for my Queen's English! Well, amongst other things!'

As usual, my darling, there is no answer to that. The Kenilworth Sundays, Joan and Teddie, remain very close to my memory's heart. Lonely Coventry Sundays brought much time for thought.

'Did you ruminate, my darling? I love that word!'

I drew many conclusions, Ronnie. From the age of eight, I had loved the Drama. It had become the central, underlying purpose in my life. What had pulled the mat from under my feet, was the life-changing reality and learning to survive as a Professional Actor. I had driven my life of Drama. I had forged decisions. Yes, my Mother had made no secret of her expectations and dreams. Her tenacity and intention had trickled like a stream through every instance of my life's unfolding and turn of events. It was unspoken, yet that compulsion returned again and again to prod and prick at my consciousness. I must never disappoint.

'To disappoint would be to choose an unsuitable partner, for instance? Like me? Oh Eck!'

Well, we've been there already! What I'm trying to say is that there had been no childhood guide, no counsellor to lay the groundwork for a Performer's way of life. My Mother had been a dancer. She must have known what could lay ahead.

'How long ago! Your Mother didn't have a clue! You were brought up to be sensitive, gentle and vulnerable. Look here, petal, has it occurred to you that if you had not had those enviable qualities, you couldn't have turned in the Performances that you did? You'd have been hard-boiled, hard-bitten and cynical! You can't have it all ways! So, Jessica turned up trumps... but she wasn't perfect!'

In a moment of despair, I contacted Harry Thompson, the lovely warm, encouraging Harry Thompson of the Gulbenkian Theatre. Here was my guru and his words became my rescue and lifeline.

"Dear Sue, the Professional Theatre is one of the most difficult environments to shake down to – like Medicine and the Law it hath its own rules and observances and these aren't quickly learned. But they are rewarding when one does begin to grasp their import – and of course they are, above all else, necessary to the Profession. It is simply a very special calling which – however hard we try – we can only begin to communicate in a place like the Gulb. The word 'experience' with which you seem to come to rest is THE word. And the only way you can finally get real experience of the real Theatre, is, ultimately, within that Theatre and nowhere else. One final thing – make sure the Audiences like you! I know you can very well do that! Love to you always, dear girl…"

'Ah…another diamond, my sweet, with a very tender kick up the bum! Now then, I've been wondering…no romances straining at the bit?'

Mine was a chaste life at that time, Ronnie. Besides, that Fifties' legacy of continence-or-else was a bugger to shake off. Ironically, Tom, even at the age of thirty-five, I'd have made a good Catholic girl! So, I had enough on my plate without attempting to complicate matters. Shall we say, there were a few fraternizations….nothing Jessica needed to concern herself with!

'Thank God I met you when you were naughty!'

'Skidaddle' closed and our small Group then embarked upon a touring Pub Show of the deserving Coventry. Jacqui Tong inferred that this was, to some degree, beneath her and spoke of being in the B Company. Poor Jacqui, you live and learn. It's true to say that I ascertained a great deal from that tour; I learned about Coventry and its people. I liked them. The Show was a varied mix of appropriate material and songs geared to the City and its history. I looked forward to meeting our Audience. Many would congregate in the Bar post-Perf and all were very appreciative, friendly and fun.

'Darling, there isn't a surer way of identifying with those whom we entertain.'

Do you know, Ronnie…one chap, who had winked at me throughout the Show, stated: "You Actors are just like us, aren't ye?'"

'Nothing like the plain, unvarnished truth pet…sounds like you pulled that night!'

It became a turning point for me, Ronnie. I came to understand what Harry Thompson had meant. I was beginning to feel anew that animating force which was the heart and life-blood of my Theatre. Yes, there would be lonely times but I would manage them. Here began a slow, emotional staying power. Was I too old to grow up?

'Never….not if you knew Susie.'

Alex was cackling and Kevin was giggling…they were coming to take me home! How good it was to see my dear, dear friends. The car was loaded and as I said goodbye to Coventry, my thoughts were of home, Christmas and joy. I was not prepared for the sorrow which followed….

'Charlie?'

Yes, Ronnie. Charlie.

Daddy was the first to greet me. He was wreathed in smiles, as ever. I couldn't wait to show him my Toe-socks!

'Dear God…what?'

Geraldine James had introduced me to these colourful socks. Each toe was a separate entity which boasted a contrasting hue. Daddy gathered cronies around to inspect. "Joe, have you ever seen anything like those? I think you can only get them in London, you know"!

I can just picture Charlie's pride, his love petal….'

Daddy died in Hospital on the 13 December. He had had a catastrophic Heart attack. The shock was devastating. There had been a warning. There had been another attack months before. He had made a recovery. He would recover again, we thought….how misguided, how wrong, how stupid, how bungling we were. So convinced that he would come back to us again…he did not….

'Tell me, pet….'

I was not with Daddy. I was sitting in The Corner with Jessica. I should have been at Charlie's bedside. I was not. He died alone….

How do you ever square that with yourself Ronnie? The regret, the wishing, the sorrow.... how do you make peace with yourself again...

'You never really did, did you?'

No.

'He knows now...he's in this Book....he's in your life.... he always will be...'

He is Ronnie. I know that now. I am certain. I do not doubt. Ever.

~

Poor Nick. He knew grief and he knew panic. Both were instantaneous. He was alone as he had never been alone before.

'Why are men supposed to take automatic control? Just because they're Men?'

There was another factor in the mix. My Father, before he died, implored Nick to "look after your Sister and Mother". No Parent should place such a burden, such a load upon the shoulders of a Child.

'They spend the rest of their lives striving to fulfil that promise'.

My Father's Funeral came and went. He would have loved the uplifting Christmas Carols, the 'Silent Night' with which he would so often try to serenade us...we, who could never understand his German rendering. I pined to hear it once more....just once more...

My Mother knew real ruin and desolation.

'So many wasted years.....'

"I didn't realise how much I loved him", she said simply. I could not answer. There was nothing to say. There was only silent weeping. Mourning for my Father involved much sitting around looking at one another. That is, until practicalities took over and decisions needed to be made.

'How much decision making had you all done?'

My Mother had played a subordinate role, leaving any complications for Charlie to unravel. Overnight, poor Nick came in for a shed-load of responsibility. He was in sole charge of running the Ferguson Fawsitt.

'No easy task if your Dad had been somewhat tenacious.'

True Ronnie. Perhaps, not consciously intending to hold back, he had, in his heart of hearts, harboured reservations about Nick's ability to carry out the job as systematically as he had done. He did not yield. It was his dominion.

'That's the crux of it, petal...'

Whatever the thought process, my Father had left a monumental accountability and a tangled web for poor Nick to figure out. Also, now as a Manager, Nick became answerable to Jacksons-of-Hull, a huge supermarket and catering Consortium; the controlling power-that-be and owner of the Ferguson Fawsitt. Enough to say, numerous Bosses of numerous Departments, held all the cards and although seemingly content for Nick to take the reins, they began to breathe very heavily down his neck.

'Poor Nick – God, you'd need nerves of steel to cope with that as well as bereavement.'

It was a very bleak time, Ronnie. It didn't help to discover that my Father had died practically penniless...

'So Nick and your Mother were totally dependent on present salaries and staying put – a bugger when your home is a tied one...'

I was relieved that Nick had the support of Angela at that time. Mum was a different matter. Naturally, she was frightened and alone. I think my Father's death hit her like a sledge-hammer.

'I suppose it was fortunate that you were at home, although trapped again...'

I knew the quickest way to pull my Mother round would be to look towards another Theatre job. Besides, it was now my living. I needed to move forward. I phoned David Scase at Manchester.

'Get back on that horse, before you lose your nerve! Did that ring a bell, my darling?'

David was very pleased to hear from me. "Leave it with me. I remember your work very well indeed...who could ever forget that face!"

'So that was that?'

Well.. Ronnie...things didn't stop there..

'Go on...don't stop...'

Tony knew I was home. He was still Lecturing at the Gulb and by then had married Vonny. She was not Drama...I think something to do with Psychology...

'Yes, and...'

I was invited to a Christmas party at their home. Tony, knowing I was out of work, had a proposition for me. Would I like to do a Samuel Beckett play at Hull's Humberside Theatre in the New Year? He wanted to cast me as Winnie in 'Happy Days'. It would be a feat of memory, strength and skill! Winnie, buried to her waist in a mound of sand, follows her dreary routine while jabbering to her husband, Willie, largely hidden and taciturn, in a second mound of sand.

'Hell's teeth, these arty-farty playwrights!'

Her frequent refrain is "Oh, this is a happy day!'"

'I've known those kind of days! Well, my darling, it would be a happy day to work with Tony again...'

Not only that, Ronnie. I discovered that feelers were being put out about the possibility of me being invited to Lecture, permanently, in the Drama Department – beside Tony and all those other clever people!

'My petal, what a choice to have to make...'

Guess what, Ronnie!

'Dear God, what...what?'

David Scase rang up!

'Yes, yes, and....'

He offered me parts in two plays at the end of his current Season!

'Security beckoned at the Gulb, or.....insecurity at Manchester!'

Tony helped me over this stile, Ronnie. "Sue, this is the Professional Theatre. It happens like that sometimes. Off you go, sweetheart. I'll find someone else for Winnie..."

'The jewels you have had in your life!'

Mum was thrilled, Daddy would have been thrilled, Nick and Angela were thrilled, but stressed; Alex and Kevin were more thrilled than anyone! Their car was at the ready. Another trip to Theatreland beckoned!

'Now then, Theatre digs or flats? Remember what I told you!'

The Library Theatre's General Manager, dear Terry Hawkins who became a loyal friend, came up with an idea.

'Terry was a mate of mine – I remember him so well...'

Terry knew of an Acting couple, Alan and Diana Partington, who had a Flat going in Fallowfield, a suburb of Manchester and within easy reach of a bus ride to the Theatre. They would be working away and needed to rent out their home.

'Now were you sure? Sure you weren't going to be lonely?'

Apparently, one of the Company's Actors, Keith Clifford and his wife Annie, lived in the Flat below. I hoped that they would be friendly...

'Most Actors are, darling!'

So, once more, I was bound for the unknown. I had never been to Manchester, was not familiar with the location and so viewed the whole encounter with my usual misgiving!!

'Now tell me, was Kevin giggling while Alex dropped the cases!'

Ronnie, they had already planned a weekend break shortly after I had been deposited, settled and working! Incidentally, they booked into a Hotel for that visit and the Proprietor Lady refused to allow them to share a room!

'Typical!'

Alex was scandalised! Kevin just giggled!

Alex and Kevin very kindly invited Mum to help on moving-in day. It all helped to assuage and soothe her heartache. Poor Mum.

'She was in a strange, untravelled land darling…'

Nick seemed quite happy to carry the Fergie millstone while we were away. The weather was fine and journeying along the motorway was untroubled. Until, that is, until we reached the outskirts of the City and poured over umpteen maps and directions in order to find Fallowfield. It turned out to be a pleasing, attractive area. We found the small, terraced house down a side street. It seemed inviting from the outside. Keys had been left with a neighbour. Mum, on initial summing up, proclaimed "Oh, it's not what you're used to!"

'Poor Jessica. First Coventry, now this… will she ever recover!'

We, or rather Alex and Kevin, assembled the gear…

'A copious amount no doubt!'

…and climbed the narrow staircase which opened out on to a landing, small kitchenette and bed/sitting room. It was really homely, Ronnie, and very tastefully furnished.

'Yes, I'm listening but at the same time, I'm visualising the expression on your Mother's face!'

"Oh, there isn't a Television!" Mum exclaimed.

'Hell's teeth, it wasn't the Ritz!'

"Oh," announced Mum, "we'll have to get her a Television when we come next time. It'll keep her company!"

'Bless!'

Kevin couldn't stop giggling and Alex hid behind a kitchen cupboard!

All was very quiet downstairs, so we presumed that the Actor and his wife were out. Mum could read her Daughter like a book. She was right. Mine was a strange, solitary countenance when my loved ones took their leave.

Smells were strange, surroundings were strange and the silence was strange.

'A tape recording of Kevin's giggle wouldn't have come amiss!'

I discovered that the bathroom was downstairs. Hmn, that could be awkward. How would I know if my house-sharing couple would want to occupy at the same time as me?

'Well, you stand on the landing and listen for lavatory noises emanating from downstairs…it's as simple as that!'

I set about putting everything straight. That included me. I was not going to be overtaken with unaccustomed circumstances. I would cry..

'Darling…you're allowed just a few tears…'

Then, I would try to sleep and think of tomorrow – my first day at the

Library Theatre, Manchester…

'I would have said "sweet dreams" – I thought of saying "mind the bugs don't bite" but realised that that could be a very dicey thing to say – Theatre digs can be lousy with them!!'

~

I stood in the Library building Foyer wondering...an Attendant directed me to a flight of steps which took me to the bowels of the building.

'Did being nervous give you wind? I always got wind...'

I followed a circular path to the Theatre entrance. Soon, I was standing looking down at the ring-shaped Auditorium and stage. David Scase and Howard Lloyd-Lewis were addressing a group of people: the cast of 'Dinner with the Family' by Jean Anouilh. I had been allotted the part of Madame Delachaume. All turned and looked at me...

'Now then, head held high – smiling please...'

Of course, Ronnie, 'twas ever thus! I admit I was feeling fazed, Ronnie – utterly taken aback as I looked down towards the Stage and all those strangers...

'Remember, be not inhospitable to them – they may be angels!'

...trust you to remember that, Ronnie...I felt as if I was about to nosedive into an abyss.

'Drama Queen!'

I needn't have worried. David Scase turned and with beaming smile and outstretched arms called "Down you come, Miss Uebel. Come and meet everyone!" I was enveloped in a bear-like hug while in the background I could hear Howard Lloyd-Lewis explaining to the Cast that I was to join them as the Parisian Mme Delachaume. I was welcomed with genuine warmth.

The Cast was about twelve-strong. Gradually, I was introduced to David Scase's wife Rosalie Williams and Howard's Wife Virginia Clarke, a very pretty woman otherwise known as Janie. I came to know later that Rosalie was more widely recognised on Film as the long-suffering Housekeeper to Jeremy Brett's 'Sherlock Holmes'.

Much later, I learned that David had brought many of his Actors from the Theatre Royal, Stratford East. Reg

Stewart and Peter Theedom had been recruited from there; both very humorous and talented Cockneys. Classical Technique was not fully their forte; instead realism, truthful emotion, Stanislavsky method and Ensemble playing prevailed.

'Dinner with the Family' was to be directed by David Tucker, an Arts Council Trainee Director. We were introduced and I settled down well into Rehearsal, gradually picking up the rhythm of the other Performers.

'It's never easy joining an established Company. The camaraderie has put down its roots...'

I found Breaks and Lunchtimes tricky, Ronnie. I didn't really know anyone well enough to join in.

'My poor darling, I know just what you mean. If it's any comfort, I have spent hours sitting on a Park bench rather than mingle at Lunchtimes...! No one believes that an Actor is shy.'

I was trying to show my independence. I didn't want anyone to take pity on me. So, I walked around Manchester for most of the time, for several lunchtimes in fact. I bought sandwiches. They tasted like cardboard.

'I hope you were dredging Harry Thompson's words from the far reaches of your memory..."experience, my dear girl, that is where you come to rest"...

"Sue, what do you do with yourself at Lunchtime? You seem to disappear!"

'I bet that came from Rosalie, David's wife..'

Now, how did you know that, Ronnie.

'I bet she was your life-saver...she wanted to take you under her wing..'

You are a soothsayer, Ronnie. That's exactly what happened.

"We all go off to the Pub, Sue. Do come along tomorrow.." added Rosalie.

That's how I came to know that her David was very fond of his booze at Lunchtime! Consequently, afternoon Rehearsals could adopt a different tone, I noticed, but were, at the same time, enormous fun. The Company atmosphere was totally relaxed, outgoing and convivial.

'I hazard a guess at things being very different from Coventry.'

They were, Ronnie. I loved it.

'How long was it before you met your Housemates?'

I met Keith and Annie Clifford after my first day of Rehearsal.

Diana Partington had made a fleeting visit to pick up luggage and introduced us. Diana was charming, sociable and seemingly very pleased that her home was going to be cherished!

Keith was very tall, angular and possessed one of the most comically droll faces I had ever encountered.

'What my Mother would have called 'a long streak'!

Absolutely Ronnie. My first thoughts were accurate; Keith turned out to be witty, ludicrous and waggish. His lithe physique enabled him to create side-splitting visual Portrayals. As a comic, instinctive Character-Actor, he was a force to be reckoned with. His domestic anchor was Annie, his young wife.

'She house-trained him!'

I could not determine how much younger Annie was. It did not matter. Annie reminded me of Kevin, for she, too, giggled. Especially when Keith voiced anything that was remotely risqué. Annie, although strait-laced to a degree, fought a losing battle. Keith was victorious! In chiding, the most Annie could achieve in admonishing, or censuring, was to collapse upon a nearby chair, giggling in despair and whispering "Ooh, Keith, you are awful!"

'What a sweetheart...how lucky you were to have them...who could be lonely with such a pair of friends.'

I grew to love them both, Ronnie. I grew in confidence, forbearing and belief through knowing Keith and Annie. I can still see darling Annie sitting beside the glowing gas-fire rolling her own fags, before she made her way, by late-night bus, to the Theatre Bar where she would meet her adored Keith.

Keith and Annie, always devoted to children, went on to have six of their own! Annie became a redoubtable, extremely capable Nurse while Keith's unmistakeable presence presented itself in 'Coronation Street' and 'Last of the Summer Wine'. I will never forget them.

'So, happy at home and happy at work! Told you so!'

~

We had a three-week Rehearsal period for 'Dinner' and during that time there was plenty of opportunity to soak up information about the Theatre Staff, other Performers and how the Dressing Rooms were arranged. I shared with Rosalie, Janie and Phylomena McDonagh.

'That's a mouthful!'

Miss McDonagh was an intriguing Actress who often seemed, while on Stage, to be bathed in a draught of dubious aroma.

'Farting!'

How accurate you are, Ronnie. It became so noticeable that in the finish I had to broach the subject to her.

'I bet the rest of the Cast thought it was you!'

Well, that thought brought the matter to a head and I gently confronted Phylomena. "Oh, they're only little ones!" said she.

'Mmn, I've 'eard that before!'

Rosalie could be most entertaining. I grew to be very fond of her. She regaled us with stories about David going to the bottom of their garden to pee on his tomatoes. Apparently, he insisted that not only did urine encourage good growth, it also saved him from a struggle to get to the house in time!

Michael Cummings, the gay Theatre House Manager introduced himself. He became a very close friend who, on many occasions, squired me over to the Oh la-la Midland Hotel for Afternoon Tea.

'This was the one in a million, unique Theatrical 'experience' that Harry had told you about...'

Yes, Ronnie. At last I had found it. I was surrounded by humorous, artistic and engaging people who produced very special work. I was home!

The Library Theatre ran in tandem with another larger one, The Forum, at Wythenshawe on the periphery of Manchester. The entire twenty-five strong Company was divided between the two. Keith was working on Alan Bennett's 'Habeas Corpus' while 'Dinner' was running. So I was informed, in hilarious, root and branch mode, of all goings-on.

'How the hell did Actors get out there to the back of beyond?'

By Theatre bus!

'I hope he was a Theatre Driver...used to a 'Fuck Off!' here and there!'

The First Night of 'Dinner' came around all too quickly. The Theatre was packed. After, the Cast made for the Bar. Unwinding is essential. Inhibitions, reticence or timidity are thrown to the winds and while the Gin flows, one learns much. Here, one clocks the signs and signals; where and how to be wary, where and how to take part.

'Did Jessica come over?'

Alex and Kevin arranged their overnight stay. So, yes, Mum was there and came back with me after the Show.

'I'd like to bet she inveigled Alex and Kevin to get hold of that Television for you. She was a woman of purpose!'

Bless them, they had trailed all the way into the heart of Manchester, tracked down Debenhams and bagged a portable Television – a white one! Mum had been hell-bent on finding a white one!

Towards the end of the Rehearsal period, I had arranged for Mum to come over by train during the day. That is, if I was not Rehearsing. She became quite used to the two-hour journey and graduated to being a slightly nervous but seasoned commuter. I would meet her at Piccadilly Station, then cart her off to a very elegant Restaurant I had found while on my scouting walks. These were lovely meetings. I enjoyed giving her such happiness. It was a pleasure to know that my Mother was really in her element; in her natural environment on those Theatre Manchester lunch days…

'Darling, she was at the centre of things. You gave her the chance to recount these happenings, to tell the story of her day…she had life's impetus once more'.

As soon as 'Dinner' was launched, our days were consumed with the next play. I was to play the ancient Mother, Maryia Vassilievna, in Anton Chekhov's 'Uncle Vanya'.

'Another poor old bugger…'

Quite Ronnie. This was a cameo role. During Rehearsal, I had a very useful window to watch the rest of the Company. Janie was playing the glamorous Yeliena to the manner born. I liked Janie. She was completely obsessed with appearance: all else to do with the character was surplus to requirements!

Janie's summing up of this Chekhov classic masterpiece was "All I can say, Sue, is that I hope the costumes are good because the play's bloody rubbish!"

'I get the drift!'

Despite Janie's dismissal of the Show, the Audiences were very receptive and houses were full. The costumes, wigs and setting were outstanding in attention paid to Period accuracy and detail.

'I trust that Janie was a sight for sore eyes?'

She was, Ronnie.

Reg Stewart and Peter Theedom, or rather 'Feedom' as pronounced by his crony Reg, brought their own measure of individuality to Performance. Stratford East's improvisational brilliance and invention was injected into both renditions. While there was intense expression of truthful emotion, both men created opportunities for subtle, jocular originality. They were blessed with ebullient, buoyant humour; a double act which made its mark wherever scope presented itself. They shared a Dressing-Room. One can only imagine the conversation; each Performance geared to their brainchild of comic contrivance. David and Howard were utterly in tune. I can still hear their infectious laughter echoing through the Stalls.

'I'd like to bet that you were not the only one who was chalking up information..'

In what way, Ronnie.

'You, your Performances, your air and impression would be being noted...oh yes, they won't have missed a trick...they don't call me Crystal Balls for nothing!'

Ronnie, much to my amazement...

'Yes...and...go on...'

David asked me to return to the Library Theatre for a full Season beginning in September 1976 and this time I would be playing Leading Parts, including Lady Macbeth!

'Surprise, surprise! My little Star!'

~

I had four months to prepare, that is, as much as one can prepare for a Theatre job.

'Back to the Fergie?'

Back to the Fergie, Ronnie. Back to Ivy's Buffet and Dina's sardonic and somewhat cynical attitude to life.

'I love Dina!'

Mum was gladdened and thrilled to have me home. The Pub seemed to be running smoothly and the Summer months were busy, crowded and constantly on the move. My Mother was more settled and engaged in the relentless pursuit of Management and Organisation. I could see, however, that Nick was gripped in a maelstrom of stress and uncertainty. Responsibility, noticeably huge, was taking its toll.

'He too was trapped; answerable, no doubt, to the demands of authority….a hellish position to be in, when one is sensitive and easily cowed by superior attitude, however phoney that may be'.

All I could do was to be as supportive as possible, while at the same time, attempting to steer my own course.

'Mmn, you always managed to steer me…even to where I didn't want to go!'

Thank you, Ronnie.

Diana and Alan Partington had returned to their flat in Fallowfield. I had been in contact with Keith and Annie and both were excited about my joining the Library Company again, especially as Keith had also been invited to take on another Season. Apparently, they had mentioned this to Diana and she offered to give me a hand in finding digs for September. My Contract would run from the Autumn until May of 1977.

"I think I've found somewhere, Sue. It's tiny, a bit like a cupboard really, but I'm sure you could be very comfortable..." said Diana when she phoned.

'Sue, you do meet some jewels in your time...'

So, Ronnie, I took time out for exploration and reconnaissance.

'Go on, then...what was it like? I hope it had a Television or Jessica will be on the warpath again!'

The bus route was straightforward and the large Victorian house easy to find. Diana had filled me in with details. Again, I would be based in Fallowfield. The house was divided into Flats and Flat-lets and overseen by the Landlady who also lived on the premises.

'You'd better mind your P's and Q's...she'll poke her nose into everything and count your Gentleman callers! You'll be known as Madame Sin before you know it!'

She turned out to be older than I had expected, Ronnie, but seemed to be very kindly.'

'Mmn....oh yes....?'

The front door opened to reveal a very wide, large staircase. Doors, on each small landing indicated others who were in residence.

'Did it smell of old ladies?'

Well, Ronnie, since you mention it, there was a mustiness about the place. It was very quiet. I was shown to the first floor. The landlady opened a door and I was shown into 'the cupboard'. Diana had been right. It was tiny, but I realised it could be made into a very cosy home. It did have a window, a sash one which looked out on to tree-tops and the street. A minute kitchenette joined the bed-sitting-room. Here was a miniature gas ring, sink and draining board – all separated by a curtain which served as a door.

'Oh Eck!'...no hanging wardrobe?!'

Now, Ronnie, you're in no position to be critical. I was being very grown-up, liberated and self-reliant!

'Darling, of course you were – but – was it what you were used to!'

Stop quoting my Mother all the time!

'Thought I'd say it before she did!'

The sitting-room did have a single bed and chest of drawers. There was a gas-fire and very small armchair.

'Just right for a very small person! No day bed?!'

Very funny, Ronnie. Well, I decided to take it. I knew it could be absolutely right for me, once all my bits were in place...

'I know how much space your bits need!'

It was an enormous relief to know that I had somewhere to live. Also, the house was near to Keith and Annie.

'Cornerstones in your life at that time, my pet...'

Now I could relax and prepare. I have always needed a structure: I do not relish the idea of leaving all to chance. My Theatre life would have been smoother, easier if I had...

'Gone with the flow?'

The familiar, the safe, the secure. Strange things make me feel strange, unsettled and lost.

'Things don't come stranger than me...and you managed that all right!'

Your strangeness always made me feel free from harm.

'Mmn, I'll put that in my Diary! Now, what happened next?'

I worked hard, provided some sort of emotional optimism for Mum and Nick and drowned some of my sorrows...

'In the Corner....Gin, and keeping Jessica company?'

I did, Ronnie. Gin was becoming something of a prop.

'Perhaps becoming part of a quiet life?'

Boredom can play its part too, Ronnie. My regular Gin n' Tonics were filling a vacuum. I very much doubt whether it ever crossed my Mother's mind that alcoholic reliance could be looming. She was content, in a manner of speaking. Mum had her security around her; her Son, her Daughter and a life she enjoyed. This was intermixed with the animating force of my Theatre life; its exhilaration, thrill and euphoria.

'As long as you returned to the fold when each trip came to an end?'

I don't remember my Mother ever asking if I was happy. I suppose I seemed to be, so probing questions were carefully avoided.

'You don't push...the truth may emerge....'

So, Ronnie, life took its course through the remainder of the Summer.

As it did, I became more on edge as I felt Manchester getting closer and closer.

'Surely you were looking forward to it?'

No, Ronnie, I wasn't. I knew I would go. I knew I would do it. I was afraid.

'Why darling?'

I felt the pull of home. I was never free of it. I kept putting myself to the test but the pull was ingrained, rooted, inbuilt and brassbound. I heard the voice of my childhood murmuring "You don't want to go, do you?"

'Ah ...I see...'

~

Alex and Kevin were on holiday when I got the call for Rehearsals to begin.

'Panic stations!'

It would have been, Ronnie, but dear Nick came up with a very kind suggestion. He would borrow the Ferguson's

Staff Transport Van and ferry me to Fallowfield. So the plan was put into motion. My Mother wished to join in, so the three of us braved the M62 Motorway.

'Still in its infancy then, I reckon?'

The racing traffic was still a daunting prospect, Ronnie. Our entourage landed in Fallowfield late on a September Sunday afternoon. We were met by the kindly Landlady. My Mother's face was a study. It was the picture of impending doom as she turned a hyper, twitchy gaze on to the oppressive wallpaper. It all seems so funny now, Ronnie.

'Now that you have grown up?'

Yes, now that I'm a grown-up old lady! I still don't like leaving home you know!

'I do know. I've always had a helluva job to kick you out!'

The Van revved up and soon it was moving away, its occupants looking anxiously ahead to where the Motorway was lying in wait. "I put a bottle of Gin in the carrier"! Jessica called through the window.

'Well, got to get your priorities right, love....Jessica's handy solution: get pissed when times are difficult!'

The little cupboard put out the welcome banner. Soon, I was getting a lamp lit and my bits in order. Thoughts were preoccupied. When would they be home? Should I ask the Landlady for the use of her phone? No, don't be daft...wait a bit longer....I waited....waited...

'Now come on, they eventually got through...?'

It was very late, Ronnie. How useful a Mobile Phone would have been in those days! Shock! Horror! The Van had broken down a few miles from Beverley and it had taken Nick ages to rustle up help. Poor Nick. After he had been so kind...

'Did your Mother give in to hysteria?'

No, Ronnie. She remained cool as a cucumber, perched up there in the passenger seat and calling out to poor Nick who may have been tussling with the Van's toolbox. "It'll be all right. As long as you have a tongue in your head, you'll be all right!"

'As long as she didn't say "Oh Nick, it's not what you're used to"!'

Stop saying that, Ronnie. That joke has worn thin!

My Landlady knocked on the door. "I'm glad all is well," she said, "they are safely home". I thanked her profusely for allowing me to take the call and made some effort to settle for the night. It was a long time before an exhausted sleep...

'AND a small Gin n' Tonic....'

....went some way towards the break of my first day at the Library.

~

Susan & Reg Stewart 'Stop it Whoever You Are' 1976 Library Theatre

The opening play 'Stop It, Whoever you Are' by Henry Livings was very much a Northern comedy. David Scase was to direct and I was to play my first leading part, Rose Warbeck, wife of William Perkin Warbeck. Perkin was awarded to Reg Stewart. Need I say more? Corrina Sklar was the only other Actress.

'So, you were surrounded by a Company of men?'

Guess who was to play Alderman Michael Oglethorpe?

' *'Feedom?'*

Perkin Warbeck, a Washroom Attendant in a factory, was a Character brimming with opportunism. Here was the possibility to outsmart, to exploit; bounty for the fertile, ingenious mindset of Reg Stewart. 'Feedom, never one to allow the golden hand of fortune to pass him by, was more than a match. Rehearsals thrived on uproarious laughter and the joy of Performing.

'True Theatre, my darling…'

During the weeks that followed, my respect for David Scase the Director grew. I loved working with him. David cut through flummery and injected pace. In doing so, he could be fierce. He believed that Acting was more about doing than analysing. Never one to lurk behind a desk, David was instinctive. Pulling furiously on a cigarette, he would enthuse about the way an Actor walked, power of his arms and grace of head, timbre of voice. His own was rich and deep.

'You must have noticed the contrast between him and Ed Thomason'.

Oh I did, Ronnie. David was instructive, incisive and well informed but, I suspect, somewhat anti-intellectual! All this was wrapped up in laughter, engaging stories and a truly infectious belly laugh. Bearded, smiling and devoid of artifice, David was an articulate, expressive breath of fresh air.

'He was fighting, in a period of increasingly University-led theorising, for the truth, for reality with an uncompromising fervour.'

Ronnie, my darling, that was very well expressed and so nail-on-the-head!

'I do try, you know! I'm not all mouth and trousers!'

David was a founder of the Repertory Movement, now so sadly gone, but his Productions live on in the memory; their beautiful simplicity, energy and zest.

My confidence soared. David had chosen me to be a member of his Library Company. He knew what I could do and took me on. In time, I came to know that many Actors had cut their Professional teeth at the Library Theatre: Leonard Rossiter, Robert Stephens, Janet Suzman, Alan Rickman and Anthony Hopkins.

Apparently, when at Chichester, Anthony based his Petruchio on David. Discerning, sharp and dazzling!

Meantime, Reg and I were getting on well. We had several Scenes to do together and I found him to be easy company. Reg was an attractive man. His bald head roused much mickey-taking and he and 'Feedom fed each other with unrestrained, reckless and rowdy gags; wisecracks and quips that reduced the Company to a wrecked, impotent heap. The Show went well and played to full houses.

Many of the Ferguson Staff had expressed a wish to see the play and so Mum and Nick arranged an excursion. Once more, the Staff Van was called into operation! They chose a night when Reg and 'Feedom's inclination towards the unexpected came to pass.

'Go on....go on....!'

In the course of the action, Alderman Oglethorpe needed to avail himself of one of the lavatories! Perkin Warbeck, mop and bucket aloft, was busily mopping the floor the while. All at once, behind the closed door, the unmistakeable noise of breaking wind reverberated around the Auditorium like a thunderclap. Reg's countenance had to be seen to be believed!

''Feedom! Who else?'

Corrina – known as Candy -and I were offstage in the Dressing-Room waiting for the Interval. We heard Audience response over the tannoy. "That scene's gone well. What have they been up to?" said Candy.

Suddenly, Dressing-Room doors were being knocked off their hinges as Reg rampaged through shouting "Who did that fucking fart!" 'Feedom had a lot to nswer for that night.

'Sue, darling...people like Reg and 'Feedom cut across pretence and posing. They were born creators...'

Mum and Nick met Reg that night and of course were slaves to his humour. Reg made several conquests that evening.

~

'How were you settling into the cupboard?'

Very well, Ronnie. It was cosy and by the time I had rustled up all my accoutrements from home, it was a real retreat.

'What about the other Tenants? Did you notice any shadowy figures creeping along the landings?'

Since you mention it, Ronnie, I did bump into one of the elderly Ladies who was very chatty. So much so, that I was invited into her room for a cuppa.

'Did it smell of old ladies?'

Ronnie, you've got a thing about old ladies and their smell.

'I know. I hope it doesn't become a phobia....'

That room, Ronnie, had to be seen to be believed.

'Had she hung her bloomers on a pulley that went up to the ceiling? Her with it...'

The whole space, every surface, windowsill or chest of drawers, was festooned with soft toys: Teddy bears, Pandas, Larry the Lambs. You name it, it was there in that oppressive room. They seemed to spring to life and eye me with an air of suspicion.

'Were they included in the conversation? Now that would have been really spooky.'

I beat a hasty retreat, Ronnie. Afterwards, I made no overtures to any other Resident and bolted before I was invited to the next Beetle-Drive!

'You never know, they may have been swingers! Think of what you missed!'

I had made the most of my cupboard. It was a sheltered, snug retreat. The nightly Gin n' Tonics served as useful anaesthesia on my return from the Theatre. I slept soundly without allowing nightmarish thoughts of freakish, off-the-wall old Ladies kipping under the same roof!

'Oh, give over, my imagination is running riot!'

Before 'Stop It…' opened, I had invited Candy to share a supper or two. We became good mates and I think my contact with her paved the way a little more comfortably when other Actresses, Corrina Seddon and Trudi Styler, joined the Company to Rehearse for the next play. Poor Candy did not take to them.

'Remember your clash with the green-fingered Linda!'

Never to be forgotten, Ronnie – one of my many learning curves…so I sympathised with young Candy. Corrina and Trudi were confident, worldly young women and well able to be a thorn in Candy's side.

~

I was on the threshold of a turning point. I was to play Lady Macbeth. Once more, David Scase was to direct.

'Not a walk in the park, sweetheart…'

It was a remarkable chance, Ronnie. David had entrusted me with a titanic venture; it was a vast undertaking.

'Not a man to gamble in vain...'

Paul Webster, an Actor whom I had not met, joined to play Macbeth. Paul was experienced, very accustomed to working with David and one of the kindest men any Lady M. may have the good fortune to work with.

"You handle the verse very well, Sue" smiled David, as he navigated me through the movement plot. David was a tactile man...

'Without being touchy-feely...'

He piloted Paul's course in exactly the same way. Three of us occupied the stage. David could demonstrate, he could show...

'Not just the gift of the gab.'

We could be reduced to giggles, to the ridiculous. David, eager to encourage Paul to take my hands, added "You can get hold of her, you know Paul. Believe me, she's just like butter!"

Production photo – 'Lady Macbeth' Manchester Library Theatre 1976

'How easily that remark could have been misconstrued in the present day...'

I never doubted David's motives, or, his respect for me. He was true blue. You can always tell the difference, Ronnie.

'Was I true blue?'

Darling, you were true blue – truly blue on more than one occasion! I do hope I came up to David's

Susan as Lady Macbeth Manchester Library 1976

expectations. Paul was a tower of strength. I remember one glowing moment of reassurance. Poised, with hands clasped regally, the Macbeth's were in the Wings about to make their grand entrance for the Banquet Scene. Overcome with nerves and anxiety, I was conscious of my cold, sweaty palms and apologised to Paul. "Never mind, my dear, I'm sure you make wonderful pastry!" was his riposte.

'What a lovely man…'

The Cast was very supportive and David was an Ensemble man. No one stepped over the line. Reg and I had worked together closely on the previous Play so our friendship went a long way towards forging a strong working relationship.

'Was that as far as it went? Was that the beginning….?'

Yes Ronnie. The seeds were sown…

'Go on then…what happened next…'

Well, I'm coming to that Ronnie. The Play ran for five or six weeks and involved School Matinees. These Perfs turned out to be a feat of endurance for us all. Phrases such as Macbeth's 'T'was a rough night' met with something of a racket, so -when I embarked upon 'I have given suck!', I fixed the audience with malevolent stare and hoped for the best. Not a sound!

Some of those Matinees were really beyond the pale. The Stage was built upon a rake so it did slope crazily down toward the Footlights. Some of the little shits thought it a real crack to take aim with Mint Imperials and watch these roll at some speed down the dipping incline.

'Devious, treacherous little buggers...'

Paul would agree with you, Ronnie. In fact, at half-time he assembled all in the Green Room and announced to poor Michael Cummings, the House Manager and my Midland Hotel companion, that in the interests of safety, he should make an announcement. A portentous silence hung over the Auditorium for the whole of the Second Half!

Poor Candy retired to my Dressing Room on more than one occasion. She was playing Second Witch and Young Macduff. Also I fear, second fiddle to Corrinna and Trudi the other two Witches. Both Rada trained, they lost no well-timed moment to warm up on Stage, displaying a repertoire of flexible bodily contortions which put the breeze up Candy and left her feeling very cowed and dispirited.

'Poor love.'

She and I made up for it in the Bar! Reg and 'Feedom couldn't..

'Give a fuck about Rada!'

Ronnie, you're a mind-reader.

I warmed to Reg and 'Feedom. I admired their deft ingenuity and total lack of hoax or deception.

'What you saw was what you got'.

Both were not handsome men, but both were attractive in that they exuded a red-blooded, hardy and bold masculinity. Threaded through this dynamism was humour, and a frank, clear-cut and artless individuality.

Peter Theedom was promised to a very pretty girl, Sheila, who worked in Wardrobe and divided her time between the Forum and Library. Friday evening, after the Show, became Clubbing night. The Company invariably retired to a Manchester Winery where numerous glasses were consumed. Also, some eccentric, energetic and gyrating dancing gave way to lack of inhibition. 'Dad dancing' would be the term used today…

'I have a feeling that Reg would feature prominently?'

He did Ronnie. I think it was 'Feedom who noticed a closer…

'Affiliation, he said pompously.'

He remarked "Everyone's falling in love with you, Sue". Enigmatic…'Feedom had seen the connection, Ronnie. That link or attachment with Reg developed into a stronger, much more meaningful affair.

'Was it an affair?'

As I look back, I try to identify with the woman I was in those days. Today – so many years later, so many experiences later, so many people later, I doubt that I would have taken that same road. So much water was to go under the bridge. I was green, credulous and untried. Oh, I would still be won over by the audacious, rash Reg…

'I sense a but….'

I would have put the brakes on, Ronnie.

'Why didn't you?'

I suppose I thought that I had found what I was looking for. I expected the heady, happy days of Manchester and the Library to last forever. Reg, unpredictable and set in the ways of the itinerant, wayfaring, jobbing Actor, came to believe he was ready to settle down. There had been other relationships.

'Had he one on the go at the time?'

If so, I was not given to understand that it was a serious one. Whatever the circumstances, Reg dissolved that attachment and proposed to me.

'Did you really know what you were doing? Had you thought it through? Were there no doubts?'

No. I was carried along. There was a kind of love; the real kind, as I thought....all that time ago. Another factor featured very prominently in the whole business.

'Yes, my darling, don't stop there....'

My Mother...

'Oh, I know what's coming!'

My Mother had met Reg on a number of occasions. She took a shine to Reg. So much so that he was invited to spend weekends at the Ferguson. Generously, my thoughtful Brother allowed me to borrow his car. Whenever free time came along, we could motor over for a day and a half, escaping after the Saturday night Show and returning on Monday.

'Tell me the tale...'

It's a puzzling tale, Ronnie. My Mother put forward no disagreeable attitude or objection. Reg became the Jester... the chosen one, the fun guy who could entertain like no other. Disarming joke after disarming joke provoked uproarious laughter in Dina's corner. Needless to say, Gin after Gin oiled the wheels.

'Kindred spirits, I guess...'

Sunday morn may have involved a country stroll or two through the village. Lo and behold, Reg was quick to point out a small cottage. It was To Let and a short distance from the Ferguson-Fawsitt Arms! He wasted no time in suggesting that we apply. According to Reg, it would be an idyllic retreat after we were married! We could commute when Theatre jobs came along.

'You were swept along....darling, didn't you stop to think? All this was so close to your Mother and home...ah well....what will be will be...'

So, my darling, that put the seal on everything. The cottage, in something of a rundown state, was rented to us. Reg, in a flurry of nesting, planned his garden, vegetables and compost heap!

'I bet Jessica was on cloud nine...'

So was I, Ronnie. Everything seemed to be fitting into place. I was happy. I had a Theatre I loved, leading parts, an Acting Fiance and a cottage.

'What did you make of Jessica's change of heart?'

I really don't know, Ronnie. I think she viewed Reg as some sort of asset. Perhaps, to her, he was on her wavelength. Perhaps Reg was affable, easy and dare I say it, malleable – putty in the hand? Little did she know....

~

'The Hamlet of Stepney Green' by Bernard Kops took over from Lady Macbeth. Set in the heart of an East End Jewish family, Mr.Kops proved that his 'sad comedy with songs' could demonstrate that community's richness, humour and zest for life. I knew nothing of such a community. My roots had been firmly set in the wilds of Yorkshire. Little did I know that Kenneth Alan Taylor, Artistic Director of Oldham Coliseum Theatre was out front on the First Night. "She's so Jewish!" had been his complimentary summing up of my Performance. Those wheels turned in a very unforeseen way some time later, when I received an invitation to join his Company for 'Celebration' by Keith Waterhouse & Willis Hall.

'That's the way Theatre can work, my love...'

By mid-December we were moving towards the Library Christmas Show.

'How did the rest of the Company react to your plans to marry Reg? I'm intrigued..'

I think some of them were very bemused, even taken aback. I sensed reaction. Were we an unlikely pairing? Reg was particularly well-known to all. Of course, at the time, one's antennae is not so sharp. It's befuddled.. I remember that David made no comment and neither did Howard. I wonder...was someone trying to tell me something?

'No one would presume, love. It might well have fallen on deaf ears anyway. You were on one of life's pathways....'

You're very wise, you know Ronnie.

'The Incredible Vanishing' by Denise Coffey had been chosen to open mid-December, David Tucker to direct. Reg was cast in the lead Bert Sparky and I gave my Australian accent for Lulu Maguire, a Traffic Warden. In the Second Half I was to take on Goblet and servant to the Goblin Queen.

'Well, you were always gobby, so I reckon that part was a piece of cake!'

All went well in the approach to Christmas 1976. Once more we played to bursting houses of Junior School children. In the Second Half, the Goblin Queen made her entrance from the rear of the Auditorium, pursued by her Goblet. We made our way through the central entrance. I was green from head to foot, Goblin-green....

'Hell's Teeth – Lady M. and now Goblet! At least you weren't giving suck!'

...face and boiler suit! The kids sitting nearest to the aisle seemed to think all this was a cue to bash me with whatever they could lay their hands on. I was black and blue....

All this came to something of a head when there was a bomb scare. My dear friend, Mike Cummings, Theatre House Manager, evacuated the whole building. We ended up in a nearby Pub, still in full costume and green hue! That certainly brought about a fun evening. Most of the customers took pity on poor little Goblet and insisted on buying Gin-after-Gin in compensation for all the inconvenience!

'Pissed again....'

Once safely back in the Theatre, we were on course for Christmas Day.

We did two Christmas Eve Shows and then were due back for Boxing Day.

A day and a half holiday!

'I hope you had time off for giving the Aunties a lift, if you follow me!'

Yes, Nick came in for that one, Ronnie. All went well and Reg bowled over the Aunties, as was his wont!

The New Year presented us with an unexpected and traumatic set of circumstances....

'Oh God, now what?'

Reg was rushed into Hospital with violent earache. Almost at once, he knew what was wrong.

'Mastoid?'

How did you know that, Ronnie?

'Premonition. ...Fortunately, one doesn't hear of Mastoids quite so frequently nowadays. They were common during my Childhood and are in the bone behind the ear...very painful.'

An Understudy had to step in quickly. Fortunately, Nick had allowed us to borrow the Morris Oxford – not the Bentley, in those days! – and so I was able to get across Manchester to visit much more easily – that is, until the car was nicked!

'No!'

I had parked outside the Stage Door. You can imagine the panic. At first, I was so stricken that I could not remember whether I had parked in that place or not! Dear Mike Cummings phoned the Police and reported the incident...

'Was it ever recovered?'

No Ronnie, never found. I had no choice but to pull myself together, tell Nick the awful truth and take the bus everywhere once more. Visiting Reg did present problems. I learned over the coming fortnight that his Mastoid had been a Childhood misery and ordeal for poor Reg. From time to time, there had been a recurrence of symptoms which had caused repeated distress. This time, Reg was treated by an Indian Lady Consultant. The Visiting Hour was taken up with Reg's description of "Punjabi" and her seemingly brutal mode of treatment. This involved the repeated packing and unpacking of Reg's ear with liberal yards of cotton-wool type stuff impregnated with appropriate medication.

'Dear God, sounds brutal...'

True Ronnie. His evaluation of this procedure by the tortuous Punjabi was something to behold! I came to realise that this was keeping the rest of the Ward entertained. Incidentally, I knew nothing of Indian people. Information about Punjabi was a complete revelation. I had no idea what Punjabi meant!

'The North of England was a different land, darling – when Susie was growing up! Remember Reg was a Cockney. He could have been raised within a mixed race environment.'

Oh, Ronnie...how lacking we are in experience. We are never fully formed when we enter this world. Our thoughts, creed, opinions, ideas and principles only develop over time. We listen to others and absorb the influence of our environment; that of our Friends, our Parents, Family and our Teachers.

'Hey up...'

Sorry, I didn't mean to go on. Eventually, Reg was released, was much better and able to return to Bert Sparky. He occupied a bed sitting-room in Whalley Range, a further suburb of Manchester. He was ecstatic to return to his outsize Television and Match of the Day!

'Nowadays, you would have moved in together, perhaps?'

I think some of our friends thought that a possibility, Ronnie. But...no.

My Fifties dogma still prevailed!

'You mean Jessica's Fifties dogma...!'

Had it not been so entrenched, Ronnie, I may well have seen the light sooner.

'Why am I worried by that remark?'

All will be revealed, my darling. Meanwhile, I have Theatre news to impart.

'About time!'

I was about to embark on my final stint in Manchester. This time I was to be based at the Forum Theatre. Much bigger than the more intimate Library space, it seated a sizeable audience. I was cast as Ursula in Peter Nichol's 'Forget me Not Lane' and spent most of my time, alone, on the Stage Apron, addressing the audience and expressing in elaborate detail the circumstances of my domestic life! It was more than nerve-wracking. Mercifully, I was partnered during the play with the selfless, big-hearted Paul Webster. How reassuring was that!

'All this versatile Casting certainly tested you, pet'.

Wait for it, Ronnie. 'Love on the Dole' by Walter Greenwood came next.

'How wonderful, petal. That became a modern classic with its harsh picture of Salford in the depressed industrial North of the Thirties. It could have been the story of my life! All about Workhouses, pawnshops, soot-covered streets, children begging for scraps...'

I was to play Mrs. Jike...

'Not the old bugger who read teacups?'

The very same Ronnie.

'All I can say is that you must have been type-cast!'

April brought along a real challenge. I was cast as – wait for it – Lucienne Homenides de Histangua in the Georges Feydeau farce 'Flea in Her Ear'.

Susan & Janie 'Flea in Her Ear' Manchester Forum

Guess who was to be my Husband and partner in crime?

'Go on, go on....I'm listening...'

Keith Clifford!

'Oh Sue, what a fabulous gift! I had been wondering how Keith and Annie were...'

I had been so busy and Keith had been just as busy working at the Forum so we hadn't really had time for a proper get-together. Now came the most wonderful break to take part in the pandemonium and rumpus of this tumultuous farce.

'Misunderstood motives, mistaken identities and bawdy humour! Just up my street – and Keith's I bet!'

Say no more. Four sets of married couples continually finding themselves in compromising situations. All set in fashionable Paris. To complicate dramatic matters further, Keith and I were supposed to be Spaniards! Added to snag and stumbling block, we had a whole Scene scripted in Spanish! A language expert from Manchester University was roped in to give us a hand. Those sessions were a hubbub of craziness. Neither of us responded in scholastic fashion!

'Fracas, knowing you two...'

It was a large Company in all. I was to work closely with Janie again and it was really lovely to see her total preoccupation with the gorgeous costumes and wigs. Janie was great fun.

First Night arrived and Keith and I forgot, totally, most of the Spanish teacher's drilling. How we got through the Scene then and on subsequent nights was a miracle. Whenever Keith was stymied and could not recall the correct dialogue, he loomed as closely as his boots and breeches would allow and whispered in thick Spanish accent: "Don't cry for me, Argentina!"

~

Reg and I were married on Sunday, 15th May 1977. Within eighteen months, Reg had left me.

'No – darling – what?'

It would be unfair of me to give a one-sided viewpoint, Ronnie. It is all so long ago now. Perhaps a brief resume?

Susan & Reg Wedding 1977

Reg and I had hoped to have a simple Wedding, but naturally my Family wished to celebrate in spectacular fashion; Brother Nick so wished to take the place of Charlie who would have revelled in his special calling as Father-of -the-Bride. Mrs. Sizer....

'Was she still on the go...'

Oh yes, Ronnie. She made my gown; a full-length, a loose-fitting vision of white silk Jersey, complete with small train, it was complemented by a coronet of white rosebuds. The making of it was Mrs. Sizer's final gift to me. She died shortly after that truly memorable occasion. The ceremony was conducted in Walkington Parish Church. Our Theatre friends and many from my Teaching or University days were there to wish us well. Reg's family: his Sister Helen and Husband Alan, Samantha, Reg's niece, Brother Johnny and even an elderly Uncle Lionel, travelled from the South to give their blessing. A lavish Reception, at the Ferguson-Fawsitt Arms, followed. There, my Mother greeted all Guests which included Aunties and Family friends.

Dear Bill Pattinson and his Wife Freda made the journey over from Norwich. They had retired there after the Kelvin days. Several years later, I was made privy to a golden, incisive comment that Bill had made on The Day: "What on earth does Sue think she's doing?"

'You'd have to be up early to catch Bill.'

So, life in our cottage began. Mum made a generous contribution to furnishing our homestead and Reg settled into cultivating his vegetable patch, picking up on his ornithology...

'Oh, he was a twitcher?'

...he was Ronnie. He was very knowledgeable. Also, I discovered that he had written several short Plays and had them published. So it all made for a varied and happy existence. We were country bumpkins! For a while...

Moreover, Mum was happy. We were on the doorstep. Our lives became inadvertently entwined with what was going on at the Pub. It percolated and filtered through our lives. Pleasurably at first, I think.

'You were drawn into the web...but was Reg?'

'Mixed Doubles'
Humberside Theatre

Life at that moment in time was a novelty, Ronnie. For both of us. It was handy to partake of a few Gins at the close of the day, once the garden was taking shape and I had turned my hand to baking the odd Victoria Sponge!

'Your Sponges were inclined to be odd! So... Gin was still playing its part?'

Oh yes, Ronnie. It was a habit, but also a boost as I engaged earnestly into married life; a married

Lady with everything to look forward to. Work came along. Within a few months, I found myself being plunged into Rehearsals for a selection of Sketches about married life, 'Mixed Doubles' at Hull's Humberside Theatre. The Show was then to tour the East Riding of Yorkshire.

'So, was Reg left twiddling his thumbs?'

No, fortune came his way. He flew to Ireland to start work on a film for BBC 2.

Late in that first year of our Marriage, I was contracted once more to the Humberside Theatre. Alan Plater, the Hull playwright, was to launch the Premiere of his new Play. I was cast in a leading Role. 'Well Goodnight, Then' played at the Theatre for three weeks before being taken on tour. Meantime, temporarily...

'At least, I expect he hoped it was temporary...'

...out of work, Reg dealt a hand at the Ferguson-Fawsitt Arms. He was a good worker and did not shy from heaving barrels and swilling cellars. We managed a Christmas within reach of our cottage, but I reckon much leisure time was consumed by Mum and the Pub. When on tour, I phoned in the evening, but when Reg was unable to take the call at the Ferguson, I guessed that he had been under the influence of a few too many jars! He was always apologetic when quizzed about his whereabouts...I guessed...

'He could have succumbed to other veiled influences... yes?'

Only time would tell Ronnie.

Reg was delighted when an availability call came from Stratford's Theatre Royal. He was offered a Contract, to begin later in the year. It would mean a long commute with the possibility of getting back to the cottage at weekends. Within the following weeks, I noticed Reg's restlessness. He was itching to get back to work.

'Perfectly understandable, love..'

"I'm an Actor, Sue. I cannot spend much more time working in that Pub. I work hard clearing the cellar – the next morning it's still in a mess. I'm fed up." This outburst did jolt and I sensed unrest. For Reg, life was beginning to pall. Gloom, dismay and a shadow fell over me. Anxiety began to disturb.

'Didn't you have a call from the lovely Bob Carlton? He who terrified you at the University?'

I did, Ronnie. He invited me to play Elsie in his forthcoming production of 'The Ghost Train' by Arnold Ridley at York's Theatre Royal in August 1978.

'Poor Arnold Ridley, he didn't make a penny on that Play. Over the years, it must have grossed thousands... let's hope his character in 'Dad's Army' brought in a bob or two'.

Nick had acquired another car. In his good-natured and helpful way, he let me borrow it for the drive to York.

'Nick's support has been a Godsend over the years, hasn't it, Petal?'

Bob had mellowed over the time since we met at the Gulb. He was a first class Director and the Play was yet another milestone in my career. Berwick Kaler played the lead and went on to give his idiosyncratic, distinctive Dames year after year in York Pantos.

In late Summer, Reg took the train to London for the last time. I remember seeing him off at the station. There was misgiving and presentiment. I think I knew...

'Darling...'

A week passed. Reg phoned....he would not be coming home....I removed my so-new Wedding Ring and laid it on the mantelpiece.

~

“Don’t live at the Pub when I’m away, Susie” said Reg. I had cause to remember that statement many times over the coming lonely weeks. I hadn’t questioned it at the time. Of course, that is exactly what I did do when Reg was in London. It seemed to be the obvious answer, rather than rattle around in the cottage all alone.

‘I would say, at a guess, that Reg preferred you to be in your own home and doing your own thing...’

I escaped everything that had become a memory. The cottage was an empty shell. I had become an empty shell, so I left it. I retreated to the place of safety: the place where all was familiar, where my Mother ruled; where my lonely Brother filled his hours with anxiety and work.

My Marriage had broken down. I did not make a secret of it. I made sure all knew. My sadness was kept in a private place; I did not divulge explanation, vindication, rhyme or reason. For Reg, the newness and originality of marriage had worn off.

‘Did you try to reason it out yourself?’

Yes Ronnie. Once the shock and loss began to diminish enough for me to grasp the reality of my life, I could make some sense of it all. Reg needed to be free. Perhaps he found the constraints and Family pressure too binding, too suffocating. He was being sucked into the demands of new relatives, a Wife and...

‘A Pub...?’

I realised, much too late perhaps, that he had found life in a Yorkshire village difficult to reconcile, to resign himself to, when the cosmopolitan sophistication and urbanity of London Theatre-land beckoned. Reg had tried so hard with a life that had begun to pall, dampen and dismay.

‘You had found a certain kind of love...that is never wasted....’

No Ronnie, it is never lost completely….

'Now, the burning question…how did Jessica react to all this?'

I wonder if Mum thought that Reg was the one to fit in with the plan? I wonder if she envisaged a time when Reg would be quite happy to spend his out-of-work times burying himself in the demands of the Ferguson-Fawsitt Arms? Often, she was heard to remark, "Oh Reg would be such a great draw here, an asset to the business…"

'And you, who could be slow on the uptake from time to time, didn't clock the surmising, the inference that Reg could strengthen her stronghold?'

Well, Ronnie, I didn't cotton on to that possibility then. I am in no doubt that Mum was Reg's champion. For me, at the time, that was a boon…

'Well, of course. Especially when all the past liaisons had come to grief. It appears that Reg fitted admirably into the slot your Mother had in mind.'

"Well, at least you didn't have any kids to worry about," observed Emily. "No," said Jessica, "that's a shame, isn't it?"

'Talk about rubbing salt into the wound. What happened to "There's more to life than having children"!'

My innermost thoughts were filled with relief. I loved children, but they could have….

'Tightened those strings for evermore…'

So, Ronnie darling, I did not lay the blame at Reg's door lock, stock and barrel. In truth, perhaps, we should not have married in the first place. That was my fault as much as his.

'Looking back, do you think that David and Howard knew that?'

Perhaps Ronnie. Their silence speaks volumes now.

'Did you ever see Reg again?'

No. Reg returned briefly to the cottage during Christmas of 1978 to collect his belongings, but I did not make contact. I had the common sense to realise that it was over between us.

'Painful, knowing he was back in the cottage. That must have been very difficult....'

I recovered gradually. I had learned much. Also, I came to be very glad that I had known Reg. He was a fine Actor, a very funny man and in so many ways, a man of principle. Until he met me, he had found his quest in life; then, for a few short months, I rocked the boat. There is always a reason why folk behave in the way that they do.

'Bit of déjà vu there, pet? Bill knew, didn't he?'

Yes my darling, he did.

There is a footnote to this story. I had to laugh. Just before we were married, my Mother said to me "What will you do? Go on The Pill?"

'What! Talk about shutting the gate after the ...you know what...'

That was the one isolated occasion when my Mother had touched upon Contraception in any shape or form!

'Just when it wouldn't have mattered if you'd become pregnant...Hell's teeth, you were married!'

Poor Mum. Was she naïve? Was she innocent, unaware and unenlightened? Was she a damaged prisoner trapped in the narrow, double standards of her early doctrines? Whatever the precept, she and possibly her peers, were guilty of shirking Parental responsibility. If things had gone awry sexually, I know where the blame, shame and axe would have fallen.

'Harsh words, petal...'

Fortunately for my Mother, she had no worries. It doesn't alter the fact that I and many of my chums suffered, caught in the bewilderment of natural feelings and inclinations.

No one explained, no one described and Sex was cloaked in a shroud of embarrassment, disgust or dirt. The youth of the Fifties found itself perched on a powder-keg of fear. Who put what, where, how and when? What happened when you found out? That's if one ever did!

'Now don't be crude – you know I blush when you are indelicate!'

Well, that would be a first!

~

Tony phoned.

'Ah...yes, and...?'

He knew about Reg. Funny how Tony was always there to salvage the bits. Jimmy knew and Jimmy always knew what to say, "Sweetheart, they come and they go...but you go on forever!"

'What did Tony do with the bits this time?'

He had written 'Child's Play' and wanted me for the lead. The play, a magical, menacing tale, ordinary in its seaside setting, pushed into the area of thriller. It traced the lives, past and present, of Brother and Sister, Lionel and Rita Jessop – Punch & Judy man and Cabaret Entertainer.

Rita Jessop was a fascinating character; indeed, all of Tony's creations were fascinating. Rita's Cabaret performance was absolutely terrifying.

'I think I know what you're going to say. Tony had you 'Performing' it.'

Exactly Ronnie. One saw two sides of the Rita coin: at home and then before her 'Audience'. Poor Rita was just about the worst Cabaret performer in existence. Her 'Show', played within a solitary white spotlight, was overblown and overflowing with appalling gags finishing up with a second rate, maudlin and mawkish farewell song! Once more, I was playing a faded, declining woman!

Shades of Beaujolais Rose. Needless to say, she was an Actor's gift... but, nevertheless, a petrifying test of memory and nerve.

'And...diversion?'

Yes, my love, a diversion. Many months later, Tony divulged the truth. I had been in a state. It had taken him considerable time to settle my wandering, preoccupied thoughts. During Rehearsal, I had been a psychological force to be reckoned with.

'Darling Susie, if Tony had known his Susie, he would have realised that emotion runs amok with her. She'd just had an almighty blow'.

I believe that the wise Tony did know that, Ronnie. Coping with it was another matter. I suffered with stage fright more severely than ever before and became beset with the thought that lines would leave me at any given moment. This scary inkling obsessed me the most when I was alone on stage; when I was Rita the 'Performer'. Transfixed by the single Spot, I felt cornered, snared. The Actor's mind works on several levels: remembering the lines, what do I do if I forget them, when might I forget them and how am I executing them until I do...

'Execute – you're so dramatic, pet.'

The worst feeling is when the words are being spoken on automatic pilot, while uppermost thoughts are lingering on the complex preoccupation of forgetting them. You feel panic rise, sweat break out and limbs weaken. I had experienced this unease before, to a lesser or larger degree. What Actor hasn't? At this time, however, the psyche was dealing with much more: was I good enough, would I ever recover from this emotional turbulence, this commotion, this sorrow.

'Sue, oh Sue...the sense of being left behind, being just left must have been very isolating...'

Yes Ronnie, it was. The support of other Actors and of course the morale boosting from home stood me in good stead. Gradually, I strengthened. Meantime, I could have done with a puff of Jimmy's Strawberry cologne. That never failed.

'Puffs never do, darling!'

Kim Durham, playing Lionel Jessop, was a thoughtful, inventive Actor. I came to look forward to our Duologues. Soon, I steadied in Performance and the old Susie began to emerge. Supporting Actors, Stephen Frost and Janet Prince, were natural comedians and my spirits lifted. They, too, were cast in the Plater play, so a consoling, meaningful friendship began to grow. I think, much to Tony's relief, I was healing....

'I bet he knew a few hairy moments!'

Funnily enough, some of the Production photographs taken at that time proved to be interesting. One can almost detect my panic, desolation and fear in the pictures.

'What did I say about the eyes being the window of the soul'.

The cottage too had been abandoned. Winter came and no one told me to turn the water off!

'Flooded?'

Flooded, Ronnie – from floor to ceiling.

'Bugger...'

Suffice it to say, that although my mind was partially occupied with repairs and restoration, it was able to focus once more on reality and progress.

'Child's Play' played to packed houses, I recovered my bits and chalked up another complicated Characterisation. Tony, my dear Tony, helped me to limp through what might have been hidden disaster; instead, Rita became an achievement, a symbol and stamp of Spiritual growth. I was very proud of her.

I had been cast in the Humberside Theatre's Christmas Show 'Arabian Nights'! This was a romp, a frivolous concoction of Sultans, Damsels in Distress, a Sinbad and guess who – the Genie, to be played by that versatile familiar local Actress....

'Susanne Ubble!'

You can imagine, Ronnie, that this extravaganza became a very necessary part of my restorative process. Coupled with the fact that Robert Schofield's Sultan seemed to pay me more than a fair share of attention. Offstage, Bob became a close, attentive friend. He was an exciting, attractive joker; a man who had worked extensively in Repertory, appearing in the hit West End Show 'Once a Catholic'.

Bob was a sophisticated Londoner and for me, a breath of fresh air.

'An Angel in disguise....? They follow you around, my darling...'

Bob came along at the right time, Ronnie. As before, this Angel, when he had done his assuasive work, disappeared...but before leaving, he mended and brought back my lost trust, my conviction. No longer restive and restless, I never forgot his parting words...."I have a great deal of love for you, Sue".

For many months, those words became my charm, my amulet.

'Your love and your hope...'

~

Alan Plater's little Company toured 'Well, Goodnight Then..' for several weeks in the New Year of 1979. We roved over North, South, East and West. The Theatre Van trundled up hill and down dale in all weathers – snow, ice, winds and the biting cold. On reaching our destinations,

Alan Platers
'Well Goodnight Then'
Humberside Theatre 1978

we camped out in various digs, built and struck the Set, Performed tirelessly and paid homage to our craft.

'That's one way of putting it, my darling...'

Needless to say, I was the most senior member of the Cast and Company.

'Could anyone be as old as you?'

This exalted position rocketed me to the most comfortable seat in the Theatre Van – the front seat, beside John the long-suffering Driver who navigated our way through the most appalling Northern Winter. It soon became apparent to me that deference or homage to my advancing years was not the only consideration. I was being utilized as Lookout.

'So – what was going on in the back?'

Pot! I didn't rumble to it at first, until an acrid smell, not unlike that of rotting vegetation was borne under my nose. Lacking in nous, I didn't catch on at first and remarked to John "What's that fucking awful smell – must be muck-spreading!'"

'You're pure as driven snow, my darling! Incidentally, I thought you didn't use that kind of language!'

On that score, I was catching on Ronnie...fast! Of course the rear of the Van stank. There they were, all lolling in the easy chairs reserved for the Play Set, practically stoned! Stephen Frost announced, "Well Sue darling, if we're stopped by the Fuzz, we knew that you could cover long enough. You're so good at it!"

'Ignorance is bliss, petal!'

So, Ronnie, we all earned our money on that Tour, but there was no time for introspection. I was cushioned and cosseted by the Company. All knew of my heartache; there was kindness and there was understanding. I was held dear and have never forgotten. They were a...

'Grand lot?'

Jewels, Ronnie.

~

I returned to the Ferguson Fawsitt. All was as it had always been. Routine followed and I took my place behind one counter or another. Just as my thoughts were once more approaching the dwelling stage, David Scase phoned!

'Yes, yes....what?'

He offered two Plays, Ronnie – 'The Diary of Anne Frank' dramatised by Goodrich & Hackett at the Forum and Simon Gray's 'Butley' at The Library.

'Sue, work just kept on coming...it's wonderful!'

It was Ronnie. I didn't have time to catch my breath and in the circumstances, perhaps that was just as well.

'Now, before Jessica starts again....where were you going to live?'

Guess what Ronnie?

'Yes, yes, go on...I'm guessing...'

With Keith and Annie!

'Oh Sue, wondrous!'

During the intervening years, Keith and Annie had produced children, Rachel two and baby Rebecca. They had set up home in a small terraced house in Levenshulme, a suburb of Manchester. I was greeted with open arms. It was a joy to see them again after such a long time. I was in seventh heaven to be with old friends and included as one of the family. Rachel and I became great buddies.

'I seem to remember you telling me that she had an obsession with your cotton wool balls!'

She did Ronnie, and kept a collection of them in her doll's house! Rachel appeared on the threshold of my back bedroom after breakfast. "What's Sue doink", said she. That was time for my make-up ritual. Rachel soon got wise to this and was there to help. I needed to allow plenty of time; Rachel was hell-bent on trying my lipsticks – mess everywhere.

"Rachel Clifford, come down here AT ONCE!!" was Annie's call to arms.

Evenings were spent in post mortems about our Theatre days. Keith was also busy and it made for engrossing, hilarious accounts of daily happenings. All this would be interspersed with Annie's determination to discipline her girls. It became commonplace for Rachel to be reprimanded with "Rachel Clifford, go and stand in the Hall!"

'Presumably a variation of the naughty step?'

It was, Ronnie. Often, Rachel, by no means backwards in coming forwards would annunciate, very clearly, from the Hall: "Rachel didn't do it!"

When 'Becca began to crawl and eventually to stagger from one table leg to another, she came in for Rachel's spleen and was blamed for any misdemeanour the cause for which couldn't be accounted for!

'Revenge!'

So, Ronnie, the house of Clifford became my launch pad. From this loving, natural home, I journeyed to the land of make-believe; the Library Theatre which I had grown to love.

'Was David directing 'The Diary of Anne Frank'?'

No Ronnie. A Diana Harker, Guest Director and new comer to me, was to step in. Dear David, my loveable Boss, was always around. His rollicking laugh preceded him, followed by bear hugs and wholesome greeting. The Forum Stage was huge. Just as well, for the Designer, Chris Kinman, set out to create an obstacle circuit for 'The Diary' and its Actors.

'Oh…one of those, eh?'

Members of the Family who spent most of their time on the 'Attic' floor, as it were, were safe as houses. I was playing the complaining Mrs. Van Daan. The quarters for my Husband and I were way up high on a very perilous platform.

Mrs Van Daan
Manchester Library 1976

'Did either of you suffer from Vertigo?'

Tough if we did, Ronnie. This raised Rostrum was accessed by an equally hazardous, precarious and chancy step-ladder. Eventually, when one had teetered or tottered to the top….

'You were sick…'

Mercifully not, Ronnie. There was quite a drop. Vomiting over the edge would, indeed, have been a disaster.

'Did you have to clamber in high heels?'

Good point, Ronnie – and yes, I did.

'Hell's teeth, Alice…'

John Jardine, a well-known Northern Actor and Library regular, was cast as Mr. Van Daan. We got on famously, which again was just as well. Once in our bedroom eyrie, there was much smothered giggling as we threw back the covers and got into bed.

'No chance of rumpy-pumpy then, Alice?'

Do you ever think of anything else, Ronnie?

'Not very often darling – especially when I'm with you!'

Ah, memories are made of this.....!

So, Ronnie, although often a shilly-shallying, rickety or wonky physical exercise, our Rehearsals were certainly histrionic. In spite of the intricacies of Performance, no one had a hissy-fit; not even John!

Sarah Greene, later of Blue Peter fame, played Anne to perfection. She was backed by a united, consistent Cast. John and I did come through unscathed; our chalk face contribution received acclaim and not least, admiration for sheer valour and pluck when confronted with mountaineering duress!

The little Levenshulme household found itself in the throes of one predicament or another over the coming weeks.

'And...you, no doubt, were in the thick of those how-do-you-does?'

I was, Ronnie. While Rehearsing 'The Diary', my evenings were free. Keith was also engaged with day-time Rehearsals at the Library. I thought it a good idea to offer to baby-sit while they had some time to themselves.

'Ah, the road to Hell is paved with good intentions, pet...'

All was quiet and under control. I was reading an idyllic Fairy tale to Rachel, just before bedtime. 'Becca was tucked up and accounted for. What I had not deemed a possibility, was a fire in the street outside! All at once, an Engine screeched to a halt outside No. 19 and a prodigious number of burly Firemen scrambled, ready to wage war on the unfortunate conflagration over the road.

'Don't tell me, everybody burst into tears!'

'Becca certainly did. It was all hands on deck to sort out the hot water I found myself in! 'Becca screamed the place down....to make matters worse Rachel kept on shouting "'Becca wettink...Sue, 'Becca wettink!"

'Of course, you had never changed a nappy in your life!'

Between us, or rather under Rachel's very helpful instructions, I managed to sort 'Becca out. I decided that the best line of action for the rest of the evening was to sit everybody on the sofa and keep together in case of further plight or pickle. Cold sweat began to bead – everywhere!

'And there Keith and Annie found you some time later – knackered!'

Rachel pointed out, very carefully I might add: "Rachel didn't do it!"

'Just as well to get that in first I suppose...'

My stay with Keith and Annie did not pass without incident; calamity of all kind descended upon us.

'The word 'experience' is where you come to rest, Sue.'

Thank you for remembering that, Ronnie. It so happened that the house next door was being partly demolished so that the owners could enlarge their kitchen. This workload caused all manner of disturbance and unearthed a plague...

'Oh, dear God no....'

...of Cockroaches! These buggers came to life at night, can you believe.

It was my misfortune to wake in the early hours on my way for a glass of water, switch on the light in time to see, crawling around all four skirting boards, a significant army of these bloody creatures!

'Did you scream?'

Well of course I did. Keith, clad only in pyjama bottoms, was framed in the doorway, sure that I had disturbed an intruder.

'Well you had, in a way....!

The whole house was in uproar: 'Becca 'woke, Rachel 'woke, Annie certainly 'woke and Keith – swore hell and damnation on next-door! To steady the buffs, the Gin bottle took a hiding at 2.00 in the morning!

'Butley' opened at the Library Theatre on 25 April 1979. It was directed by David Scase. For once, I was playing 'straight' in that I was not smothered in green greasepaint or masquerading as a Traffic Warden. It was a change to be plain Mrs. Butley.

'Not plain darling – just interesting...'

I was to work with David Calder. He was a leading Actor and had appeared in just about everything and all over the place.

'Easy to work with?'

Well, different Ronnie. It was a good Cast and I was delighted to see John Jardine and Sarah Greene on the List. Most of my Scenes were with David. As far as I was concerned they were successful.

'I sense some reticence?'

No one really knew what must have been rumbling under the surface, but all came to the crunch when, at one Performance, David must have had a do, so to speak; he was unable to continue with the Second Half.

'Oh Eck!'

That was the first time I had encountered the possibility of the 'Show must not go on' after all! It remained a mystery and 'It wasn't Susan's fault'!'

'Butley' was to be my last Show at the Library. Towards the end of my stay an offer came from Oldham Coliseum. Would I like to play Rhoda in Kenneth Alan Taylor's production of 'Celebration' by Keith Waterhouse & Willis Hall, to begin rehearsals in May?

'Another brilliant Northern comedy...and more work, darling!'

I knew how fortunate I was, Ronnie. I also knew what a wrench it would be to leave Annie and Keith. The absence of Rachel's "What's Sue doink?" and "Rachel didn't do it!" would create a lonely, silent gap in my life. Once more, I had set down roots – in Levenshulme.

On the morning of my departure, Keith, who was a gifted Artist, gave me a pencil etching which he had modelled from my Front-of-House photograph. It was a startling likeness. "For all your First Nights, dear Sue" said he simply.

'You promptly burst into tears...'

Ronnie, how did you guess. It was a tearful, heavy-hearted parting. Keith, Annie, Rachel and 'Becca were my little Family and I had grown to love them all very much. As I climbed into the taxi which was to spirit me away, I felt utterly bereft.

"Where's Sue goink?" whispered Rachel.

Leaving David Scase was to bring its own sadness. He and Howard had trusted me with some exceptional opportunities. I had grown so very fond of both men. They were special...

'Angels......well, you know the rest....'

~

I did not have time to return home before moving to Oldham. I had been put in touch with an elderly couple, Esther and Clifford, who lived in Chadderton. Apparently, they enjoyed having Actors to stay.

'Up your street, darling...someone to watch over you!'

It just seemed so very strange...

'Well of course it did. You were about to settle into a normal home! Presumably light years away from Keith and Annie's Theatrical refuge. Just remember never to say 'Fuck'!'

I did Ronnie. I managed to adjust, but it was all so proper! Esther and Clifford were the kindest couple and made me very welcome. They had recently said farewell to Timothy, a young man who had also worked at the Coliseum. He came up in conversation repeatedly; it was obvious that they had grown very fond of him indeed. I felt I was a poor substitute...

'Give over, I'm sure they would soon get used to your strange ways!'

Needless to say, I was busy almost at once and so Esther and Clifford were, in the main, evening companions.

'What were they like?'

Clifford was rather large, about seventy I would think; he had a shock of white hair and a faintly sallow complexion. This seemed to match rather well with his reserved, somewhat unforthcoming countenance. I think I'm right in saying that he was a man of few words.

'He might have been shy. You're enough to make any man bashful and retiring!'

Thank you, Ronnie.

Esther was, in contrast, garrulous. I think she was filling in for Clifford much of the time. I did wonder if Clifford had had some sort of accident at work, for he sported a noticeable scar across his head.

'That could explain his manner...'

Much to my embarrassment, they flatly refused to accept any payment for Rent. I attempted to insist, but all to no avail. So, I was in a fix.

'I bet you soon came up with the key to that one.'

I did Ronnie. One night, after our evening meal, I was helping Esther to wash up.

'One of my favourite pastimes, you'll remember!'

Afterwards, I was intrigued with one of her regular occupations – putting tea-bags into a large kitchen container, marked 'Have a Cuppa!' While chattering away to me, she would meticulously separate the tea-bags that were joined, dropping each very methodically into the aforesaid receptacle!

'Pretty spicy, heady stuff, Sue!'

I thought it was an ideal moment to hand over a cheque which I had at the ready. It was for a hundred quid which went some way to covering several week's Rent. Esther, for once, was speechless before calling for Clifford. "Well, Clifford, we'll be able to go and have a real buyin' in at the weekend".

'A what?'

It turned out that 'a buyin' in' was a very large shopping quest, where one accumulated several week's supply of groceries and the like.

'More tea-bags I bet!'

So, to say that my stay with Esther and Clifford was different, would be an understatement. Having said that, they were the most thoughtful of people and my whole stay at their comfortable home was just what the Doctor ordered.

'Did you start work straightaway?'

Yes, Ronnie. The centre of Oldham was only a short bus ride away and there I found the Coliseum. In the late Seventies, the Theatre was still one of those fashioned for use in Music-Hall and Variety; you know, opulent velvety boxes, plush seats and an Auditorium that consisted of Orchestra Pit, Stalls, Balcony and The Gods.

'Real Theatre, darling...'

I didn't know any of the Cast for 'Celebration'. I didn't really know Kenneth Alan Taylor, the Artistic Director. I had gleaned a little information from Keith who had come across Kenneth from time to time. I gathered that he was much revered in Oldham, where he had garnered a keen, ebullient reputation for producing legendary, traditional Pantomimes. To cap all, he was renowned for his saucy Dames. So, in all, my first encounter was another journey of discovery.

I arrived on the dot and found most of the Company were congregated in the Stalls where Kenneth was holding court. He nodded to me, smiled and invited me to join the others. All seemed to know each other very well.

I discovered that most of the Cast had, at some time or another, played in 'Coronation Street'. I came to learn that the grassroots of their Theatrical experience had begun to flourish at the Oldham Coliseum. Now, it seemed, however, that the Theatre was undergoing a sea change. 'Celebration' was to mark the end of its first season.

'Were you about to meet some of the fledgling Performers of 'The Street'?'

I was, Ronnie. Do you remember Lynne Carol?

'She was Martha Longhurst, the snipey gossip and Snug regular at The Rovers along with Ena Sharples'.

All seemed very friendly. I was to take on Rhoda Lucas, Mother of the Bride! The First Half of the play, set at the Family's Wedding Reception, proved to be a load, burden and onus for me.

'If I remember clearly, Rhoda has to set up God knows how many tables!'

Ronnie, it was a nightmare: cloths to spread, cutlery to set, glasses to position and to crown all, the Cake to arrange – three bloody tiers of it!

'All that and the lines as well! That cake warranted danger money!'

The Second Half was less of a liability. The same Family was presiding over a Funeral commemoration! At least the refreshments were much easier to cope with and the play was a riot of Northern witticisms. Rehearsals were fun.

Lynne was, of course, a fount of Street information. Others who had taken part, were also armed with intriguing stories.

'What was Kenneth like as a Director?'

He was orderly, precise; also, graced with chichi manner and pattern of speech. He was a card, a caution. His routine was punctuated with riotous anecdotes and comments on behaviour. I recall one yarn very vividly.

'Yes, I'm waiting with bated breath – you always stop there!'

Kenneth was calling to mind an occasion when Theatre friends were visiting his home. These people seemed to be well known to the 'Celebration' Cast, so there was much "Mmn…ing and Aahing…" as the story progressed. According to Kenneth, there had been a lull in conversation, perhaps when boredom crept in. All at once, a member of the throng announced, "Oh well, does anybody fancy a fuck?"!!

'No!'

Well, you can imagine, everyone on Stage just collapsed. Funnily enough, I remember being really shocked. My Theatrical education was still in its infancy! I couldn't believe what I was hearing!

'You've got to admit, that was funny Sue!'

Now, as I look back, I realise how hilarious it was…at the time, it stopped me in in my tracks.

'Sweetheart…you were still adjusting to the rough-hewn, crude and bawdy. You hadn't met me then!'

You were just homespun and earthy!

'You never let on!'

Once the Play was running and Audiences were rolling into the Coliseum, my confidence was soaring. I had enormous fun and the Company was a real…

'Tonic?'

Oh yes, Ronnie. I found myself working with an Ensemble Cast. No one was out to seek glory. That generosity produces its own rewards and I was quite downhearted when the Production closed on 16th June 1979.

'Was it home to Fergie and don't spare the horses...?'

It was, my darling, but not before I had said my Goodbyes to dear Esther and Clifford. They had taken their place among my favourite people. Needless to say, I made sure there was to be another 'buyin'-in' after my departure. Little did I know then, that that Goodbye was not a final one. I would encounter Esther and Clifford again several years later...

'Had I come on the scene then?'

Now that would be telling!

~

It was Mid-Summer at the Ferguson-Fawsitt Arms.

'Back in the old corral, eh?'

It was good to be back on familiar ground again, Ronnie. There was time to relax – but, for once, no work was coming in...

'Don't relax too much, pet...'

I didn't Ronnie. I was still very much on the ball. For some time, I had hoped to work nearer to home.

'Oh no, darling...was that a wise choice?'

Perhaps not, Ronnie...with hindsight...

'Bloody 'ell, not that stumbling block again?'

I had been harbouring the thought of working for Alan Ayckbourn at Scarborough.

'Well, that's a turn-up for the books, pet...'

I thought that if there was a chance of joining his Company, it would be a further boost to my career. To tell the truth, I didn't know where I was. I was in limbo ...

rudderless again…waiting, I suppose, for the next push. In the meantime, it as good to be home. Once more, I revelled in its sanctuary, cover and retreat.

'Was the impetus, the force of Theatre still there?'

Oh yes, Ronnie. It nagged at me all the time. It was continually paired with the thought "Now come on, Theatre is what you should be doing".

'Ah, but did you really want to?'

I did, Ronnie, but the fear never left me – fear of meeting strange people again, fear of the pressure, the strain of it all…fear of pushing myself over the edge; facing the summons to combat that fear. Yet the invisible thread kept tugging …the urge to move on to the next acid test.

'What were you looking for?'

You're going to laugh…

'Have I ever laughed at you, my darling…?'

I longed for happiness, to be settled and secure.

'That's not something to laugh at – it's something we all crave…'

I was struggling with this dilemma. It was time to take my own advice; the counsel I had always given to frightened children in my care.

'The only way to deal with fear is to face it head on!'

So, I did. The application for Audition went off to the Stephen Joseph Theatre in Scarborough, where Mr. Ayckbourn called the tune.

~

'Now, how was that Jessica faring these days?'

As soon as I was home again and all her chicks were back in the nest, she seemed to be in very good spirits. She presided over the Dining Room with polish and finesse. She was communicative, approachable and stylish. An impressive anchor-woman and Hotelier, she impressed all with her subtle Mine Hostess composure. Customers warmed to her, her humour, inclination to oblige and willingness to turn her hand at the wheel.

'Wheel and deal might be nearer the mark!'

Her appearance was unsurpassed. She was the articulate, aesthetically dressed boss and boffin. My Mother could never be accused of an inclination to dodge or duck out of duty or the job in hand.

'I can't resist the temptation to add that she was artful, foxy!'

Oh, true Ronnie. I did, however, take my hat off to her for sheer perseverance within a situation that, without my Father, must have been scary to say the least. She was feisty.

I remember, with such fondness, that Mum had a repository of 'sayings' which could be levelled at those who insinuated slur or affront. These descriptions could be wickedly accurate.

A regular diner at the Ferguson had an unfortunate physical build in that her bottom was of gigantic spread. This Lady could be difficult to please and so Jessica, by way of covert settling of her hash would mutter under her breath "Oh, she's 'ere again, 'ere's me 'ed me arse is comin'!" or, "She's seen 'er arse and doesn't like the look of it!" Other forms of address, presumably inherited from Gran and Grandpa, would crease all within hearing: "Fanny Fanacka Pan", "Titty Fa Loll", or "Madam Fancy-Knickers" could be applied to any doomed or sour woman who had the gall and effrontery to antagonize my Mother.

'Imagine the shock! Here was the Lady of the Manor, immaculate of Performance and courtly of manner polluting the air with mild expletive! I love that Jessica!'

She would then lean in towards the indomitable Dina and declare "You can't catch old birds with Chaff!" What the fuck did that mean!

'Language! Like Mother, like Daughter! I reckon you were running to Ivy's aid while all this was going on?'

Yes Ronnie. The Pub was busy, in fact heaving during the Summer months; there was not time to draw breath. Saturdays were particularly frantic: Weddings were booked and these could present us with unforeseen aggravation in spite of meticulous planning.

Again, my Mother offered the ultimate in self-sacrifice when she offered our main bedroom for the Bride and Groom to change. Most were attentive and careful, but...

'Didn't one couple attempt to try out the bed?'

Just so, Ronnie. Later, my Mother, feeling like a couple of hours respite, retired upstairs only to find the room trashed – one leg broken off the bed and the floor covered in confetti!

'Perhaps the Groom was pissed – or, the Bride told him to piss off!'

Poor Mum was horrified. Later, when she spilled the beans to the devout, irascible Dina, the pair of them were locked in ire, umbrage and a surge of incredulity. Dina was heard to sum up the whole dire, deplorable escapade with "I can remember a time when such things were kept under wraps!"

'I love that Dina!'

Stories of those Wedding Days were numerous – legion in fact.

'Oh go on...one more...!'

One Saturday morning, more or less at the crack of dawn, the Bride's Grandmother arrived to deliver the cake which had been lovingly created by her own fair hands. We were given strict instructions on how to assemble each layer. My Mother's unease was palpable, as Dennis, Chef, eager to take charge and pot-belly to the fore, was seen to lean heavily against the confection's silver salver. There was a slight wobble – Dennis' stomach, fortunately, not the Cake – and all seemed to bode well.

The Bridegroom turned out to be a Naval Lieutenant and so insisted on cutting Grandma's pride and joy with his Ceremonial Sword! Grandmother's icing turned out to be a brittle as hell and as soon as the blade sliced into it, slivers hurtled across the Dining Room like splinters and splits from a hurtling, charging glacier.

'Did Grandmother have the vapours?'

All I can say, in conclusion, is that Dennis was nowhere to be seen and Dina summed up the whole unfortunate incident as "An act of God!" God certainly had nothing to do with it! The blame was laid very firmly at the door of Grandma. Mum discounted all guilt or culpability and hit the gin bottle!

~

'How was Nick panning out?'

I think with a great deal of stress, Ronnie. He had been Assistant Manager before my Father died, so, to be catapulted into overall accountability, suddenly and fearfully, must have been awesome. The angst was showing and I overheard the word Valium bandied about very often; I found that alarming.

'Poor Nick. Needless to say, with no Partner around, Jessica would also be reliant and demanding. I don't envy the poor bugger…'

Nick was solicitous when it came to my place in all this. He was heedful, as always; I was put on the payroll while working. Granted, I worked hard, but would have helped out regardless of remuneration. Nevertheless, that extra cash maintained some independence. All the while, Nick continued to be very popular with Customers, both regulars and casual visitors. The process did, however, take its toll.

Then....guess what happened Ronnie?

'I can't guess...go on, go on...!'

I received word from the Stephen Joseph Theatre!

'The Man Himself?'

Not quite, Ronnie. Via his P.A. I was given an Audition date to report to the Theatre-in-the-Round in the middle of July. I was asked to come armed with the usual pieces for Performance.

'Same ones as before – you know, Tony's Beaujolais Rose?'

Ronnie, I would never go anywhere without that!

'Were you nervous all over again?'

That was a foregone conclusion, Ronnie. I borrowed Nick's car again and drove myself over to Scarborough.

'Go on, describe everything – as if I had never come across the Theatre before and didn't know this famous seaside town!'

I discovered that the Theatre-in-the-Round was down a small incline at the end of Valley Bridge Parade. I came to know later that the Bridge had been a chosen suicide venue in the past, which did explain why there was such elaborate gratings and deterrent rails. The Theatre carried the title of Westwood Theatre. The building was a close neighbour of the Technical College in the early Eighties. This was the home of Alan Ayckbourn...

'No 'Sir' in those days...'

The entrance vestibule was really a corridor. Once through the front door, I came face to face with the Booking Office. The passage to the left led to the Bar and small Restaurant. I parked myself on a nearby chair and waited for someone to come along. There were double doors to the right which I presumed led to the Main House Theatre.

'I bet you were there early... as usual...'

Of course, darling. The minutes ticked by and I became more and more on edge. In fact, my hands felt as if they had been glued together. The double doors opened and a young man, who introduced himself as the Stage Manager, Sean O'Neill, appeared. "Hello Susan, do come this way".

'Did he see you trembling?'

I think he must have done Ronnie, for he said, "Oh don't worry, he'll be more nervous than you!".

'Now what was that Theatre like...remember, it's as if I didn't know...!'

The seating was circular and rose in tiers round the central Acting area. At regular intervals, what looked like small passageways could be seen. I came to know these as Voms, short for Vomitory, used for entrances and exits as in an amphitheatre.

'Anything suggesting vomiting for the First Night Actor would be appropriate!'

Mr. Ayckbourn was sitting on the front row! I was introduced. He was very different from what I had expected.

'Mmn...say no more...'

To say he was a man of few words, would have been an understatement. Oh, how I pined for David Scase and his chuckling bear hugs...

'Oh darling...never mind, life is made up of the unexpected...'

Alan Ayckbourn was a big man. His gaze was searching; it certainly didn't give anything away, not even a smile. As for a grin, well...forget it. He had a very high and expansive forehead. In those split seconds of weighing him up, I remember being reminded of The Mekon, arch enemy of the British Comic Book hero, Dan Dare. The character appeared regularly in the 'Eagle' Comic that Brother Nick used to pore over every week in the Fifties; he had been created by scientific experimentation, engineered for a very high intelligence.

'Hell's teeth, Sue. All that summing up in the blink of a practised eye!'

Well, I must have taken it all in for I thought about it in microscopic detail on the way home.

'How different did you find the Acting area? So at odds with a Proscenium Arch...'

You're right, Ronnie. Once in that 'Round' the Actor can be seen from all angles. The Audience would be close enough to touch; daunting, at first.

'Did he give anything away?'

No Ronnie. He didn't. But....he half smiled as I was taking my leave...it was impossible to detect which way the wind was blowing. I did, however, overcome my nerves. I know I didn't fall by the wayside!

'I'd love to have been a fly on the wall, after you'd left!'

I knew that I wanted to work at the Theatre-in-the-Round. I was very affected by the Theatre and all that it promised.

'So, it was back to my beloved Dina and the rich excesses of the Ferguson-Fawsitt Arms?'

At least I didn't feel as though I was sitting on my hands, Ronnie. I was doing something. I was forging ahead...even if, on bleak days of anxiety, I was filled with foreboding...'

'Now that's interesting...you have never actually applied the word anxiety to yourself before...'

No Ronnie, but it was there...always...hovering....

'I meant to ask earlier – what was happening to the cottage and were the Aunties still around?'

They were, Ronnie. Their visits were spasmodic, but I fulfilled all my exemplary, upright and transport obligations...and...I hasten to add, cleaned out all the flat's cupboards before Jessica went on the rampage in a fever of anticipation, sure that she would go to the bottom of the class as far as cleanliness was concerned.

'You are evil!'

I'm afraid that the cottage was off bounds, most of the time. It had become something of an ongoing liability. I did pay it attention as far as maintenance was required, but that's were my compulsion ceased. I did, however, hang on to it for the time being. Something told me that it could come in handy...God knows what for....

'For your Mother and Nick, perhaps? Just a thought... one for another day, I reckon...'

You're just an old Gipsy, the teller of cryptic messages!

~

Within days, I received a phone call from the Theatre-in-the-Round!

'Yes, yes....what?'

I was invited to play old Rebecca Nurse in an Ayckbourn production of 'The Crucible' by Arthur Miller. Rehearsals would commence in the Autumn with a Read-through of the Play in October.

'Darling, that's wonderful...but...er...were you thrown into a frenzy of preparation?'

There would be an important consideration, Ronnie. Where would I live?

'Oh Eck! That's always your first thought, Alice'.

The Theatre's Production office were not very helpful, I'm afraid. A digs list seemed to be non-existent. I was going to be thrown on to my own resources.

'Take heart, Alice. You know who helps those who help themselves...'

True Ronnie, but cold comfort when one doesn't know where the bloody hell to start. At that time, I was foolish enough to think that no other Actor worried about lodgings. I thought I was very peculiar, green and ingenuous.

'Well – you were!'

You know, now, what I'd say to that...!'

'Bugger off Ronnie, I expect!'

I happened to have a confab with Dina, the oracle and wellspring of all knowledge. She came up with an idea of sounding out the possibility of off-Season Scarborough Holiday Flats!

'Trust that Dina come up with – hindsight I state pompously – the obvious!'

Well, it should have been plain to me, Ronnie, but it wasn't! After much rooting and delving around, I managed to find a Flat which was nearly opposite to the Theatre entrance path.

'That was lucky, pet...'

It could have been, Ronnie.

'Oh God, that doesn't bode very well...'

The Play Read-through loomed menacingly close and I began to get the wind up. All the familiar terror-stricken feelings were unearthed again and I wanted to run. I didn't know any other member of the Cast. What would they be like? Would I be good enough? The thought of facing Mr. Ayckbourn and his intimidating eagle eye every day, put the fear of God into me.

'Darling, didn't it ever occur to you that you had a track record – a good one – you were more than qualified to join his Company'.

Yes, in my heart of hearts I knew that, but I also knew that I was going to long for people like Keith, Annie and darling Jimmy.

'Now, what would Jimmy have said about Mr. Ayckbourn?'

Something like "Oh Aileen Ayckbourn – come on, pet, She's only a Director!"

'So, you did get yourself to the Read-over. Now what happened that day?'

Fortunately, old Rebecca Nurse featured in very scattered exchanges. It was a cough-and-a-spit part. That gave me plenty of scope to observe.

Mr. Ayckbourn seated his Cast in a circle. I soon realised that many of the Performers had worked with him before. I guess that roused a certain presumption and 'in' jokes soon began to rattle back and forth. I'm sure that added to the discomfort of many, not just me. Several Actors were vocal, bold and blatant. Mr. Ayckbourn reciprocated, responded with a few Theatrical reminiscences of his own and was rewarded with the clamour of obsequious merriment.

'Ugh! Just do your own thing, pet. Let 'em get on with it...we always come across a few...'

There was not time on that occasion to make meaningful contact with the more open-minded and receptive Actors, but their expressive smiles and unreserved manner promised a future connection where the down-to-earth among us could come together.

I did notice that Mr. Ayckbourn made little or no attempt to put those of us who were newcomers at ease. Again, I compared the David Scases of this world. One could only assume that Mr. A. thought an introductory ushering in was of scant importance; perhaps he would suffice it to say that as you were there, in his presence and had been employed by him, it was quite enough.

'You had a few week's grace before the onslaught began?'

Mum and Nick were resolute in their determination to see me settled in the aforementioned Holiday Flat. Rehearsals began at the beginning of a week in October 1979, so moving-in day was a Sunday. Armed with accoutrements – duvet, supplies and of course a stash of Gordon's – we unloaded. You would think I had learned a valuable lesson at Coventry, wouldn't you? Again,

I had not taken on board that, owing to the possibility of Rebecca's infrequent Rehearsal calls, I would not be summoned very often. So, for the whole of a three-week stretch it would have been possible to commute by car to home in Walkington!

'Instead, you were to be condemned to the flesh pots of Scarborough!'

Well, Ronnie, that's where it all started.

'What started?'

Little did I know that I was in the early stages of a breakdown...'

'Darling...surely, it couldn't be as bad as that?'

Everything came to a head when I stayed, alone, in that Flat...that one ghastly night. I wandered from bedroom to kitchen, bathroom to bedroom and back again to sit in despair on the armchair. I remember only its threadbare moquette upholstery. I drank Gin but never came under its influence. I was lost. I didn't weep. It was as if I had forgotten how to weep. Nothing released the fear. All was a sinister, forbidding, baleful blank...of course I didn't know I was depressed. I didn't know I was anxious. I could not rationalise this state, this spacing out. Foremost in my thoughts, was the worry of not being able to function the following day.

'Why didn't you call home?'

I was afraid, afraid to tell anyone how I felt. How would they understand?

What could they do? I was a child-adult and how could I admit that? I lay, fully dressed, on the bed. My eyes wouldn't close. They stared and the ceiling stared back through the peeling paint and cobwebs. I suppose I must have slept. I don't remember. I remember getting up, in the dark. I remember looking out of the window into the street. That night was the most petrifying of my life....as

I looked out, out into the blackness, I couldn't breathe. I felt my heart bursting from my chest as the panic rose and I sank to my knees. In that dreadful moment, I almost wished I was dead....there, as I lay upon the floor...I no longer cared...I just wanted to be free....free from caring, free.... to run and run and never stop.....to scream.....to scream for the love I so desperately needed.....

'My darling...all the while, I was but a few streets away, a new life away...but we had to wait... as they say, wait until our souls were ready to meet....'

I knew nothing of that then, Ronnie. I was lost. I could sink no further....

'I think, my love, that you were very ill'.

Thank God I didn't realise that then, Ronnie.

Somehow, I must have slept – on the floor. As my eyes opened, I realised where I was and felt the panic rising again. I cannot really remember how I washed, dressed and walked over to the Theatre that morning – but, I did.

'Did you telephone home for help?'

I did, Ronnie. Nick said "Phone again, when you're finished. I'll come and get you". It was that promise that saw me through the morning. As fortune would have it, I was not needed all day. The Call Sheet revealed a free afternoon and the day to follow.

'How did you cope with the Rehearsal and Himself?'

I suppose on automatic pilot, Ronnie. I walked through all as if in a hypnotic trance, a fog. Faces were transient, as if they were fleeting, ephemeral. My lips were moving. I hid behind my Script, hoping that no one would see the wide-eyed distraction, the troubled confusion and dread – the dread of losing my nerve.

'How very odd that all this came to a head when you were Rehearsing a Play about one of the strangest and most awful chapters in human history...'

Yes Ronnie, I've often thought about that since – a strange turn of events.

Nick came. Mum came. They were frightened too. I escaped. Once I was home, I wept. I wept without ceasing, for a very long time. I gave in completely. I was incapable of any rational, lucid bearing. Now, so many years later, I can look upon the aftermath with some sense of the ridiculous!

'Yes, go on...'

It will come as no surprise for you to know, Ronnie, that Mum's comment was "Well, I never thought that Flat was what you were used to!"

'Bless, oh bless...'

My family did realise that urgent help was needed. Much to my amazement, I learned that, unbeknown to me, Nick had been seeking help for his own mental state.

'No!'

It seems that he had been introduced to a most unusual man, a Parapsychologist. Of course, that meant nothing to me and I was afraid. I trusted Nick. He explained that this gifted man had reassured and supported him at a time when he felt utterly vulnerable and paralysed with defenceless instability. The Ferguson Fawsitt Arms and all that it entailed, had nearly finished Nick. I agreed to meet this rescuer.

'Did you need to miss Rehearsals?'

Providence stepped in, Ronnie. I received a message from the Theatre cancelling my Call. I was to appear two days later.

'Who was this stranger? What was his name?'

You are always speaking of my Guardian Angels, Ronnie. So, shall we call him Dr. Seraph? As with all my helpers, he remained until his job was done and then as time went by, he faded away, knowing that I was strong again. His Teachings have endured the test of time. I have never forgotten his wisdom, kindness and altruism. He saved me.

'He saved us both, petal...'

Dr. Seraph listened. He waited. He watched. He hardly spoke. In the first few moments of our meeting, I wept. Again, I could not stem the weeping.

"Let's get you through the next few weeks, Sue. Then we'll put you together again....do not be afraid...I know you...I know you better than you know yourself...".

I was advised to cancel the Flat and commute to Scarborough by car. Home was where I needed to be. Arrangements for staying over could be made later. I was to phone Dr. Seraph each evening to strengthen the threads of help.

'Darling, the relief must have been unbelievable...to know that someone was listening...someone understood...'

It was, Ronnie. I was still very nervous and shaky. Trembling became the order of the day! But...I was being set free and I could take strength from that.

'Needless to say, Nick came to your rescue...you could use his car...'

I did, Ronnie. Nick was good to me. So good that he actually found me a little Mini Minor car...I knew he paid a pittance for it, but how I appreciated his caring generosity. The bloody thing broke down within a week and poor Nick was unable to do anything about it. Once more, Mum capped the whole miserable business with the comment "Oh well, I did say he might be buying a pig in a poke!"

'Now which worthy Car Maintenance Brochure did that come from?'

I had faced a mammoth shock, Ronnie. I was mentally ill. I felt great sympathy for my Mother who found the whole experience incomprehensible. It was unimaginable, unthinkable, out of the question. Why was her Daughter plunged, suddenly and without warning, into a pit of despair when her life seemed to be a bed of roses? Well, in time, we all come to realise that the mind is a very powerful thing...it can only take so much. One's mental balance, judgement, reason, senses and wits can kick against demands, strain and relentless influence. In the blink of an eye, all can collapse.....

'...and....it did....'

This breaking downfall affected me physically. My limbs seemed to be working independently; were ineffectual and weak. This was an entire breach, a rupture of my whole being. It was terrifying....

'For God's sake...what happened?'

I had a few days for someone to apply a short-term plaster. That's the only thing I can say. I couldn't be cured instantaneously. So, Ronnie, Dr. Seraph appeared and carried me, but it was all very close to the wire. I had several meetings with him. "Sue," said he, "tell me, tell me everything. Some things I already know. Those are the things you may care to keep hidden. Never fear...I know what they are anyway...."

'How did he know?'

Ronnie, he was a Psychic. I didn't find it strange. All I felt was trust. He had such a simple way of explaining. "Sue, think of a kettle full of steam. Something is stuck in the spout. Release it and out pours the steam. Not unlike our mind, when someone opens the floodgates".

As I spoke, some peace began to be restored. The balm, the relief, was soothing. Here was the deliverance, ease and comfort that only specialist palliative care could bring about. I was being prepared for a temporary return to life and work. I was constantly assured that it would be all right. I would not fail. I was being guided, shown how to begin my healing.

'Did you feel you could go back to work?'

Not at first, Ronnie. Only when I felt the cushion beneath me, did I know I had been saved.

I was fearful. The drive over to Scarborough seemed to be filled with thoughts of disaster and loneliness. Instead, the countryside, in its Autumn light, brought hope. I was beginning to feel aware again; aware of normality, regularity, usualness and naturalness. Yes, I was nervous, but now there was an element of control because there was an escape route.

'Dr. Seraph'.

Yes, Ronnie.

I was greeted very warmly on my arrival at the Theatre. Mr. A. smiled. Several smiled, so all was well! My Rebecca scene was short, mostly spent at the bedside of the inert, comatose Betty Parris. Ironic that I was playing the character who was, to all intents and purposes, able to inject a modicum of discernment, calm and tranquillity into an atmosphere of lunacy, delusion and mania!

'Easy to see that now, pet. Not at the time…'

It's extraordinary, Ronnie. When you know someone is on the end of the telephone should you start to panic again, you can summon the tools: nerve, fortitude and guts.

Other helpers materialised. Lavinia Bertram, playing Mary Warren, came over to have word. She had heard that I had worked at the Library Theatre. It transpired that she had once been the Partner of – guess who?

'Yes…yes…'

'Feedom!!

'No!'

Small world, isn't it Ronnie? So, here was someone I could relate to. Lavinia and I had many conversations between Scenes. I felt that I could confide in her. She was gentle and understanding. So sympathetic that when she heard of my travelling difficulties, she said, "Sue, don't worry, I have a car here that I'm not using. For goodness sake, do borrow it and go home when you are not needed".

'The kindness of strangers, who are really not strangers at all, are they my love? Do you think that Dr. Seraph could be telepathic as well? Lavinia's helpful suggestion was such a coincidence in the circumstances....'

All this began to steady me, Ronnie. I began to recover a little faith in myself again. I still felt scared, estranged, and distanced from what was going on, but there was a small element of control.

Mr. A. seemed conscious of the fact that some members of his Cast had not worked in The Round before and in the course of Rehearsal his anecdotes not only raised a laugh, but also, gave some indication of just how close the Audience was and how different responses could be.

I found out that the first fortnight of every Season, in the late 70's, beginning in May, was devoted to Pensioners. Consequently, tickets could be reduced in price and full houses guaranteed. The close proximity of the spectators occupying the first row, enabled Actors to be in full hearing of any passing comments. One choice example was, when the Stage lights faded up: "Doris, it's in colour!" Also, remarks – some hardly flattering – referred to an Actress's appearance: "I don't like 'er 'air this time. It were better blonde in the last Play".

'Glorious! Of course, long before I met you and working at the Theatre, I can remember how easy it was for us Actors to see all the old ladies' bloomers! They would sit on the front row with their legs wide open – never aware that we were close enough to see!'

So, Ronnie, those first few days did pass. I did Perform. I did stay calm. Being able to return home each evening and spend the odd day there when I was not called, restored capability and means of control. The nightly phone calls to Dr. Seraph and weekend meetings with him, began to steer me on a more even, rhythmic course. Certainly one that could get me through...

The coast road from Scarborough lay, in those days, very close to the cliff edge. That, I found to be treacherous. I dreaded approaching that stretch; it hovered, soared like a spectre: hazardous, precarious and – dangerous. Fortunately, if traffic was sparse, I could veer over to the other side of the road, concentrate on the white line or the cat's eyes, until the direction changed and fields, hedges and trees could compose and make me still.

'Why, darling, were you so afraid of the cliff?'

It was the bogeyman that would lure me over the verge...

'Dear God, love....'

Yes, Ronnie, it was a terrible time...I have done my best to explain how ill I must have been....but, all passes with time... bye and bye, happier days came along and I was the stronger for it....I became a very different Susie in later years.

'Did Dr. Seraph know the enormity of it, do you think?'

Oh yes, Ronnie. "Well, Sue, now you have reached rock bottom, your soul can begin to grow...." I couldn't understand then, but when the mists cleared, I knew he had been right. I was growing up – at last...

'The Crucible' was scheduled for a three-week run. It became obvious that travelling home every night, after the Show finished at 10.00 p.m., could be a headache I needed to deal with. The coast road, in the dark, was not a factor to be contemplated in my present frail and flawed state. I happened to drop this into conversation with Sarah Bennett who was playing the somnolent, dead to the world child, Betty Parris. I liked Sarah. She was unperturbed, unruffled and in no way highfalutin or grandiose.

Sarah went on to describe where she was living. She was renting a room in a large house on the Valley Road, a stone's throw from the Theatre. I learned that there was a free room going there, if I was interested. The Landlady lived on the premises. I was keen to know more. It would be good to have a companion when walking to and fro; especially a friend who was nearby at night. My demons could lurk in the hours of darkness!

When we were both free from Rehearsal, Sarah introduced me to her Landlady, who took me on a tour of the vacant room. It was small, but cosy and inviting. I settled on it there and then. I phoned Dr. Seraph. He was delighted.

'Oh my darling…all without any handholding…'

Ronnie, you would have been most intrigued with that Valley Road house.

'Oh God, now what's coming?'

It had an indoor Victorian Garden!

'No! Sue, those are really rare…what was it like?'

On first visit, Sarah and I approached the house by a side entrance, way of a an uphill path. A door on the left opened on to a leafy interior. Almost at once, you were engulfed with a steamy, humid aerosphere. Plants of every description were encased within a vast floor-to-ceiling glass Conservatory: Ferns, palms, Hoya Carnosa…

'My Uncle Sandy had one of those…don't you remember, pet?'

Of course I do, Ronnie. I could just about identify many others in that wondrous collection: climbers such as Bourgainvilleas, Stephanotis and Plumbago! Over all, hung the breathtaking scent of the sub-tropical. It was…

'Like a Nurseryman's catalogue by the sound of it!'

And, darling, a little water butt bubbled and dripped. The sound seemed to echo the hush, stillness and serenity of this wonderful place.

'Therapy for the troubled soul?'

I grew to love that garden, Ronnie.

'Did Nick and your Mother see it? I reckon they came over to get you safely in?'

Yes, Ronnie, they did. Some time ago, we had already vacated the other Flat, scene of so many dismal, cheerless trials. I think that Mum and Nick were worrying, but relieved that an ally was only a short distance away.

'I'd love to know what your Mother thought of the indoor garden!'

She did look nervously about her, Ronnie, as if some phantom force was going to creep up from behind!

'Now I do hope she didn't say….!'

No, Ronnie, this time she refrained from saying "well, it isn't what you're used to!" but…

'Odds on that's what she was thinking!'

I think she was so thankful that I was a little better. She was prepared to put a good face on present circumstances.

'How did she react to Dr.Seraph?'

Well, she didn't give much away. In fact, nothing at all…but there was certainly a reticence; she was guarded.

'Ah…Mmn…'

I think there was suspicion for, unusually for me, I did not confide. I was not forthcoming in any way about my healing. I had an instinctive feeling that my confidences were now my own. Dr. Seraph had charged me with a secret task; that would be the bedrock of my recovery.

The play opened. I performed. Alone, apart from the friendly Sarah, I existed in my one-room cocoon and lived from day to day. I did not venture into the future. I had had strict instructions not to go there, but to remain only in the present. During the day, I took the car on slow, leisurely journeys to the Ferguson. Those were the days when restorative time with Dr. Seraph was fixed. My life became an ongoing therapy of faith, belief, dreams and longing....

I looked forward to chats with Lavinia. She knew the Library Theatre so well and it was a treat to remember the fun and gossip; most of all, the laughter generated by 'Feedom and Reg. I wonder, how would Mr. A. have coped with their 'method'?

'There might have been a bit of toe-curling going on!'

Like those two, Lavinia was also a product of E15 Acting School and very familiar with its technique, so our harking back to Library incident and experience was a welcome solace for me. She knew I was keen to be invited for a further full season at the Theatre-in-the-Round. "Sue, I know you've been ill, but try to make it through. I'm sure Alan could make you an offer a bit later on".

'Bless...'

Yes, Ronnie, it was such a lift to know that another Actor saw your potential and wished the best for you. Her hope was borne out when I received a card from Mr. A. It was his custom, I was told, to send a First Night Good Luck card to each member of the Cast. Mine read "Dear Susan – have a very happy and successful time with 'The Crucible'. Thanks for what I hope will be the first of many... Love Alan".

'A bonne bouche, as they say in France!'

Lavinia Bertram was a lovely, most talented Actress. I worked with her many times and was so impressed with her attention to detail, her realism, Professionalism and infinite kindness towards her Associates. I was deeply saddened very many years later to hear that she had died... much too soon.

'We never forget, do we darling, those who have left a trace upon our lives...'

THE SEARCH FOR THE TRUTH

1980

> *'You don't have to see the whole staircase,*
> *just take the first step'*
>
> (Martin Luther King)

I did not work in Theatre for a further five months. I had no inclination to chase further jobs. I was utterly drained, weary and used up. I needed to accept that rest for my body and soul was imperative. I speak of rest, but sleep was fleeting, erratic and fitful.

'Were you frightened?'

Yes, I was Ronnie. I could see no end to the turbulence and chaos; no end to the bedlam and disorder of my thoughts.

'Now come on…there must have been a turning point…'

There was, Ronnie, but it was so gradual that I wasn't really aware of any change. Christmas 1979 came and went. No one asked any questions. I must have seemed to be normal. Aunties came and went, Gin came and went and activities came and went.

'Did you start to feel better?'

The focal point of my existence at that time was my meetings with Dr. Seraph.

'Ah, I thought so…and…?'

The nurturing, the explanation of cause and effect began to make sense. Most of all, I began to realise that my illness was not my fault. I was not to blame. My body had responded to intolerable strain in the only way it knew how. It became traumatised. It caved in.

'But why had stress affected you so badly?'

I came to understand that influence may be embedded within us for a very long time, even from childhood. Environmental, Parental influence – for good and bad – can play its part. We can be totally unaware of its power, but it becomes habitual to respond to it. I found out that trouble starts when that goes against our true, unique, special, innermost nature; distortion is the result. When that bends, twists and sculpts, our whole essence can become warped. We are not being true to ourselves. The mind senses that...

'And...it rebels...reacts physically...'

As soon as I realised that the mess could be un-knotted, disentangled and made free, my healing began in earnest. It was intense, searching....

'How could that happen?'

Through talk, Ronnie. I confided. I shared my secrets. I spoke the truth about my fear, hope and loss; the mists started to clear and I left all those things on the table. They would not torture me again, for truth became my mantra.

'I think of Buddhism when you say that...'

Truth is something I would never try to hide from again; being true to myself. Tears were shed; guilt, misery and hopelessness left behind.

'Why guilt, Sue – for Heaven's Sake, why guilt?'

I felt guilty for most of my early life. It never left me: guilt for not looking after Nicky properly, guilt for being attracted to unsuitable partners, guilt and shame for my puberty and blossoming feelings, shame for their natural expression, the curiosity, the sexual awakening....'

'My darling, it was all perfectly natural, normal...'

No, Ronnie, for me it never was. Fortunately, the guilt never hindered my development, but, as Dr. Seraph disclosed, it had come dangerously close. He gave me permission to rejoice in the normality of it all, albeit a bit late! That imposed guilt, the emotional blackmail, could have affected the rest of my life, making me unable to respond within a loving Relationship.

'So, my love, a new life began, didn't it?'

Ronnie, I learned so many things; about love in particular. I will try to explain. Once one's feelings are true and pure, they never change. No matter what the distance, the strength of that love can never weaken, but only grow stronger, providing it is not confused or measured by the need for physical possession. No person can ever possess love; it must be given freely and accepted with grace. It must not carry ties or chains, for if it is given and received in the purest way, it does not require any. If it is demanded, its pure flow is taken away and it becomes strangled. It must be given space to flower and grow. No one can help falling in love; it does not have laws or fences to stop it happening, but when it does, it must be nourished on trust and truth.

'Was that your first grown-up lesson?'

It all came in one package on the day I met you, Ronnie.

Initially, Brother Nick helped with Dr. Seraph's fees. I had a little money left from 'The Crucible' but not enough to foot the bill indefinitely. The time came when I needed to confide one more thing to Dr. Seraph. I could not afford any further Therapies. "Sue, you are very nearly there. I find that I could now do with a little help from you." I was mystified. "Sue, you are sufficiently advanced for me to mention Role Play. I'm talking about Psychodrama. Here, you can give me invaluable help. I am not a Drama Specialist. You are. Will you help me and other Patients by sharing your expertise? That way, we will both be learning and fees will fade into non-existence!"

'Oh, Sue....so it became a two way process between Masters?'

I think I found my true self then, Ronnie. I could help those who needed the guidance that I had received. Just as I had helped all those Children to face their fears so many years before. The days were filled with reward.

'You were nearly better, weren't you?'

Well, nearly Ronnie. I reckon, I was just work in progress!

~

I had met Tony several times during my time at home. He buoyed me continually with his cleverness and stirring ideas for the Gulbenkian. It was at that time, about a couple of months after my Therapies and work with Dr. Seraph began, that I was presented with the possibility of two turning points in my life.

'Yes, yes...go on...you always stop there!'

One: to Lecture in the Drama Dept. at the Gulb. Two: A full Season with Alan Ayckbourn at the Theatre-in-the-Round beginning Rehearsal in London, May 1980.

'Dear God, what a choice to make! Did Dr. Seraph help you make it?'

Oh no, Ronnie. This was the first test to be true to myself. I do believe that Dr. Seraph secretly hoped that I would stay...but knew that the best thing for my continual advancement would be to stand on my own feet, to practise being my strong self – no influence, no boundaries, only the truth. "It's your decision, Sue. You're a big girl now...." said he.

I sent my letter of acceptance to Play-as-Cast for a full Season at the Theatre-in-the-Round, Scarborough.

There were no strings attached when I said farewell to Dr. Seraph. It always was, however, my wish to include him in every turning point in my life from that time and for many, many years to come, until he died. The life I now have is the life I owe to Dr. Seraph and his Spiritual wisdom. His legacy was supreme, infinite. I miss him.

'Never be inhospitable to strangers...'

~

'Did you feel different petal?'

Yes, Ronnie. For the first time I felt an inner peace. I knew there would be times when nervousness would present itself, but I learned that there was such a thing as 'healthy anxiety'! I would be in control of it.

'Now you would be in the driving seat!'

The weeks of Therapy had brought about change. I knew a confidence that enabled me to steer my own life. The Theatre-in-the Round beckoned and I was ready for it.

'What about that Jessica? Did she sense the change? I'm interested to know how she reacted.. not easy, I'm sure...'

She was very pleased about the Scarborough job, Ronnie. I'm sure she was happy to see me on the road to recovery. She did not, however, take kindly to another influence playing its part. She did not like Dr. Seraph, mistrusted him and could see that my dependence on her was slipping. He, in Mum's opinion, was to blame and I don't think she ever forgave him. Dr. Seraph had been instrumental in bringing about my separation, freedom and self-government. I was no longer a child-adult. If this had not transpired, I am convinced that I would not have survived.

I continued to care for my Mother, to love her as always and involve her in all aspects of my life; she was never shut out...but... guilt was no more.....

~

In May of that year, I was London-bound to begin three week's Rehearsal for Alan Ayckbourn's Production of Priestley's 'Time and the Conways'.

We would be working at the National Theatre where Alan was overseeing one of his blockbusters.

'Were you frightened?'

Yes, Ronnie, but I thrived. This time, Dr. Seraph received a progress report every evening! That string did bind and guide. I was not alone....

'Sue, my darling, I sense that we are coming to the end of our talking together....we are coming to our time in the story...are you going to remember how we met or is that for another time...?'

Well, yes, darling Ronnie, it is...but if you like I will repeat a few lines from the other Book...just to please you!

> "I had gone to the Wardrobe Department for a costume fitting.
>
> I was to play Rebecca Nurse in 'The Crucible'. Ronnie remembered that first meeting. I found the memory vague and uncertain. He said I appeared to be careworn, pensive and sad. He was quick to add "until you smiled". Ronnie, spoke with pins in his mouth and said I was done.
>
> Ronnie appeared (in London, during 'Conways') towards the end of the Rehearsal period. We had stopped for tea. Suddenly, the Wardrobe man came through the door. Of course there was no recognition of me so I was able to observe him. I wondered why he was there. He looked different for he was not fitting costumes, pins in mouth. He was interesting,

quirky. Someone said, "Oh Ronnie, it's good to see you" and laughter began. I weighed him up. First, my attention was drawn to a large brass safety-pin attached to his leather belt – on it hung a bunch of keys. Extraordinary. He was wearing twill trousers with myriad pockets. Ronnie was popular....funny. He was entertaining a very receptive group. He had curly hair and a fetching, disarming smile. I found myself on the brink of a new, affecting and accomplished life...and...Ronnie...

The brass safety-pin now hangs on the wall of my kitchen."

'And that's where it all began...another part of the story... when I came to know Susie! May I suggest a quote for your ending? I think it's got to be Bette Davis!'

Go on then...

'Slow curtain......The End'

IF YOU KNEW SUSIE

Popular song written by
BUDDY DeSYLVA and JOSEPH MEYER
(Published by Shapiro, Bernstein and Co. in 1925)

Sung by Eddie Cantor, Dean Martin and Frank Sinatra

I have a sweetie known as Susie
In the words of Shakespeare she's a "Wow"
Though all of you may know her too
I'd like to shout right now ...

Susie has a perfect reputation
No one ever saw her on a spree
Nobody knows where Susie goes
Nobody knows but me ...

If you knew Susie like I know Susie
Oh! Oh! Oh! What a girl!
There's none so classy
As this fair lassie
Oh! Oh! Holy Moses, what a chassis!
We went riding, she didn't balk
Back from Yonkers
I'm the one who had to walk!
If you knew Susie like I know Susie
Oh! Oh! What a girl!